OUTDOOR ADVENTURES
in the Upcountry

edited by Michel Stone
with Lydia Dishman

Photography by Ted Borg

HUB CITY
PRESS

SPARTANBURG, SC

OUTDOOR
ADVENTURES
in the Upcountry

edited by Michel Stone
with Lydia Dishman

Photography by Ted Borg

First printing, November 2010

Editors: Michel Stone and Lydia Dishman
All photographs by Ted Borg, except pages 10 (Michel Stone), 24 (bigstockphoto.com) and 60 (David Scott)
Book Design: Brandy Lindsey and the Graphics House, Roebuck, SC
Cover photo features Tom McInnis of Clemson, SC, a representative of Trout Unlimited
Proofreaders: Megan DeMoss and Betsy Teter
Printed in China by Everbest through Four Colour Imports

Library of Congress Cataloging-in-Publication Data

Outdoor adventures in the upcountry / edited by Michel Stone with Lydia Dishman ; photography by Ted Borg.
    p. cm.
 ISBN 978-1-891885-75-4 (alk. paper)
 1. Outdoor recreation--South Carolina. 2. Hunting--South Carolina. 3. Boats and boating--South Carolina. I. Stone, Michel, 1969- II. Dishman, Lydia.
 GV191.42.S6O88 2010
 796.5--dc22
                    2010023253

Hub City Press
186 West Main Street
Spartanburg, SC 29306
864-577-9349
www.hubcity.org

VI. EXPLORING:

VII. OBSERVING

ANIMAL ENCOUNTERS

BIRDING

PLANTS

THE HUB CITY WRITERS PROJECT THANKS ITS FRIENDS WHO
MADE CONTRIBUTIONS IN SUPPORT OF THIS BOOK:

SC Arts Commission
George and Sissy Stone

Stan and Paula Baker
Jim and Carol Bradof
Mac and Margie Cates
Paul and Tara Desmond
Andy and Lynne Falatok

Mr. and Mrs. John Faris
John and Nora Beth Featherston
Donald L. Fowler
Stewart and Ann Johnson
Julian and Dorothy Josey

Bob and Ruta Allen
Mack and Patty Amick
Tom and Ceci Arthur
Greg and Lisa Atkins
Robert and Susan Atkins
Andrew and Kitsy Babb
Bill and Valerie Barnet
Tom and Joan Barnet
Charles and Christine Bebko
Carl and Deborah Beck
Clarke and Martha Blackman
Shirley Blaes
Markus and Heidi Bollinger
Don and Martha Bramblett
Bucko and Mary Nell Brandt
Susan Bridges
Jack and Myrna Bundy
Dr. and Mrs. William W. Burns
Fred and Joan Butehorn
Fritz and Lori Butehorn
Marvin and Katherine Cann
Terry and Janis Cash
Peter Caster
John and Lisa Chapman
Martha Cloud Chapman
Robert and Janeen Cochran
Justin and Anna Converse
Tom Moore Craig
Nancy Rainey Crowley
Bob Cumming and Rosa Shand
Ted and Becky Daniel
Wilhelmena Dearybury
Fredrick B. Dent
Mr. and Mrs. Magruder H. Dent
Bernie and Anne Dunlap
Ray and Kathy Dunleavy
Dan and Fran Dunn
Dr. and Mrs. William C. Elston
Bill and Cheryl Epton
Max and Ann Fain
George and Mildred Fields
Lib Fleming
Ashley and Kimberly Anne Fly
Will and Liz Fort
Denise Tatum Frazier
Elaine T. Freeman
Sam and Sarah Galloway
William and Cha Gee
Jimmy and Marsha Gibbs
Ernest Glenn
Barney and Elaine Gosnell

Jim and Kay Gross
Carlos and Barbara Gutierrez
Roger and Marianna Habisreutinger
Lee and Kitty Hagglund
Benjy and Tanya Hamm
Mr. & Mrs. Robert A. Hammett
Ibrahim Hanif
Tom and Tracy Hannah
Robert and Carolyn Harbison
John and LouAnn Harrill
Peyton and Michele Harvey
Eaddy Williams Hayes
David and Rita Heatherly
Gary and Carmela Henderson
Marvin and Pat Hevener
Tom and Max Hollis
Doug and Marilyn Hubbell
Mr. & Mrs. Kenneth R. Huckaby
Jim and Patsy Hudgens
Woody and Carol Hughes
Monroe and Debra Hutchins
David and Harriet Ike
John and Sheila Ingle
Dr. and Mrs. Vernon Jeffords
George Dean and Susu Johnson
Tom Johnson
Wallace Eppes Johnson
Betsy and Charlie Jones
Frannie Jordan
Mr. & Mrs. Daniel Kahrs
Jay and Pam Kaplan
John Lane and Betsy Teter
Cecil and Mary Jane Lanford
Wood and Janice Lay
George and Frances Loudon
Robert and Nancy Lyon
Ed and Suzan Mabry
Jim and Heather Magruder
Nathaniel and Gayle Magruder
Zerno E. Martin, Jr.
Connie McCarley
Levi McLaughlin and Lauren Markley
Ed and Gail Medlin
Larry E. Milan
Scott and Diane Milks
Bob and Karen Mitchell
John and Belle Montgomery
T. Craig Murphy
Douglas and Maxine Nash
Kam and Emily Neely
Nick and Missy Nicholson

Mark Olencki
Don and Erin Ouzts
Alva and Janice Pack
Geneva F. Padgett
Mr. & Mrs. W. Keith Parris
Bill and Mary Pell
Carolyn Pennell
Richard Pennell
Pat and Ann Porcher Perrin
Bob and Dixie Pinson
John and Lynne Poole
Harold B. Powell
L. Perrin and Kay Powell
Harry Price
Rebecca Ramos and Kelly Lowry
Eileen Rampey
Ron and Ann Rash
John and Allison Ratterree
Chuck Reback and Melissa Walker
Naomi Richardson
Ricky and Betsy Richardson
Rose Mary Ritchie
Regis and Elisabeth Robe
Martial and Amy Robichaud
Renee Romberger
Steve and Elena Rush
Kaye Savage
Garrett and Cathy Scott
Danny and Becky Smith
Emily Louise Smith
Lenette Sprouse
B.G. and Sandra Stephens
David and Tammy Stokes
Eliot and Michel Stone
Phillip Stone
Chris and Jessalyn Story
Bob and Chris Swager
Nancy Taylor
Ray Thompson, Sr.
Bob and Cheryl Tillotson
Aaron and Kim Toler
Gregg and Mary Helen Wade
Jay and Jenny Wakefield
Bill and Peggy Wakefield
Bill and Mary Walter
David and Kathy Weir
Dave and Linda Whisnant
John and Karen White
Chuck White and Ruth L. Cate
Hollis E. Wilson and Emma Chisolm
Elizabeth H. Young

INTRODUCTION
Michel Stone

ONE CRISP FEBRUARY MORNING IN 2009 A SMALL GROUP OF FOLKS MET OVER COFFEE TO DISCUSS THE IDEA OF A BOOK ABOUT OUTDOOR ACTIVITIES.

Hub City Press had tossed around the idea of such a book for a while, and that morning, as a consensual vision of an anthology of essays set in the Upcountry emerged, I jumped at the opportunity to shepherd this project. Our call for submissions went out to newspapers in communities large and small: Greenville, Pickens, Spartanburg, Clemson, Laurens and others. We put flyers in outfitters and bike shops and anywhere else nature lovers congregate across the region.

As we shaped the concept of this book, I recalled my early days in the woods or on rivers, hunting and fishing with my parents. The deer, doves, ducks, or fish we took home were not the dominant part of my recollections. What I recalled most vividly was the time spent with loved ones outdoors, regardless of the activity or the "success" of the hunt. I imagine that

feeling holds true for most outdoors enthusiasts, and I was eager to capture in this book the universality of that experience.

I've discovered that outdoorsy types often are writers as well. What is the connection? Perhaps just as an outdoor jaunt often proves to be serendipitous, so is the process of writing: you never know what you'll discover or what you'll realize in the process.

Renowned nature writer Rachel Carson said, "If a child is to keep alive his inborn sense of wonder, he needs the companionship of at least one adult who can share it, rediscovering with him the joy, excitement and mystery of the world we live in."

On a recent spring day my young son Will and I took a walk in the woods in southern

Spartanburg County. The day was ideal for an outing, and the land was rugged, hard packed clay littered with shards of Indian arrowheads. The Enoree River borders the property where we strolled, winding beneath towering syca-mores. My son loves the notion of hunting, and so on this day he brought along his cap gun and proclaimed that he would hunt a turkey. Will's enthusiasm reminded me of my own as a youth, trudging through woods and fields to see what I could see.

Will and I rounded a bend in the road and five white-tail deer darted before us.

"Did you see their tails," I asked? "Did you see what color they were?"

"Yes," he said. "They're white!"

The rest of our day unfolded like that with little teachable moments presenting themselves. As we walked along a path toward a small pond, I cautioned Will about the animal droppings lit-tering our way.

"What do you think that is?" I said, pointing.

He shrugged his shoulders. "I don't know."

"It's…" I hesitated for dramatic effect, then whispered, "Coyote poop."

His eyes widened, and he grinned.

A little further down the path we encountered deer scat and raccoon droppings, and I pointed these out to Will with equal zeal. Along with the scat were tracks, lots of tracks, including turkey tracks. Will understood this discovery to be evidence of past visitors.

"Where are they now—the turkeys and coyotes and deer and raccoons?" he said, looking to the surrounding woods, now suddenly more intriguing and mysterious.

"Maybe they're watching us," I said. "Maybe they'll come out here to look at our tracks after we've gone."

"Yeah," he said, now whispering in his new-found reverence for his surroundings.

He shot a hand upward. "Look at that flower," he said, pointing at a pale yellow and orange blossom drifting down like a pinwheel, twirling toward us from the canopy above.

I caught the flower and handed it to Will. This came from that tree. It's called a tulip poplar," I said.

"Tulip poplar," he repeated. "I like its flower, Mama."

"It's pretty, isn't it?" I said.

I think of Rachel Carson, and her notion that a child needs the companionship of at least one adult to keep alive his sense of innate wonder of nature. I say sometimes an adult needs the companionship of at least one child to reawak-en her own sense of innate wonder and appre-ciation of the outdoors.

Carson also said, "It is not half so important to know as to feel when introducing a young child to the natural world."

I think Will and I felt each other's joy that day, shared a sense of awe and wonder and excite-ment about nature's mysteries. By the end of the day, he seemed to have forgotten his desire for a turkey hunt, but he recalled the tracks, the twirling poplar flower, and the animals who'd walked our path before us, animals hid-den in the dark edges of the nearby woods, perhaps watch-ing, wondering, waiting in their own ways, just as Will and I were, for discovery.

"It is not half so important to know as to feel when introducing a young child to the natural world."

As essay submissions from across South Caro-lina and the region filled my in-box, I encoun-

11

eye and sense of what works in an essay were invaluable as we pared submissions down to the thirty-four included here.

When I began looking for a photographer for this anthology, my search ended at Ted Borg, a master nature photographer. For nearly thirty years the gorgeous images in *South Carolina Wildlife Magazine* were captured through Ted's lens. I recall seeing his name in tiny print beside the photos for much of my life.

As soon as I explained to Ted the point of my phone call, the voice on the other end came to life. Ted's love for photography and the outdoors energized him, and I'm certain I could hear him licking his photo-journalistic chops across the miles.

When I said, "My budget is pretty small," he said, "Ma'am, I'll do this. Your budget doesn't worry me."

You're holding the result of this collaboration. I hope you discover something unexpected and pleasing on these pages, something that inspires you to create your own outdoor adventures in the Upcountry of South Carolina.

tered many diverse voices. Each relayed an experience both unique and universal, something familiar yet surprising. The editing process proved intense at times; how would my co-editor Lydia Dishman and I choose among so many interesting and varied essays? We wanted the book to be both entertaining and literary. In the end, the essays selected for this anthology were chosen because they were literate, descriptive, and reflective, and they referenced the Piedmont landscape of South Carolina in an interesting and entertaining way. Lydia's keen

FISHING

Scott Gould

Wilson Peden

Ron Rash

Pat Robertson

Charles Henry Sowell

Emma Chisolm

A LETTER TO THE SUNDANCE KID

Scott Gould

Enjoy! Sam G. Nov '10

TO: ROBERT REDFORD
        SUNDANCE INSTITUTE
        PARK CITY, UTAH

Dear Mr. Redford,

My stomach hurts, so I will get right to the point. Several years ago, specifically 1992, you put a blight of Biblical proportions on fly-fishing in South Carolina, and I have kept my anxiety bottled up for so long, I have, at this time, started to experience abdominal pains because of my silence. I should have said something a long time ago, but I gave you a flyer solely on the merits of *Butch Cassidy and the Sundance Kid*, more accurately the scene with Katharine Ross and the lacy shirt that falls to the floor of her cabin. That couple of minutes within the darkness of her boudoir was a formative cinematic experience for an eleven-year-old, and I gave you partial credit for my adolescent epiphany. However, I can no longer keep quiet. I'm getting old, and I only have so much time

left in my waders. That and I'm tired of having cramps.

I'm sure you that when you directed *A River Runs Through It* in '92, you didn't expect to breed a whole tribe of faux fly-fishermen—men who saw the movie, tossed their American Express cards down on the closest fly-shop counter, and begged the salesperson to turn them into Brad Pitt With A Seven Weight Rod. I remember heading for the Chattooga River a few months after the movie premiered. It was mid-fall, but most of the leaves had long fallen and been carried downstream weeks before. The water, especially upstream from Burrell's Ford, was clear as cut glass, not a trace of autumn mud or milkiness. At the first big bend upstream from the parking area, I knew of a deep cut at the backside of a riffle where the rainbows rafted up just under the surface, fluttering in the current, waiting for the rare hatch that comes here and there during Indian summers. On the tailgate of my truck, I pulled on my hip boots, tied my leader with something my father had concocted from deerhair and pheasant tail, then headed up the trail for the bend in the river. (I tell you this because I know, from watching your movies, that you appreciate good backstory.) I did not notice the Audi and Suburban taking up space on the shoulder of the road.

Even in the fall, the bare trees and the rhododendron were thick enough to make seeing the river difficult, so it wasn't until I broke from the trail to the bank that I saw the man standing in ankle-deep water, thrashing the surface like a mad animal trainer with a new bullwhip. Save for the learning-disabled casting, he looked like a page from the Orvis catalog. His vest hadn't been out of the package long, loaded with every accessory he could shove in a pocket or clip on a seam. Even from where I stood I could see a water thermometer, a pair of sparkly hemostats dangling from a zip-line, several bottles of line flotant, a half dozen spindles of tippet, a high-tech telescoping wading staff, and a net that appeared to be made of teak or some such exotic wood. I tried to pick out what kind of rod he had, but the thing was moving too fast. His backcasts were almost angry. His arm flopped so far behind his head that his line lay on the surface for what seemed a few seconds before he snatched the rod forward, creating a rooster-tail of ferocious water to his rear. The line slapped forward, landing in a strange calligraphy in front of him, the fly hiding somewhere in the coils and s-curves that began to wriggle in the current. He didn't leave his fly on the surface long enough to make a difference to anything, especially the fish. He was more interested in casting, in churning up the water in front and behind. He didn't know that he'd probably already scared off every trout within a hundred yards. You see, Mr. Redford, in South Carolina, you spook a trout and he'll disappear under a rock for days. He'll go hungry before he tests the surface again. Our trout aren't like those pond-raised petting fish you used in the

movie. These are real fish. You know what I thought was so ironic at the time (and I know you love irony, as well)? Here this guy spent a few hundred dollars on waders that would keep him bone dry in a fifty-year flood, and he's standing in water so shallow you couldn't drown in it.

I glanced upstream, searching for an escape route, I suppose, and I saw this fellow's twin, another man swaddled in khaki and neoprene. He wore a felt hat, a fedora cocked over his eye. I imagined he had flies hooked in the sheepskin hat band. He wasn't whipping the water like his buddy, though. No, he was doing that insane "shadow casting" thing you showed off in your movie. I admit, yes, it looked good on camera, with the Montana sunlight glinting through the spray off the line and those big loops cutting wide figure-eights in the air, but shadow casting is all about looks. It's nothing but imagery. Mr. Redford, with all due respect, the fish don't care. And my guess is they were laughing. Why? Because they know that real fly-fisherman would rather fish than cast, and if you're casting, you aren't fishing.

I left the river right then, without wetting my line. On my way back to the parking area, I saw fish lying in the shadows of the bank, browns and rainbows bullet-like in the current. I saw them dimpling the water in the big pools, but I didn't have the heart to drift a fly over their noses. I realized then that a new type of fisherman was walking up and down the banks of the Chattooga, fishermen who thought they could buy a five-hundred-dollar rod and thrash their way to peace and tranquility and enlightenment, all the while screwing up the river for people like me, men who think the most perfect shape in the world is a big brown rolling white and pissed over on a dry fly. These

> Our trout aren't like those pond-raised petting fish you used in the movie. These are real fish.

other guys, they'd caught the fever, but they wouldn't catch any fish, at least not until they figured out that you tricked them with editing and camera angles. And maybe they never would figure it out. Maybe they'd spend the rest of their lives whipping fish into a froth and wondering why they never caught trout like Brad Pitt did.

It took years, but I eventually ventured back to the river, and I learned to stake out some new territory that the Orvis models wouldn't go near, like the East Fork on the Chattooga, where the undercover is so thick, casting is akin to throwing darts, and where the fish are native and mean, like the little brookies that possess a bad attitude. And I decided to go back to the big river, too, and try to come to terms with the faux fly-fishermen who were still here and there, beating the water like they were whisking scrambled eggs. But one day, something changed again. I guess it was inevitable it would happen.

Just when I was beginning to find some sort of peace on the river, I came upon a sight that chilled me down to the felt soles on my boots. It happened just last month. I went back to that honey hole on the bend, but I didn't get there first. In the ankle-deep water too far from the fish to reach even with a decent single-haul cast, stood a man in his expensive waders, waving his bamboo rod over his head. It was one of your tribe, one of your *River Runs Through It* groupies, still casting like he didn't have a functional rotator cuff. And there, by his side, stood his little son, dressed just like dad, in little waders and a little vented fishing shirt. A little miniature Orvis boy. Together, they whipped the water into an honest-to-god roil, snapping their leaders across each other's ears.

You see, Mr. Redford, enough time has passed that the faux fly-fishermen, the bad casters,

have bred and created the next generation of shadow casting show-offs. And I, frankly, don't see any end in sight. Because men will be men, they will continue to propagate, creating generation after generation of boys who don't know a nail knot from a half hitch. I have dreams, Mr. Redford, nightmares actually, wherein I see the banks of the Chattooga River packed shoulder to shoulder with perfectly dressed fly-fishermen who are casting into a completely dry river bed, having the time of their lives shadow casting into the rocks. In my dream, I scramble across the rocks toward them—to stop them, I suppose, or maybe kill them—and suddenly I hear you scream out from the river bank, "Cut, dammit, cut! You're in the shot!" I don't think you have to be a genius or a film director to interpret that dream.

My simple plea is this: Make another movie. That's right. Another movie. We—and when I say we, I speak for the real fly-fishermen, who know how to unfurl a thirty-yard cast and let a Parachute Adams float to the surface of the water as light as lint, who could land a nymph dropper on a thin dime, who know what it means to stalk a trout for season after season and never catch it, who know how to spot a mayfly hatch before the sun goes down, who know how to roll cast in a stream the width of a hallway—we need another *Deliverance*. That movie cleared the river for years. Fear kept the poseurs out and let the fishermen in. We need a river-bank horror film that empties the Chattooga of everything but trout. I realize that horror is a genre that you've rarely explored, unless you count that film with Demi Moore and Woody Harrelson which was scary beyond belief, but I ask you to consider it. It's the least you can do for the people who would rather fish than shadow cast.

Yours truly—a fan and fisherman,
Scott Gould

MY MOTHER'S FISH
Wilson Peden

I SHOULDN'T HAVE BEEN SURPRISED WHEN MY PARENTS ANNOUNCED THEIR INTENTION BUY A CABIN IN THE WOODS. NEITHER OF MY PARENTS WERE WHAT YOU'D CALL CITY PEOPLE, BUT THE CABIN IDEA STILL CAUGHT ME OFF GUARD.

At fifteen, I had yet to read Thoreau, but if I had, I would have noted that we really weren't Thoreau-type people. My parents were not the kind of people who broke the law, not even in noblest act of Civil Disobedience. They were thrifty, yes, but not Spartan; they owned a very expensive vacuum cleaner. And they definitely weren't the type to quit their jobs at the pencil factory to go live in the woods.

But my mother was set on having a cabin, and we all knew—me, my sister Sydney, my father—that in the end this would be my mother's decision. It was my mother's finger that dialed up realtors, traced the routes on maps, and directed us into the station wagon my father piloted from Greenville up Highway 25 and 276 into the Blue Ridge foothills. My mother pointed us toward the mountain ridges, and to valleys looking back up at the mountains. But this was a place of vacation, our little slice of paradise, and you can't have paradise without water. So when my mother saw the waterfall, she bought the cabin that came with it.

It wasn't really a cabin, just a regular house, though it was tucked out of sight between two steep hills. The mechanical thrum of Highway 11 was less than a mile way. But the waterfall was truly spectacular. It was hidden in the back of the property, where the land was crumpled and ridged, like a piece of paper someone had wadded up and then attempted to smooth out again with dubious results. An unnamed creek flowed past the house and dropped twelve feet over an outcropping of black rock, splashing into a round green pool with a single boulder in

the middle. From the edge of the plunge pool, you could just stretch a foot out to the boulder in the middle, and if your balance was good you could step/hop onto the boulder and stand right in front of the falls—an act performed first by my sister, then me, and finally even our mother, jeans rolled up and shoes clutched in one hand, the other hand pin-wheeling for balance while my father took pictures from the ridge above.

The waterfall was perfect, though nothing else about the cabin was—especially not the furniture, which was grossly-oversized and upholstered in a coarse, purple-and-green fabric. But earthly paradise must be worked for, so work we did, my sister and I perhaps a little less cheerfully than my parents. Summer came, and with my mother no longer teaching and my sister and I out of school, we could spend whole weeks at the cabin. We carried out the ridiculous furniture, tore down the old dog fence, and repainted the chipped siding. Most important, we built a new porch on the front of the house and reworked the one that stretched from the side of the house above the waterfall. Even before the railings were finished, my mother drank her morning coffee out on that porch, tilted back in a plastic deck chair and staring at the white water.

June passed, July—lush, high summer in the mountains. Air temperatures were five to ten degrees cooler than in Greenville, and the foliage had grown so thick there was no sign of any other houses. Even the sounds of Highway 11 were muffled, only the occasional motorcycle or semi engines generating enough noise to reach us through all that vegetation. The abundance of life in that little patch of mountain forest was becoming more and more apparent to us every day. A number of animals lived inside our four walls, but they mostly announced their presence at night, when their scuttling kept us awake, or when they died and their corpses turned up in unusual places. The scorpions ended up in the ceiling fixtures, their distinctive silhouettes clear against the light globes. The anole lizards had chosen the carpet under my parent's bed as their dying ground, where their corpses became desiccated in the dry air around the baseboards. And the mice died anywhere they pleased and stank like hell till we found them and threw them off the porch.

These are the kinds of neighbors you deal with when you live in the woods—this is what my mother said when Sydney and I complained. And for every stinking mouse corpse and mummified lizard, there were plenty of quiet and beautiful neighbors. A five-foot black rat snake took up residence near the hot-water heater, and suddenly the number of stinking mouse corpses started to drop. Ruby-throated hummingbirds began to frequent the red feeders my mother hung near the deck. And always, there was the waterfall.

There were already creek fish in the spill pond, little chubs and suckers that swirled around the boulder, but my mother wanted trout.

"I'm sure it's cold enough, and when they get big we can eat them," she told me, practically hopping with excitement. "Come on, you like to fish—wouldn't you like some trout in our waterfall?"

I did love to fish, but something seemed odd about raising trout in the waterfall pool. I wasn't bothered at the thought of killing our own food—I was an avid fisherman and a competent gutter of trout. Maybe if I'd grown up on a farm as my mother had, I wouldn't have been bothered, but the waterfall seemed an odd place for agriculture. The waterfall was too pristine a piece of water to sully with human engineering.

My mother asked around about acquiring some trout fingerlings, but soon she abandoned the idea, realizing there really wasn't much space. Instead, she decided to use the little pool as a natural aquarium, stocked with some of the more colorful native fish species.

Because I was the fisherman in the family, I was sent to acquire the fish. Taking my fishing rod, a metal bucket, and a stale piece of bread, I followed the unnamed creek upstream from the falls, out of the woods. The creek flowed out of the little pond where I liked to fish—a grassy dam that trapped four acres of still, clear water, stocked with bass and catfish and a half-dozen varieties of bream. The bream were small and hungry, quick to bite on a pinch of bread. The first that I caught was small enough to fit in my palm. The scales on its side changed color in the light, shifting from green to violet flecked with gold; the belly was solid yellow-cream. The bream in this pond were hybrids, a mix of local and stocked sunfish species that had comingled since the creek was first dammed. That first little bream had the red ear of a shellcracker, but the golden flecks on its sides spoke of pumpkin-seed heritage. I set it in the metal bucket, which I'd filled with pond water. Then I set another pinch of bread on the hook and cast it back into the water.

I caught four bream, each a slightly different hybrid. Their sides were green, teal, orange, but always there was the yellow-cream belly. One by one I pulled their flat, leaf-shaped bodies from the water, and one by one I held them across my palm and watched their scales change colors before setting them in a bucket that was turning warm in the sunlight. When I emptied the bucket in the plunge pool, the fish swam immediately behind the boulder, where the water churned and I couldn't see them. I waited in the hollow under the falls until the spray beaded in my arms hairs, until the droplets grew fat and ran down my wrists, but I never saw the bream.

My mother could bring them out, though. She crumbled dry cat food and soaked the pieces in water to soften them, then carried her tray of wet brown food down to the base of the falls and scattered the mush across the surface of the water. At first only a few creek fish came out, brown fingerlings that snatched up the food and disappeared back against the overhanging banks. But when she returned to the cabin each weekend, she threw food to the water, and after a few weeks the bream learned: soon they, too, came out from the behind the big rock and joined the creek fish at the surface, snatching food off the surface hard enough to pop and splash. The bream and creek fish alike grew long and fat, which delighted my mother—she could see them much easier, watch their scales change color as the fish spun after food. In a few weeks they learned to recognize her shape, and when they saw her coming they would form a swirling cloud just beneath the surface, waiting for manna from heaven. Even from the porch you could see the surface churn as she tossed out the first handful. From a distance the water was still green, but if you walked down to the plunge pool you could see flashes of color in the water, yellow and purple and orange—all the bright residents of a little mountain Eden that my mother had created.

Time passed and our lives changed. Sydney finished high school and left town for college; two years later I did the same. For Sydney and me, time was passing quickly and our lives changing significantly. It was the same for my parents, too, I suppose, though I didn't think

of it that way at the time. They worked the same jobs, lived in the same place—they were at home, and it was that home that formed the basis of my progress, the point from which I measured the distance I'd gone. I just assumed, unconsciously, that my parents had reached a point of stasis in their lives.

It's a natural part of growing up—returning to the places you knew and finding everything different. But with the cabin, the process seemed accelerated—a few weeks, a month, and everything was changed. "The place looks completely different from the last time I saw it," I would exclaim every time I visited the cabin.

"Yes, doesn't it?" My mother or father would respond, delighted at what they'd accomplished. There was a tomato garden, a new screen door, my father's antique shotguns hanging on the wall. There were new, shallower stairs, and a new bedroom off the back deck. That nice, stable place was in a constant state of change as my parents barreled ahead toward their newest vision of perfection.

The surrounding woods weren't holding still, either. The dead scorpions in the light fixtures were soon joined by dead bees in the bedroom—insects that my father couldn't let be, as the expired corpses were still equipped with stingers that ended up in bare feet. My father finally succeeded in caulking out the bees, but the caulk didn't stop the squirrels, who decided that they, too, wanted in, and they were adept at chewing their way through the siding. The squirrels were joined by a new generation of mice who not only died in the walls, but left scatterings of their tiny feces everywhere. The thick coat of mouse droppings on top of the hot water heater led my mother to conclude that the black rat snake had moved. She was dis-

> It's a natural part of growing up—returning to the places you knew and finding everything different.

pleased with this development, even more so when she saw his new home.

"I had to move the hummingbird feeder," she shrieked. "That snake was curled around the same branch, just waiting for the birds to land. That snake!"

And so the feeder was moved, the walls were patched, and traps were set. As soon as the current critter crisis abided, my father began tearing up the bathroom floor and laying down new tile.

Watching this work happen over months, a year, two years, I saw that the work would never end for them—between my parents' changing vision, and nature's changing species, a stable cabin environment was impossible. That's the trouble with paradise—the unearthly is awfully hard to find on earth. The pursuit of Eden moves like the curve of a hyperbola that swoops higher and higher, approaching a straight line but never quite reaching it. Even stability was a foolish pursuit—after all, the whole point of owning a cabin was to enjoy the surrounding nature, and the natural world is anything but stable. Plants grow, mountains crumble; an animal dies and a new tributary splits off from the river. My parents could keep working on the cabin forever and never reach a perfect, stable place—both their platonic vision and its earthly foundation were changing all the time.

This was, of course, why they'd bought the cabin in first place. Paradise wasn't a location to them—it was the act of living there itself, a style of living they could carry out in the hills. My father didn't cut and chop wood because we worried about heating the house; he just liked doing something useful with his hands. My mother's projects, too—the tomatoes and gardens and even the bright fish in the waterfall—these were the things she did.

I made peace with the constancy of change—in the cabin, and in my life. During a summer between semesters of graduate school, I returned to Greenville and moved back in with my parents for several months. With my father retired and my mother finished teaching for the summer, we went back to the cabin. My sister, who'd been away in graduate school herself, was living in the Southeast again, just a few hours away across the Georgia border. I wasn't happy, at first, to be living with my parents, but I quickly settled into the comfortable rituals of my family.

The summer passed with its usual mix of steadiness and flux, and I fit my days into the season's rhythm. In the mornings I drove to Greer and taught classes at a summer art program; in the afternoons I returned to the cabin and took my laptop onto the porch, where I sat back in an Adirondack chair and worked on my thesis. I spent the long evenings out there reading and writing and napping, looking out at the churning falls and listening to the hum of moving water.

One morning, my mother saw something else from the porch—a great blue heron perched next to the falls. She rushed back inside to tell me about the bird, *sotte voce* even in the house, and gestured for me to join her again outside. The heron must have stood three feet tall, with a grey pick-axe head and folded slate-blue wings. The heron took a few tentative steps into the water and paused on one spindly orange leg, neck coiled in an "S" and beak pointed at the water. The heron waited and we watched, till our necks were stiff and our coffee was cold, but we never saw the heron strike.

A telephone, lunch—something called us inside, and when we came back the bird was gone. My mother took her tray of cat food down to the falls again, and at the bottom she scattered the entire tray across the surface all at once. The surface of the pool bubbled immediately.

"They're still here!" she shouted up. "The heron didn't get my fish."

But a week later, only two bream came to the surface. And the week after that, we saw the heron again, flying up out of the hollow just as we arrived. This time, when my mother threw food into the pond, only the creek fish came to feed. When they'd snatched up the largest pieces they disappeared again. She waited, but the colorful bream didn't come out to feed. She kept feeding the creek fish for several days, waiting to see her colorful hybrids emerge, but they never came.

The heron made a few more appearances over the next week, perched on the same rock near the water's edge. My mother kept up the feeding, but she didn't enjoy it the way she used to—it was rote now. When I watched her from my chair on the deck, she threw all the food at once and barely glanced at the creek fish before she turned and walked back up the hill, up the steps to the porch where I sat.

"My bream are all gone," my mother said. "That heron ate all my fish."

She paused. "You'll have to go to the pond and catch me some more."

EXOTIC FISHING

Ron Rash

BARRY HANNAH IS CORRECT IN CALLING FLY CASTING THE EPISCOPAL METHOD OF ANGLING. WHEN I WAS GROWING UP IN BAPTIST WESTERN NORTH CAROLINA, NO ONE I KNEW ACTUALLY CAUGHT FISH THAT WAY.

Fly-fishing was exotic, something you heard about, maybe even saw a picture of, but still couldn't quite believe—like Louisianans eating crawfish or Alaskans living in igloos. Nevertheless, the pictures in my uncle's issues of *Field and Stream* intrigued me. In those photographs and cover paintings, fishermen held fly rods flexed like hunting bows; on the other end, lunker trout leaping skyward or about to be netted, a colorful fly embedded in the fish's jaw. I'd been catching trout since I was four years old, using hickory branches first and then a Zebco 33 spinning reel. At the end of my line were red worms and crickets, an occasional Panther Martin spinner, but by mid-summer of my twelfth year I was lobbying for a fly rod and reel, first for my September birthday, and, when that didn't work, Christmas.

When I woke up Christmas morning, there it was. A spool of bright-orange fly-line lay next to the rod and reel as well as a box of trout flies, their pattern names printed on squares of paper beneath them. Trout season did not open until April, so I practiced casting in the field next to our house. At night, I'd oil my reel and practice tying leaders made from line off my Zebco. I'd also take out the trout flies and study them, matching their patterns to their names. I sometimes wonder if my love of poetic language was ignited on those winter evenings. I would pick up the flies and say each name softly: Gray Ghost, Royal Coachman, Quill Gordon, Silver Doctor, Parmachene Belle, the bright beauty of the fly and mellifluous name merging into one.

I had no one to teach me how to fly-fish, so I

taught myself, learning quickly that the long, elegant casts shown in the magazines were impossible on rhododendron-choked creeks. I taught myself something between a roll cast and a lunge. I didn't carry a net because the one time I did, it constantly snagged on briars and limbs. No waders or wicker creel, no hat with flies. I waded in old jeans or khakis and canvas tennis shoes, my flies and leaders inside a Prince Albert cigar can. There were no attempts at matching the hatch. I just tied on whatever felt right, and tried to cast it into pockets of water often no bigger than a tractor tire. In the rivulets I preferred to fish, the trout didn't have the luxury of being picky. If the trout didn't see me and the cast was accurate, I would usually get a strike. I suppose you could call my method a low-church response to the Episcopal method—eschewing ritual and formality for the inelegant and individualistic, and no qualms about getting wet, even dunked, having been theologically prepared at an early age for immersion in cold water.

I soon lost all the original flies in trees and deep snags. The fly-line itself cracked like old leather. Eventually, the rod broke. Only the reel remains. I still use it and I still fish much same way I did at twelve. Fly-fishermen and fisherwomen are a common sight on Carolina trout streams these days. Most look as though they are posing for an L.L. Bean catalog. I recently saw one of these folks talking midstream on a cellphone. I suppose in a few years there will be a fly reel invented that will allow an angler to text message on it, but I won't be buying that reel, because what I love most about my fly reel is its culturally obsolete simplicity. Nothing on it beeps or flashes. Its sole function is to allow line to be taken out and then taken back in, and my Pflueger has done that for forty-two years. I'm not sure how much longer the reel will work, but I do know that when it quits I quit as well. ✍

NOODLIN' AND CANOODLIN'

Pat Robertson

CANOODLE: *V.* KISS AND CUDDLE AMO-ROUSLY —*Oxford Complete Word Finder*

NOODLE: *V.* THE ART OF FISHING WITH YOUR HANDS —*www.catfishgrabblers.com*

Ol' Carroll felt the catfish first, and then invited me to move in and put my hands on the big cat's head. I slid in beside him in the waist deep water and let my hands explore the opening in the bank, a foot and a half beneath the surface of the water. The fish's head was more than I could hold in one hand, so I hooked my fingers in the gill flaps and tried to pry its mouth open so I could slip my thumbs in for a better grip. The huge catfish was having none of that and clenched his jaws.

Ol' Carroll—and I called him that because he

was three or four years older than me—had quit school to spend his time squirrel and possum hunting and fishing. I had no intention of quitting school, but when I got home from school in the afternoons I often joined Ol' Carroll in his pursuits. On this warm, spring day, when I was perhaps all of fourteen or fifteen, we were catching catfish—by hand. Carroll called it "gravelin'," and later I would learn that in other regions this unique fishing sport was often called noodling or grappling.

That spring in the early Fifties we were not so much concerned about what it was called, but the results it produced. Carroll and I would go to a certain pasture where a deep ditch dug off the Middle Tyger River provided a water source for the cows that grazed there. The catfish loved this ditch and had wallowed out pockets all along its banks to hide in. In the spring catfish move into shallow water to spawn. The females look for sheltered locations to deposit their eggs, and the holes and depressions in the bank of the ditch provided ideal spawning areas. After the females deposit their eggs, the males come in to guard them. They will stay in the nest to aerate the eggs and protect them from predators until the eggs hatch into fry and the fry leave.

I am sure gravelin', or noodlin', has been around since man first discovered how good fresh-caught catfish taste. All it takes is enough bravado to reach into underwater holes and grab the fish with your bare hands. We usually returned home from an afternoon of gravelin' with a croaker sack half full of eating-sized catfish.

Noodling is not for sissies, says fishing writer Bob Bledsoe. This, he writes in the *Oklahoma Game & Fish Magazine*, "is *mano y mano* fishing—grabbing catfish from their dens or spawning lairs by hand and wrestling them to the surface … Stories abound about noodlers encountering beavers, snapping turtles, snakes and other terrors. I've never actually talked to a noodler who has been bitten by anything other than catfish while noodling, but I've known several noodlers over the years whose wrists and forearms were scarred by wounds received while wrestling a big flathead."

I was still holding the catfish in the hole with both hands, while Carroll surveyed the situation. Finally, he decided the fish was too big for us to wrestle out of the hole entirely from the front.

"I'll climb up on the bank and punch a hole down to the fish and grab it by the tail," he said. So, I held on while he dug the hole and then reached for the fish.

When Carroll grabbed the catfish's tail, the big cat decided it was time to leave his hole. He burst out of the hole, slamming me out of the way and into the opposite bank. His slick skin slipped easily through my grasping hands and he swam down the ditch and to freedom.

On the way home that afternoon I thought long and hard about this sport of gravelin'. That hole in the bank or any of the other holes I had bravely thrust my bare hands into time and time again, I surmised, could just as easily have held a mad muskrat or an angry moccasin.

> I am sure gravelin', or noodlin', has been around since man first discovered how good fresh-caught catfish taste.

The next time Ol' Carroll came by and wanted to go gravelin', I remembered a big pile of homework that I had to get done. My noodlin' days were over.

A year or two later I turned sixteen and took up a much more enjoyable pastime—canoodling. ✍

HOW GOOSE GOT HIS NAME
Charles Henry Sowell

GOOSE GOT HIS NAME ON THE WEST FORK OF CHATTOOGA RIVER, OVER IN GEORGIA WHERE THINGS CAN GET TESTY. IT HAPPENED YEARS AGO ON THE OPENING DAY OF TROUT SEASON, APRIL FOOL'S DAY.

Appropriate, all things considered.

Goose, known as Carter to his mother and various Baptist relatives scattered around the Great Pee Dee Swamp near Florence, was a lanky kid nearing his twenty-fifth birthday when we ventured into the wilds of East Georgia in search of rainbow trout. He came from Baptist Missionary stock, a rock-solid background that tends to produce saints of distinction and hell-raising kids who attend Clemson University and change majors five or six times before the end of their sophomore year.

If politics makes strange bedfellows, then fly-fishing goes it one better. On the Havilah Babcock scale of strangeness few things could be odder than the twenty-something Clemson grad and a middle-aged Gamecock parked in

streams from one end of the Blue Ridge Escarpment to the other.

We even managed to catch a few fish.

At the time I was making a living as an editor and columnist for an Upstate daily. Carter was just done with Tiger Town; he'd had one summer in Montana wrangling for a fly-fishing outfitter and was torn between taking off for Alaska to catch king-sized salmon, and settling down and marrying the love of his life. Hormones being what they are, the smart money was on marriage and a lifetime of lawn maintenance.

The jaded journalist in me enjoyed jabbing at Carter when we visited various fly-fishing hotspots around Lake Jocassee.

"Are we having fun yet?" Carter screamed to me over the howl of an outboard boat motor as we skipped across the emerald surface of the lake.

"You'll miss all this one day," I screamed back to him, breaking the crust of freezing fog from the bill of my ball cap with numb fingers. It was mid-February, and sane people everywhere in the Upstate were snug at home, sipping their first cup of coffee as dawn broke over the frosted mountains.

"No I won't!" Carter shouted. Pinching his cheek between thumb and forefinger, he continued, "How do you tell if you're getting frostbite?"

I glanced over at my junior partner. Carter's face had a ruddy sandblasted sheen; his lips were a healthy blue color and frozen tears crusted his eyelashes. "You're doing great!" I shouted. "The big 'bows ought to be stacked like cordwood up the Horsepasture."

Carter looked more than just dubious before he ducked his head to ride out the rest of the trip shivering behind the windscreen of our rented powerboat.

Amazingly enough, the big rainbows *were* stacked at the mouth of Horsepasture that morning and for the next couple of days, too.

There is nothing like trout straight from the rod to the pan for breakfast. Fish so fresh they're wiggling when you plunk them down to fry in hot, melted butter. A tasty breakfast serves to lessen the impact of minor discomforts, even major ones.

The scenery at the mouth of that river is nothing less than spectacular—at least it was once the fog lifted and we got our first good look at the swinging bridge that carries the Foothills Trail over Horsepasture.

"So, what's next on our fishing agenda?" Carter asked, admiring the bridge in the late afternoon sunlight as we sedately motored back to the main landing on Jocassee after two days in a gray cotton hell.

"Oh, I don't know," I said, carefully rubbing my frostbitten cheek. "I've heard there's some good fishing on the West Fork of Chattooga."

Carter looked at me strangely. "That's in Georgia," he said in a tone that suggested a need for Sherpa porters.

"It's not the far side of the moon," I said in a chiding voice. "Where's your sense of adventure? What would your uncle say?"

Carter's uncle had been the subject of long, passionate campfire discourses during our two nights on the river. An Albert Schweitzer-like figure, the missionary uncle had braved the mysteries of the African veldt and come out singing "Onward Christian Soldiers."

"Oh, yeah," Carter muttered and snuggled down behind the windshield. "I'll let you know."

A secret smile tweaked at the corners of my mouth. Carter didn't know it, but he'd already let me know.

Onward Christian soldiers.

*   *   *

The great American expatriate poet T.S. Eliot knew a thing or two about April. In his epic *The Waste Land*, he wrote:

"April is the cruelest month, breeding
Lilacs out of the dead land, mixing
Memory and desire, stirring
Dull roots with spring rain."

April also stirs those who are old enough to know better and those too young to know much of anything with the prospect of rising fish at the end of a winter-long respite in the wilds of East Georgia.

East Georgia's mountain wilderness has problems that challenge the most seasoned fly-fishermen, issues unique to the hinterlands of Atlanta's suburbs, like half-million dollar condos made out of old barns and throngs of would-be trout fishermen being ferried in and out of the best spots on the river by the Georgia Department of Natural Resources' shuttle bus service.

Being the purists that we were, Carter and I eschewed the mall promenade crowd down by the Highway 28 bridge and made our way upstream to the unsullied waters found about thirty yards off Highway 28 on a graveled Forest Service access road where the West Fork and the main branch of the Chattooga meet.

Carter examined the vacant parking area with a troubled look on his face.

"Sure is quiet here," he said as I hastened to assemble my fly rod.

I paused for a moment. All that was audible was the burble of the Chattooga and a strange hissing and clacking sound. "Sure is," I said with admirable wilderness fortitude. "There's nothing like getting away from the crowd to find some good fishing."

Carter lollygagged for several minutes, putting his rod together and settling into his waders.

When we stepped off the bank and into the West Fork we were confronted with at least a gaggle and a half of geese—big, honking Canada geese that watched us with little beady black eyes and sullen expressions.

"You start with this pool," I told Carter, generously letting my junior partner have a go at the primo water. "I'll ease on upstream."

Carter shot me a look of surprise. Generosity has its rewards.

"We'll leapfrog one another. Watch where I step in, and when you get to that spot, step out of the river and go around me," I told him, explaining the strategy.

I left Carter to deal with the geese and scurried upstream about eighty yards. Stepping into the Chattooga, I watched Carter gingerly ease around the raft of geese that were hogging the middle of the stream. Waterfowl have no sense of sportsmanship.

The big birds bobbed their heads and watched Carter intently. Faintly, over the burble of the river, I could hear a clacking and hissing sound but dismissed any concerns about Carter dealing with the geese. After all, he was from missionary stock and could handle anything nature chose to dish out.

I'd just caught and released a small rainbow when I heard Carter's shout.

"Charlie, check it out!"

My friend was hard against the right-hand bank of the stream. Surging upstream, about five feet above the water, was the whole gaggle and a half of geese. They took up the entire center and left-hand side of the river, landing and spreading out in an arc between Carter and me.

Carter looked upstream to me with a pleading expression in his eyes. With no regard for my own safety, I indicated with hand signals that Carter should get out of the river and come to me.

He nodded and I sat down on a rock at midstream to watch him avoid the feathered flotilla.

"I will show you fear in a handful of dust," Eliot wrote in *The Waste Land*. He may as well have added "or in the beady eyes of a gander."

Distantly, downstream from Carter, a gray-feathered dart whizzed upstream. My partner's attention was focused on the birds in the water, and he didn't notice the winged missile headed for his head. Before I could shout a warning, the big gander clipped Carter in the back of the head, nearly knocking him down, sending his cap skittering into the water, and dashing his fly rod to the bottom of the stream. The gander gracefully landed in the water to the hissing and bobbing applause of his compatriots.

Unseemly though it may be, the airborne gander attack elicited several gusts of laughter from me as I watched Carter retrieve his hat and fetch his rod from the river bottom.

The winged hero was the focus of excessive amounts of female goose adoration, lots of head bobbing and hissing, which the gander received with due modesty. Carter, by now, had his sopping wet hat perched back on his head and his rod in hand. He started edging his way upstream against the right-hand bank, having ignored my sage advice to get the hell out of the river.

He'd nearly gotten past the raft of birds when the attack gander spotted him and lowered its head in a hissing challenge.

Befuddled, Carter froze in place.

As the rest of the gaggle urged him on, the gander started a charge across the river to attack Carter again. The gander became airborne about halfway across the stream. Carter leaned back into the laurel-choked bank in fear.

With an open mouth and an outstretched neck the gander closed in for the kill.

It was not looking good for my Tiger Town fishing buddy.

Just as the gander was about to strike again, Carter's missionary genes cut in; he dropped his rod and met the bird's beak with a perfect right cross.

The gander hit the water like a sack of wet rice.

In an extraordinary show of fly-fishing solidarity, I slid off the rock and let my waders fill with icy water as my gusts of laughter filled the air.

The gaggle and a half of geese silently set sail downstream to beleaguer us no more that extraordinary day.

Later, as Carter dried his hat over a smoky fire, I dubbed him forevermore to be the "Goose of West Fork," a nod to the American Indian tradition of naming people for the animals that most closely resemble them in spirit.

There is nothing like trout straight from the rod to the pan for breakfast.

FLY-FISHING AND THE ART OF A WOMAN'S HEALING

Emma Chisolm

EVERY ARTIST NEEDS A MUSE, AND THROUGHOUT LIFE, THROUGHOUT ONE'S GROWTH AND CHANGES, MUSES COME AND GO.

They appear in different forms and aspects, in music, in nature, in books, in paintings, in friends and lovers, even in a beloved sister's dying. They appear in cats and dogs, in rainbow trout, in summer flowers and winter's snow and ice. They're constantly around us but we must learn to sense their presence, and to do that we have to transcend the mundane earthly things of this life and allow ourselves to lift into oneness with the spirit-world.

I've always given my heart too soon and too quickly but it's always been impossible not to. I have as much love in me to give out and share as there are bubbles in all the soap jars and bubble baths known to womankind. It's like daily I dip my wand into the soapy foam and blow gently to see where my heart's going to go this morning, this day. It's the way I've learned to live in the Now. It's my Zen metaphor for Life.

I know it's important to listen and be aware of all the signals that come one's way, that point to change in direction or manner of being. But sometimes they have to pound me over the head to get my real and steady attention. Like with fly-fishing. And how all this magical plunge into a world of living, shining, glistening, rainbow-hued Christmas ornaments that I can hold for a moment in my hand and then let go—only to know that forever and ever I can hold such glory yet again in my hand— came about.

The Cruel Fairy Tale

It all started a year ago when I was tricked out of my house by my husband and his three wicked boys. It's the stuff of fairy tales. Childhood stories are full of violence and wickedness but somehow in the end the princess is spirited up to a place of safety and protection, far above the tawdriness she left behind. And that's what happened to me. Blessings, first disguised as, and then discovered in, misfortune, have become my abundance. And the husband got his comeuppance, too, for he died. And those red-headed, spotty-cheeked boys are aging terribly, sporting lined faces that look haunted and haggard, framed now with white hair and paunched bellies. Signs that assure me that from the inside they're being eaten alive. Which is fine by me. The worst part of it all is the lawyers, of course, and the money or lack of it. But that's where the Zen comes in now for me, and how fly-fishing has come to be my spirit-healer.

I walk the woods a lot now, following old trails up the mountain, trails that wind alongside the river. Occasionally I pass other hikers but I'm always alone. Deep in thought, I'm content and peaceful, wrapped in the dark green leaves of my laurel thicket—"laurel hell" as it's called by the locals up here. Sometimes I pass familiar faces. We recognize each other and have eye talk, but very little conversation. But yesterday as I was walking up and they were walking down, I overheard one say to the other, "Every time we see her there're tears drying in her eyes." And we all kept walking.

The tears are always hot but rarely now do they burn a trail down my cheeks. They usually just well up behind my eyeballs and seep out in little eyedrop squeezes. I know they take my eyes from clear-water to smoky-blue because I've seen the change myself. For me it's a natural occurrence and one that happens so frequently and so expectedly that I'm no longer aware of the tears themselves, only the hot lava building up behind my brow. That's why I know that what they were saying is true. And though the tears represent my own personal and cumulative sorrows, they are, even more, an atavistic response to the deep abiding sorrows of all life, more so than mine own in particular.

But ironically, that's a happy thought, as Jane Austen would say. At least it is once I've begun to wrap my mind around it. Because that's the point when I begin to take control, when I begin to take those tears, those sorrows, and make something else out of them. That's when I begin to create something that did not exist before from my experience, my sorrow. That's when I follow Merlin's advice to the young King Arthur: When you find your heart broken, it's time to learn something new.

So that's the first curve in the path of how I came to fly-fishing. Through my tears and sorrows. And a new job that required me to write about fly-fishing. Big fly-fishing. About which I knew nothing. Never been fishing in my life, thought of it as boring, as in who in the world would ever want to sit on a hard little hot boat seat in the sun and catch smelly fish when they could be doing—well, almost anything else on earth.

And that's when I met my Muse.

Now, as I've said before, Muses come in all shapes and sizes and peculiarities. What I haven't said is that they're usually dangerous to me because my full-bodied woman's heart likes to fall in love with them. And that's so utterly reasonable from my point of view, the artist's point of view, because it's all based on *passion*. Without passion nothing gets created, nothing happens, it all stays the same. So my Muse need never worry that I'm falling in love with *him*. It's all part of the story, the journey. It's all part of the song. I want my Muse to play me like the fish: reel me in and then let me run—but don't net me up and bring me to shore.

Big Medicine

Before I ever got to the river, though, I had at least to be conversant with the sport of fly-fishing. So my good Muse took me on and with lots of patience and even more forbearance brought me from totally ignorant to only partially so. I thought of fly-fishing as a dance, with rhythm and grace—sort of like rhumba and tango combined. But in reality my first attempts resembled a classic spinout gone wrong, for the line and my forearm tangled up in what can only be called every fisherman's nightmare—the dreaded "bird's nest." But, with time, Grace prevailed; and Simon, with his gentle forbearance, forbore. And I began to take my first steps out of Piscean darkness into the bright confusion of too much to think about and do and coordinate all together. My admiration and awe of the sport and sportsman went from zero to sixty in a heartbeat.

And I was hooked. I had to learn it. I had to learn to be good at it. I had to take all this pent-up energy and channel it into a four-count rhythm of God … SAVE … the …. Queen. And I had to set the hook and place the fly gently over there in the darkest corner just underneath the bank. Did I get there? Well not wholly yet, but at least I got a couple of "Perfect! Good cast!" interspersed with lots of silences and "will you stop *waving* the rod!" One thing, though, about being a woman who knows heartbreak—I don't give up easily.

On the River

As we headed to the river, my heart grew more and more tremulous. My throat was dry and my blood thumped a strange rhythm and I was seriously nervous. I didn't want to get in that river and be wooden. I longed for the natural rhythm and grace I saw in my imagination to electrify my body. But as Churchill reminds us, nothing worthwhile is easy. Especially fly-fishing for the very first time in the presence of and under the tutelage of a seriously profound and expert teacher. Who was fast taking the shape of a Muse.

But to misquote Macbeth, I knew I might as well get on with it. I'd already come this far. It was equidistant to go back and I'd be throwing away

everything I'd learned and earned along the way. So I let go of fear. I swallowed it whole (along with lots of pride) and turned toward the river bank with Simon—and the sweet brown rocky bed of Looking Glass Creek.

"You honor a trout when you give him a good fight," Simon said, opening the secret compartment in the back of his truck, pulling out a clear vial tinted with Woodford Creek Kentucky bourbon and anointing his tobacco. "God made this world the way He wanted it to be," he continued, positioning the tobacco somewhere in his mouth, I couldn't be sure where, trying hard to listen and watch and think at the same time, and to not be unduly curious at the same time. "It's not cruel—no, it's not—" he said to my quick look. "Rather it's the way He meant it to be. It's the dynamic He wanted to exist between his creatures, between man and beast. It's all good." And he put the golden vial back into its secret compartment.

"Now get on down here—you're in Simon's Southern Appalachian Spirit-Fishing Place and we're gonna try (a bit of emphasis on the 'try,' I noticed) to catch some fish. These little trout, they're like lightning—quicksilver in a race to the moon. Introduced here at some time by some unknown fisherman. They're not native, but they've adapted to their environment. Beautiful little things but elusive and very, very quick—you'll see."

And I did see. How quick and how beautiful they were. For when Simon caught one, he gently pried the hook out and held the translucent rainbow in his hands long enough for me to see the pinks and lavenders and silvers, the orange fins, and the gills, on the bigger ones, turning from silver to champagne. Then he gently slid the fish back into the water where it was off like a shot.

I never did catch one of the little darters, but little did it matter to me then. I was spellbound by where I was and what I was doing and feeling. Simon, quietly from behind, corrected my cast, and just as quietly adjusted my over-informed eyes and brain by reminding me to roll or drop cast to avoid an overhanging branch in our upward wading progress. We'd walk and cast, walk and cast. I loved being in the water in felt-bottomed boots, learning to feel secure on the slippery rocks as we walked against the current. Though I thought I would have been just as happy sitting on the rocks watching Simon cast and catch, every now and then coming over with a bejeweled offering to show me.

But in the end naturally it was more fun to join in with the dance, for truth be told, I've never been much good at spectator sports. And once I began to feel the rhythm of the sport, my confidence grew. And once my confidence grew, I found myself forgetting myself, which was a good thing, though Simon still persisted in warning me "not to wave that thing around."

I loved learning to skim the fly across the water in the still waters, learning to spot the little wisp of fluff that looked like every other piece of floating detritus in the ruffled waters. I learned to lift the rod tip and re-cast before the fly tumbled over the spills. I tried to put the fly where Simon told me to, and wished for months of aiming at pie pans before having to do the real thing.

"Follow that line of bubbles over there. Now, cast between the white shoals into that tongue of quiet." Leaning into the rod, I tried to dance to his calls.

I loved the sweetness of it all. The quietness. The companionship. The relaxed but tense awareness of being ready for the moment when it came. But I never hooked one of those six-inch quick-silvered rainbow trout. Somehow they just wouldn't nip the fly and then gently jerk the line to say, "OK now, quickly lift your wrist and get me." There were still too many synapse-gaps between my brain and my fly arm. But the adventure and spirit of it all had begun—and I loved it.

Sharing the Words

When the fishing was over and the day was waning, we made our way back to the truck.

Took off our boots and socks. Because Simon (gentleman that he is) had offered to his neophyte his own neoprene socks, and she'd accepted them unabashedly, his toes were red wizened nubs. Mine were silky dry and smooth. I felt really bad. But I hadn't known any better. Simon nonchalantly wrapped his feet up in the white bar towels he had in the back of the truck, pulled out his fishing chair and picked up one of the books he'd had stashed on the dashboard all day. I sat on the tailgate of his truck. He asked me if I'd brought *A River Runs Through It* with me. I said as a matter of fact I had. And pulled it out from my bag.

He opened it and began reading aloud.

"Now nearly all those I loved and did not understand when I was young are dead, but I still reach out to them … and a four-count rhythm and the hope that a fish will rise. … Eventually, all things merge into one, and a river runs through it. … I am haunted by waters."

When cars passed by he'd stop and wait. When they'd gone by us I leaned forward so as to hear every word, to hear his voice say the words he'd read to his heart over and over and over again; to hear his voice read them to me, as if for the first time in eternity. Like it probably was once … in the Garden of Eden.

Tears came to my eyes. I tried to squeeze them away. By now, gentle Reader, you know that I cry easily and obviously, and but what you may not know yet is that I'll cry at the same passages that move me over and over again, each time I read them. And I'd already cried at those parts Simon was reading me now because I'd read them on my own. Cried by myself, with myself. So no wonder I cried again now, with him reading those words to me. For I'll ask you, oh most discerning Reader, how

> I want my Muse to play me like the fish: reel me in and then let me run— but don't net me up and bring me to shore.

long has it been since someone who was ONE with the WORDS read such words aloud to you? Believe me, when it happens—stop, acquiesce, and give yourself over to humbleness and tears, all to the sweetening of your soul.

There by the tailgate of Simon's truck, head to head, heart to heart with the words, my Muse imparted to me his spirit. I was hushed and quiet. Wouldn't even breathe while he was reading lest I miss a word, a turn of the phrase. For the moment we'd first been on that river together, albeit totally unequally matched, we were kindred spirits. And our hearts knew it, rejoiced in it, and reveled in the daring sweetness of this moment when we could share words about the river—as well as the river itself.

Departure

Once Simon's feet had resumed normal color, we packed our things and made our way back down the mountain. Not much was said on the way home. I had way too much to think about. Simon's phone rang with problems from work. I was able to Zen my way back to Looking Glass Creek while he talked plane fares and schedules. I felt exhilarated, released, wildly free and happy. I'd been received and blessed by the Southern Appalachian Spirit-World and would never be quite the same again.

At the parking lot where we parted ways, I touched the forearm of my Muse and thanked him. I wished him Godspeed on his journey to a faraway country. And if I never see my Gospel River-Muse again, my heart will always hold him fast in the moment—the moment he shared with me his Southern Appalachian Spirit-Fishing Place on Looking Glass Creek. And taught me to love and honor the graceful sport of fly-fishing. He passed on the great baton. Soon enough, now, it's going to be my turn. With gratitude, I thank you, Simon, Fly-Fisherman Extraordinaire. The healing has begun.

HUNTING

Rob Brown

J. Drew Lanham

Hunter Bridges

John Faris Jr.

HUNTING MAGNOLIA
Rob Brown

I LONG FOR WILDERNESS—THE KIND OF PLACE YOU EXPECT TO FIND LEWIS AND CLARK OR JIM BRIDGER, SOMEWHERE WITH VERY FEW FOOTPRINTS BUT A GREAT MANY GAME TRAILS.

I love wide prairies, forest covered mountainsides, whitewater trout streams, rolling hills, salt marshes, slow moving black-water rivers—all of them underneath a clear night sky, unobscured by city lights. I long for wilderness, but what I have is access to two hundred and fifty acres on the Pacolet River and an occasional invitation to hunt on a friend's property in southern Spartanburg County.

When I was a child, a drive down Highway 56 was a trip into the country. Farmers on tractors and logging trucks carrying cut timber slowed traffic to a crawl. My father, who was not usually the most patient of men, never seemed to mind. He took the added time to tell me stories about his childhood—kicking up quail along the fencerows of his uncle's farm in McCormick or working the horses his own father kept down in Britton's Neck near the Great Pee Dee River.

The slower pace of our country drives appealed to him, and I could feel him relaxing as we got farther away from town, one arm propped on the open window of our old Ford Falcon, the other draped across the steering wheel. With cigarette in hand, he pointed out the progress of the crops that grew alongside the road and disparaged the spread of kudzu. He smiled a lot on those drives and was even prone to laugh out loud at his own stories. It was like he was exhaling tension along with his cigarette smoke.

Some forty years later, Highway 56 is still only two lanes wide, but the journey now has a more manicured feel. New homes and businesses have marched south to the intersection with Highway 215. A Dollar General sits near another intersection, and you can buy designer coffee at the corner store. But farther out, there are still remnants of the rural world of my youth.

On a Sunday afternoon in early November, I drive south with my son Zach. He is a year away from entering college, and I know these trips will soon become rare. It's the kind of fall day people describe as crisp—a hint of cold in the air mixed with the smell of smoke from woodstoves and fireplaces and leaf piles being burned. A few miles below Pauline, we pull off the road and stop at the entrance to the Magnolia Tract. It belongs to my friend George, and to fit the name he has planted magnolia trees on either side of the gate. They are still young trees, but I can see them one day standing tall with waxy green leaves and broad white blossoms. We wait at the gate for Wayne, who manages the property. A moment later he drives up and unlocks the gate, swinging it wide for us to drive through, then locks it behind us. Wayne is a tall man with glasses and a graying beard, and he is fast to smile. He is ready for us to hunt and moves with quick efficiency.

Getting out of the truck I tell Zach, "Get your things ready, son."

Stepping up beside us, Wayne grins at me as he speaks. "I ain't never heard of no preacher huntin' on Sunday. You Episcopalians must be a little different."

I try not to rise to the bait but can't help encouraging a little back-and-forth. "Well, you know preachers only work two hours a week and that's just Sunday morning. As long as my assistant covers tonight's youth group, I'm free."

Prodding a bit more, Wayne says, "I thought a man was supposed to rest on the Lord's Day? Maybe spend the day in prayer and con-tem-play-shun?"

"The Book says, 'The Sabbath was made for man, not man for the Sabbath,'" I say, smiling. "Actually Jesus said that. Now, you don't want me arguing with Jesus, do you? Besides, the best praying I do is while I'm sitting in the woods."

His look changes a bit and is serious for just a moment as he meets my eyes and nods. "I know what you mean."

We walk around to the front of Wayne's truck. "I'm gonna put the boy in Number One. It's right down this dirt road here on the right." Turning to my son, he says, "Zach you're gonna walk about two hundred and fifty yards. You'll see the road curving just a bit and then there'll be food plots on both sides. Mostly winter wheat and some rye and maybe some clover. The stand is gonna let you see down both those food plots and the short pines on the edges. Deer been working out o' those pines before dark and into the food plots. A buck's gotta be eight and outside, but we need to take some does. So if you get a shot, fire away. Any questions?"

"No sir," Zach says.

"Awright then, I'll be back after dark."

"Where is my dad going to be?" Zach asks him.

Wayne nods to the left and gestures with the bill of his cap. "You see that ridge with all them oaks?"

"Yes, sir."

"He's gonna be up there. Y'all are gonna be about a half-mile apart. So if you both get lucky, you'll hear each other shoot."

Zach grins, shakes Wayne's hand, shoulders his rifle, and starts walking. We watch as he disappears around the bend. "He's a good boy," Wayne says.

"Thanks," I answer. "Now, how do I get to that ridge you mentioned?"

"You see how the road bears off to the left from the main gate?" he says, pointing. "Follow that on around those pine trees and you'll start headin' downhill. There's a bit of gravel but it'll peter out as you reach the bottom of the hill. When you get to the bottom there'll be a culvert and a bridge across a small creek. Head up the hill from there and you're gonna be walking into the hardwoods. Lotsa oak and maple. That's what's givin' that hillside all that red and gold right now."

As Wayne talks I look toward the ridge, an explosion of color in the middle of a sea of pine trees. The dark tones of the evergreens are like shadows all about the feet of tall oaks and maples and the occasional beech. There is a slight breeze stirring the leaves.

"As you go up the hill, keep your eyes open for an old tumble-down chimblee off on the left," Wayne adds. "It'll look like a pile of rock but you oughta be able to make out the hearth. It's still black from the fires it held. After the chimblee you'll come to the flat at the top and that road is gonna keep winding on past the old graveyard. It's on the left too, but you don't wanna go that far. There's a big oak you can't reach around about a hundred and fifty yards before you get to the graveyard, and the stand is right in front of the oak. It's a tower so you oughta be comfortable."

"Sounds good. Thanks." I like the way Wayne says "chimblee." It reminds me of when I was a boy and the older folks pronounced "Mrs." as "Miz Riz." It sounds warmer and less modern—less homogenous.

"I seen deer tracks crossing between the stand and the graveyard. The rut's still on so anything's possible, and there's plenty of acorns to hold 'em along that roadbed. I think you should take your truck on around the corner a ways and park it behind some trees."

"Are you going to hunt?" I ask.

"Nope, gonna do a little tractor work on the other side of the property."

I smile. "You think you ought to be working on Sunday?"

"Ain't hardly work in the new tractor," he says, grinning. "Got an enclosed cab, heatin' and air conditionin', and a stereo. Hell, at my age that's better'n sex."

"I can't believe you said that to a man of the cloth," I joke.

With a smile he gets in his truck, says, "Good luck," and pulls away.

I get back in my truck, too, and drive left until I find a small stand of trees where my vehicle is safely out of sight. I get out, check the pockets of my jacket to make sure I have everything, drape binoculars around my neck, pick up my rifle, and start walking. As I ease down the old roadbed I keep an eye out for movement. It's still early afternoon, but during the rut deer can move at any time. There are tracks crisscrossing the road at regular intervals. Clearly, the deer are moving back and forth from bedding to feeding areas. I hope the deer are still farther back in the woods and unaware of me moving toward a prime feeding area. It is a common practice in the Upstate to plant food plots to supplement natural browse, but given a choice, deer will choose acorns over just about anything else.

I stop at the bottom of the hill and examine the banks leading down into the creek. There are tracks in the soft mud—deer, raccoon, and what looks like coyote. Coyotes are a growing problem in the Upstate and in some places you can hear them howling like they are on a South Dakota prairie. It is a wild sound and I love it, but I know they are too good a predator for the turkeys and fawns of the Carolinas.

The road curves gently left then right as I slowly walk up the hill. Just-fallen leaves rustle underfoot and it's an effort not to make too much noise. I pass quickly out of sunlight into shadow and the temperature noticeably drops. Glancing left and right, I see a long, stretched-out line of rock scattered across the ground and realize I have found the chimney. The large stones are covered here and there with patches of moss, and stooping down I can see the soot-blackened hearthstones. I run my fingers across the rock, but hundred-year-old soot doesn't rub off. At some point in time, a farmhouse stood on this hillside with a fine view down to the creek. No doubt the oaks around me had been saplings then. It has been a long time since a fire burned in the chimney.

I pause when I reach the top of the hill. The scene is beautiful: the leaf-covered road meanders among tall trees in a long arc that curves past a cluster of old headstones before it disappears into the distance. Except in the graveyard, heavy woods stand a thick dark watch no more than ten or fifteen yards back from the road edge.

The deer stand is exactly where Wayne had said it would be and offers a clear line of sight in three directions. It's about twelve feet up to the floor of the camouflaged fabric-sided box blind. The bench seat puts you about three feet higher and gives you an even better view. I climb up and in, load my rifle, and take a first look at my surroundings through the binoculars.

It generally takes a while for the woods to calm down after a person has walked through. No matter how quiet we think we have been, it is impossible not to announce our presence with every footfall. Add to that our human scent, and we are sending out a powerful warning that the planet's most successful predator is nearby. A successful hunter plays the wind and counts on stealth and more than a little luck.

Ten minutes pass, then twenty, and finally thirty. My well-equipped pockets include a paperback book and my journal, filled with observations from dozens of other journeys to the woods. The paperback is just the latest in a long line of "something to read in the woods that will fit in my jacket," usually a collection of outdoor essays, or poetry, or the occasional devotional. I set my rifle aside and read, glancing up every minute or so to look down the road and to either side.

A sound catches my attention, a light crunch from the woods on my left. Even though my head is covered with a camouflage mask, I turn very slowly and carefully. At first I see nothing, and then, stepping out of the shadows at the base of an oak is a doe. She hasn't the slightest inkling I am there and is eating acorns. The

sound was not a stepped-on fallen leaf, but the crunching of acorns as she chews. As I watch, another doe moves in the shadows, and then another. Soon six deer are moving and eating along the wood line beside the stand.

I have doe tags, but I am waiting for a buck. It is a rare thing to get to hunt this property, and I have heard rumors of big bucks equal to anything on the Outdoor Channel.

Over the next two hours deer move all around me, even through the graveyard. At one point I watch a young spike buck stand and seem to read the headstones over the waist-high metal fence that surrounds the little family cemetery. The graves are old, and some of the markers are cracked and broken; others are so worn you can only make out a letter or two. In some places you can't see any markers, just indentations in the ground where wooden caskets have obviously decayed, causing the ground above to collapse.

As the afternoon passes and the sun moves toward setting, it becomes colder. I shift a bit in order to reach my gloves, and that's when I see him. He has crossed the road behind me, taking advantage of the one blind spot in my field of view. His walk is heavy and stiff legged.

"He's gonna be up there. Y'all are gonna be about a half-mile apart. So if you both get lucky, you'll hear each other shoot."

His hide and fur show signs of battle. The fur is turned up and ragged in a few patches, and one of his brow tines is broken off an inch or two above the base. Bucks fight for dominance during the rut. The winners get to breed the does. He walks like he won.

I place the crosshairs of my scope on his shoulder and follow him as he paces toward a stand of short pines and heavy brush. I easily see his antlers, and he more than meets the eight-points and outside-the-ears rule. The buck pauses, lifts his head, and sniffs the air. His big head turns left, then right, and he stands absolutely still. My gaze ranges over him, and I notice the swag in his back and his heavy shoulders, the Roman nose and sagging belly. He is old, very old for a Piedmont deer. A six- or seven-year-old deer is old anywhere, but in Upstate South Carolina it is like watching a ninety-five-year-old man stroll through the woods.

His tail flicks and he lowers his head, only to quickly raise it again. He's winded me, I think, and click off the safety. But he continues to stand still and is now looking behind him. A doe moves out of the woods and begins nibbling on the grassy verge. My big buck is old, but I know as I watch him that the magic of the rut still inspires hope for one more conquest, one more opportunity to propagate his line.

The doe moves up to him and passes, paying him no attention at all. *A bit of an insult to the old gentleman and a definite challenge*, I think.

I click the safety back on and watch—not out of sympathy so much as respect. If he had one more in him, who was I to stand in the way? I sit still as he follows her into the brush. They both disappear.

✻   ✻   ✻

It is a powerful thing to have life and death in your hands. I take a deep breath of the cold air. It feels good and carries with it the smells of fall—pine, smoke, and the dusty odor of fallen leaves. The hunt is always about more than the kill. I put down my gun and take out my journal. I write down all I can remember about those country drives with my father. I make notes about my son who is sitting just half a mile away, waiting and watching with the intensity of youth. I write about fallen chimneys and old deer and why I wish for woods untouched by man and what I think is waiting there.

I long for wilderness, and perhaps in the tame woods of South Carolina I can still find a vestige, a hint of what I need. After all, for the Israelites, wilderness was as much a state of mind as a place. It was where they went to encounter God. 🖎

HUNTING DEER IN BROKEN COUNTRY

J. Drew Lanham

THE PIEDMONT IS BROKEN COUNTRY. FOR THE MOST PART, ONLY FRAGMENTS OF THINGS REMAIN. MANY OF ITS FORESTS ARE ISLANDS IN THE MIDST OF THINGS MOSTLY UNNATURAL.

There are pieces of what used to be: a sliver of swamp here, a remnant of woodland there, a sea of suburbia everywhere. The wild things that call the midland places home must by necessity be comfortable at the transitions between nature and be able to survive in the perforated landscape lying between the mountains and the sea.

Whitetail deer are the quintessential edge beings. Endlessly adaptable, they were once a rarity after almost being hunted out in the early parts of the twentieth century. After successful restoration efforts, they are everywhere now. The in-between places so abundant in the Piedmont seem to favor the species. Rats do not rate poetry, and many see *Odecoileus virginianus* as not much more than the hoofed version of such. Breeding at prodigious rates, eating expensive shrubbery, and driving insurance rates higher

with their jaywalking indiscretions, they warrant admiration in the eyes of a diminishing few.

But for those who are willing to see the wild superlatives beyond the plight of a pest, there is much to admire. The almost infinite plasticity of adaption means that whitetail deer live in tropical forests, deserts, mountains, swamps, farms, and inner cities. They are super-beings, bounding and leaping and running and smelling and hearing better than almost any other wild thing. And then there is the super sense of prescience. They know you are there before you arrive— know where you are likely to be before you decide to go. Most of the admirers are hunters, like me. We arise early, stay late, and most often leave the whitetail woods with the deer still alive and one day wiser to our ways than when we arrived.

And so I hunt for deer in the bits and pieces of habitat that are left because in many ways the species represents wildness in a place where humans have tried their best to do away with it. It is hunting on these edges where I find me while looking for something else. It is a quest, not for killing but rather for life that takes me into the broken places.

October 9

The evening pursuit begins as I chase the westering sun to beat the night. It is the transition, the golden time of shape-shifting and light-play. The sun is sifting through legions of loblolly and burnishing the languishing leaves of the hardwoods when I step off the little dead-end dirt road through a wall of woods—and disappear into the deer world. My attempt at moving stealthily along the old logging trail now tunneled in with trees and carpeted with crispy, drought-dry leaf fall is folly. Despite my best efforts the try is really more riot, and the wary surely hear the heavy footfall fracturing the silence. The deer folk await dusk, chewing cuds in briary beds, and I'm sure their sensitive noses note the olfactory intrusion. They let me pass without snorts or wheezes to warn the woods of my presence. They know that stillness is true stealth. I imagine them lying and looking, waiting for the wrens and cardinals to sing vespers. It will be their time then.

Opposite the morning, when darkness wanes and sight with it, the eve's dying light and falling night press opportunity tightly between shadows. Opportunity likewise tightens within the dreary confines of dusk and dark. A brief breeze rattling rusty red oak leaves sends the scents swirling; the licorice-like aroma of sweet gum mingles with the sharp clean aroma of pine pitch, and my distinctive human stink drifts into flaring nostrils. I climb high to see low, settle in to watch the dayshift go to bed and the night-shift punch in to work. A hermit thrush nestles in somewhere below me, clucking itself softly to sleep. It is more peaceful up here than anywhere I can think of. It is prayer and meditation and supplication—church unlimited by walls or ceilings or guilt. Although I sit in a third-growth forest reclaiming old cotton fields, I don't feel the fracture here. Some might see the loblollies and sweet gum that dominate so much of the Piedmont as poor substitutes for forest, but at least it is not pavement. The squirrels here do not wait for handouts, and the deer find no leisure on manicured lawns here. It is sometimes more home to me than home. Things broken inside me are repaired out here. This wildness, not quite wilderness, is enough for me to know my humanity and the smallness of it.

I sit and wait and watch. Sometimes, it is so peaceful I slip into brief bouts of unconsciousness—and sleep. The cacophony of acorns dropping and squirrels caching their newfound treasures beneath the fresh leaf fall sound like more than that and for a while every scurry is something else. There are moments when the right pattern of scamper, stop, and dig could be something with hooves. In those moments, my heartbeat accelerates, and a spike of adrenaline sends my nerves to a palpable edge. My pulse pounds and my eyes narrow to catch things sliding through the periphery. And then the discovery of what it is not sends every nerve and tension back to a calmer standby.

I sit and wait and watch. My brain somehow finds a different place to be. It is in the present but not the one that connects me to ordinary obligation or mundane duty. It is in the ultimate here—the most precious now. The left-sided regions of my brain bound to calendars and schedules switched off not long after I stepped onto the wooded road. Time now is governed by the sun and the moon. On the journey to the stand, I leave burdens behind and pick up my instincts. Up here I can truly see, honestly hear life beyond my own human heartbeat.

Amidst the birds' and squirrels' last stirrings of the day I hear different sounds as the woods give way to night things. Somewhere down in the creek bottom a barred owl sends shivers along some rodent's narrow spine. A coyote yips and the deer's ears swivel nervously to catch the sound. And then softly, almost imperceptibly within the evening's goings-on, I hear something different—grunts and clicks, strung together like no other animal does. A branch breaking gives away the voice's origins as the deer folk move to the moon rising and the insistence of empty rumen. Nearly unintelligible, totally unmistakable, intriguingly undecipherable—deer talk. This is it.

When "it" happens, when the deer are moving, the awakening instinct clears everything else away, and something deep within the gray matter clicks on. It is my weak human woods-wit against a superior sylvan wisdom that knows infinitely more about this place than I can ever hope to. I accept the challenge, though, in spite of my disadvantage. My instincts to seek and maybe kill within the context of all this peace are as cleanly derived and justified as anything I do. I am at a bare essence of who I am out here. The desire to hunt is a thing born honestly and is deep-seated in the hard-wired brain place that will not allow me to deny it.

The light is decaying and my sight with it. The clicks and grunts pass around me. It is as if I am at an intersection of some ghastly quadrupedal procession. I hear but can't see because the jungle tangle of saplings and vines are dog-hair thick. The brush barely moves and I think I glimpse a flash of gray brown—maybe shoulder, maybe haunch, maybe not. Legal light dies and my hopes with it.

It is another lesson in the deer woods; tonight the same test taken unsuccessfully. Like most forays out here, I fail to kill but succeed to be. I was privy tonight to whitetails whispering and that is enough. The deer folk know the woods and feel it in ways that I never could. They live within the creases of wood shadow and wait on the edge between nerve and instinct. Though they thrive in the brokenness of our Piedmont progress, there will always be wildness in their eyes. Our attempts to foil their wisdom are often folly, success frequently relying on luck more than skill. Trails I follow they abandon. Perfect plans at ambush they outflank. The wood lore engrained in their cervid psyches is something I can never possess. But as night

falls, and deer folk stroll to dinner on moonlit paths, I look forward to the next lesson and another evening's pursuit.

Thanksgiving

To this point the hunting has been just that—hunting, no killing. The bucks and does slip and slither in places where I am not. They sleep during my tree-borne vigils to rest up for love play in the cool moonlight. The tracks and trails, scrapes and scat tease like calling cards. Maybe I'm trying too hard to think like a deer. My study is merely guesswork. The predictions are purely speculation. And so the deer win almost every time, laughing in muffled grunts and guffawing in snorts and wheezes.

Today is a new day and a new experience. It is Thanksgiving week and there is much to be grateful for. Even in the midst of venison drought, the season's first real chill to the bone is respite from a fickle fall—mercury more up than down. Is this the same warming that makes the polar bears sweat and ice caps melt? The cold rain and a crisp north wind have driven the leaves from the brush. The jungle tangle is less so now. Will the game of hide-and-eek now become a little fairer?

The sun rises reluctantly behind a blanket of clouds, and the morning light subtly breaks the mist. There is no gilded dawn-break today but rather the quiet emergence of something less than full day. The brooding morning is heavy with wet and cold—perfect hunting weather. The slender pines are shrouded in the fallen clouds. Some say that they are sad replacements for what should be big timber, but this morning they may as well be giant sequoias bathing in Pacific coast fog. The creation here, today on the old Ninety-Six homeplace, will not likely draw reverence from anyone but me.

The dawn brings the chatter of the morning's first flock—hermit thrushes awakening in half light, the faint flicker of a kinglet's wing, its ruby crown glowing like an ember against the gray day. The whistling warbles of fox sparrows cut the rising mist as towhees formally attired in black, white, and tan punctuate the chorus with panache.

I can see the world from here. It is home and wildness and meditation in all its imperfection. It is a creation of pines and pokeweed, red clay and cardinals. It is a forest trying hard not to be old field again. It is life and death on a hundred acres, and I am a privileged witness. I see a dingy yellow bobcat, stumpy tail twitching and pointed ears erect, make its way across an old logging deck. It pads over the fallen timber and through the weedy jungle, intent as I am on the morning's pursuit, but perhaps without as much distraction. It is on the hunt and everyone knows. It measures its survival in mice and perhaps a cottontail caught. I measure mine in simply being there and seeing it all unfold.

The male cardinals—vermillion, scarlet, indescribably red—threaten the brush with their fiery wings. They almost do with feathers what the sun cannot with light. The chirping and chasing in and out of the brush mean that there are seeds at stake. Even outside of the fever pitch of making more little cardinals, there is territory to defend.

And then I see something that is neither bird nor bobcat in the periphery of my forty-something year-old vision. In the midst of the being, there is a glimpse of movement through the still timber. From afar, a gray form is there—and then not. Something sleek and slender and swift darts like quicksilver through a break in the brush like mercury through a needle's eye. Atop the vision's head—forks of polished white. At least that's what I think I saw. Mental trickery, desire of imagination, or real—the answer matters very little this morning. The apparition offers no possibility of confirmation, no chance of congruence with crossed-hairs. My satisfaction lies somewhere between the dumb luck of being in the right place at the right time, the wonderment of how many such spirits slip undetected outside my imperfect sight—or occasional slumber— and how the choice to kill means so much in the grand scheme but so little right now. This morning, the hunting has been good. Thanksgiving,

venison-less though it may be, has come early. My soul's cornucopia is full to overflowing with the morning's feathered bounty and the fleeting glimpse of future possibilities.

Dogwood

And then the day comes when luck falls your way. The deer are careless or just unlucky and maybe your skill plays a minor role. As I sit watching hermit thrushes gorge on the persistent scarlet dogwood drupes and listen to the whistling wings of wood ducks arrowing straight-away to some wooded slough. In the riot before the awakening I detect a difference—feel some presence. And then from below, I hear them coming before I can see them coming. It is not the teasing play of squirrel or the scratching of brown thrashers. No, this time the clamor is unmistakably significant. Fallen limbs and slash cracking under heavier, slower, deliberate steps on the old, overgrown, skidder trail mean that the deer are moving this morning. In the right place at the right time, luck or skill does not matter at this moment. I am here. They are here. Thinking will now have to become action—or not.

And then: the gray ghosts simply, suddenly appear.

Two does—one large and lithe the other not— move cautiously but confidently, following the overgrown logging trail that is now the deer road. The leader moves into a crosswind, giving away her olfactory advantage. The pair advances, as if drawn by some magnet. My pulse surely audible, it seems as if it will send them flying away on wagging whitetail wings. I am naked sitting before them. My instincts are exposed. No camouflage cover could conceal me. My trembling hands will surely betray me.

The slender one, leading—grunts softly, nibbles at a briar and then suddenly raises her head as if on alert. Her woods wisdom tells her that something is not altogether right. Her big doe eyes, dark orbs on a narrow face, search for something she cannot quite discern is there. She bobs her head like the deer folk do when something is amiss—maybe to gain perspective or to feint the unknown into giving itself away somehow. The wind across her narrow muzzle and my frozen face don't bring my presence to her, but she remains apprehensive, cautious—the woods are full of things to take flight from. She must decide if my strange form is one of them. What she sees—or cannot see—conflicts with what her nose isn't telling her. I cast my eyes elsewhere to allay the predatory stare. She stomps and her companion is suddenly suspicious too. The slender doe quarters away to ask the wind for guidance again, and in that instant she presents herself to me.

I exhale.

The rifle's report shatters the woods for a millisecond and then everything is oddly quiet; everything except for the sound of the doe crashing through the brush chasing her life's blood away. When all is still, I climb down. Four panic-stricken whitetail bound from the place she last drew unfettered breath; the doe's white belly shines like the moon in the dark morning woods. She lies there on her side in the midst of her last stride in a little opening along a narrow draw full of red oaks dropping acorns— her likely destination before my decision. The scarlet drops spilled on the dusky leaves look like the dogwood fruit, but they are sticky-wet and still warm. The other deer, long since gone, is alone now but wiser and warier in its woods ways. At the expense of her companion's life she survived another day to learn on the keen edge between instinct and ignorance.

At the moment of killing, the decisions are never easy for me. Common though the deer may be, I always see a life before me, wild and free. My choice at taking that life is a privilege but a necessity too. The predators that would otherwise wield the lethal knife against burgeoning populations are largely gone. They are gone because of us, and so we bear some of the responsibility for killing cleanly and with purpose. At the instant of the decision I am simply a part of the web. It is special even when I hunt in imperfect places where nature is not so big or far away. The woods do not have to be dark and deep for me to revere them. The Piedmont scars— scrubby old fields, planted pines, and muddy creeks—are at least signs that there is some hope left for recovery amidst the paved-over wounds of development that have little hope of ever healing. The whitetail deer that make do in spite of the chronic conversion from wild to tame deserve counterbalance to their craftiness. I try hard not to forsake my responsibility. I thank the slender doe for her life and the privilege to remain a part of the cycle. In this piedmont place, imperfect in its wildness, I learn hard life lessons in hunting and, in so doing, try to mend the things that are broken. 🖎

Nearly unintelligible, totally unmistakable, intriguingly undecipherable—deer talk. This is it.

ROLLING GOBBLES IN THE FOOTHILLS
Hunter Bridges

SCREEN DOORS ONLY SQUEAK IN THE SOUTH. THIS IS NOT TO SAY THAT NEGLECTED HINGES DO NOT BEMOAN THEIR LACK OF OIL ABOVE THE MASON-DIXON LINE.

But rather that their bemoaning is acknowledged here in the South, in the sound's ability to beckon a sense of belonging to the region, and to the land. That distinct whine cannot be adequately defined through grammatical doctrine, but may be illustrated through analogy by the fine distinction that it shares with bare feet, fireflies, and very sweet tea.

That old familiar sound was the first to greet me on an April morning in the foothills of South Carolina. It was the first day of South Carolina's turkey season—my favorite day of the year. It was very early, and the damp coolness immediately permeated the layers of my drab-green flannel shirt and faded canvas coat. The deeply blued barrels of my father's L.C. Smith side-by-side shimmered in the moonlight as I walked toward the truck. There seemed to have been more stars than sky that night and a

brilliant crescent moon was already far west of the zenith, letting me know that I'd better get moving.

Before long I was pulling the truck off the shoulder of an old gravel logging road at a familiar trailhead. After a brief check of my gear—a handful of No. 4 shells, cedar box call, and a camouflage bandanna—I stepped out of the truck. A whippoorwill beautifully narrated the setting with his endless chorus as I began my walk. The trail began on the top of the ridge, cutting through a stand of Virginia pines and sparkleberry, then turned downward, working diagonally, across steep slopes of oak, poplar, hickory, ash, and buckeye toward a rich cove, nestled on the bank of the Eastatoe. I was confident that somewhere in that valley, the turkeys were perched in the dormant canopy.

I had covered a short distance when I surprised few deer. They blew just before fleeing, and I cringed as the sound of loud, raucous wheezes filled the hills. Then the sound of hooves pounded the terrain as they dashed through the tough brambles of heaths. When the sound ceased, I continued onward.

The sound of my footsteps changed as the stand of pines abruptly gave way to hardwoods, which were not as forgiving to footfall as a layer of brown needles. Moonlight filtered through the bare canopy and filled the slopes with a silvery glow that was both elegant and ghostly. Despite the uncertainties underfoot, and the risk of a misplaced step, I could not bring myself to spoil that glow with the harsh yellow beam of a flashlight. As the crow might fly, I was not especially far from any town or city. But as I negotiated those soft slopes under the elegant moonlight, I felt free to envision a vast forest of rolling hills—the kind William Bartram knew—separating me from civilized places.

Finally, I came to a small branch, and after a few nimble steps from one stone to another, I emerged on the other side, and, to my satisfaction, with dry socks.

A rich cove forest stretched out before me, and my breath hung in the heavy morning air while I listened to the lonely hoot of a barred owl echo through the hollows. I stood stock-still for a moment, knowing that the leaves would announce my approach to all within earshot; finally, I made my way toward a lofty yellow buckeye. I took a seat at its trunk among a sparse stand of doghobble and felt the cool mellow loam through my faded camouflage pants. The cedar box paddle scraped the box as I fumbled through my pockets for the camouflage bandanna, betraying my secrecy with a raucous squeak. After cringing in embarrassment, I set it gently in the leaves beside me; I dropped a shell into each one of the Damascus barrels and smiled at the hearty *clunk* when I closed the breech.

The temperature dropped a few degrees as a gray light began to fill the forest. It was that distinctive, pre-dawn light, indifferent to detail and shadows. A flock of dark-eyed juncos fluttered nervously about while a lone towhee scratched in the leaf litter; I sat shivering at the base of that tree waiting for … something. High in the canopy, a yellow-throated warbler greeted the morning, and a ruby-crowned kinglet fluttered weightlessly from the end of one delicate branch to another. His exuberant chatter sweetened the air, and I grinned at the little fellow's confidence while the rattle of a woodpecker echoed through the cove. I felt well concealed, nestled tightly against the trunk as the eastern horizon began to glow. I let my head lean back on the tree and dozed off. Then, from high in the canopy, just beyond the opposite ridge, a single cluck cut through the forest.

My heart skipped a beat. With my left ear cocked skyward, mouth slightly open, I listened intently. Within moments another cluck rang out, followed by a few sleepy yelps. After a few minutes, the flock was engaged in spirited chatter, filling the canopy with the sharp, melodic notes of spring.

Then I heard the muffled, chesty rhythm of beating wings as the first turkey descended from its lofty perch. The next turkey to pitch landward proclaimed its descent with an enthusiastic cackle. And then it came. A deep, thunderous gobble rolled down through the primordial hills like a freight train—his majesty was awake. Perched in his lofty throne, he signified his presence and established his dominance over everything in range of his magnificent voice—he knew that spring belonged to him. I reached for the old box call that had betrayed me earlier that morning, and with trembling hands, managed to respond with three timid yelps, wincing as they drifted across the forest. But almost immediately, another thunderous gobble rolled down in approval. Feeling consoled, I laid the box call in the leaves beside me and listened. In the distance I could hear distant purrs above the swishing of leaves as the birds began to raid the forest floor for breakfast. Again, but this time with more confidence, I sent forth a series of shorter, more excited yelps. The sound fell upon the forest with no response and I grew very uneasy with the stillness.

By then, the sun was rolling lazily over the horizon, casting the first shafts of golden light into the canopy, falling gently on the vernal ephemerals. Mayapple, Allegheny spurge, bloodroot, Catesby's trillium, and catchfly were all taking their share of sunlight before mid-April woke the canopy. A white-breasted nuthatch darted nimbly down the trunk of a sweet birch, and I wondered if he was a little smug over being the only one of his passerine peers with the dexterity to run down a tree. A wood thrush dashed from limb to limb on a nearby sourwood, and a brown thrasher stood poised on a pine snag, then quickly descended upon an unsuspecting insect. I was amused at his enthusiasm for breakfast.

The sounds of turkey had become a memory, and after a while, I began to consider that old tom a lost cause. I could imagine his tail feathers, raised high and confident as he followed his hens toward, well, wherever the hell turkeys go. At the moment, I was content to think about the mountains and enjoy nature's indifference to my presence.

Suddenly, another thunderous gobble rolled through the woods, but this time it was so close that it seemed to rattle the very hills. My heart began to race, and my eyes cut to the right. I dissected the forest but I could not see anything that was not there before. A pileated woodpecker cackled in the distance and another deep, commanding gobble rattled through the cove. I pushed myself tight against the trunk. It felt like years passed as I stared in the vicinity of a large hemlock, which, as it seemed to me at the moment, had taken root in the most inconvenient damn place in all of the foothills.

My heart skipped a beat. With my left ear cocked skyward, mouth slightly open, I listened intently.

My heart raced. Logic melted like wax. I could not see him, but his presence pervaded the cove. A house sparrow scratched in the leaves only a few feet from me. Out of the corner of my eye a dogwood bloom swayed in the breeze. But there was no breeze. A second look revealed that it was the old tom's clammy, white forehead. He was in half strut when he stepped into view.

I moved the safety on the L.C. Smith forward, muffling the click with the back of my thumb. With another thrust of his head the tom took a step forward, and then another, while the morning light danced on his iridescent feathers. His path led him behind a hefty beech, affording me just enough time to shoulder the heavy L.C. Smith and nestle the dark walnut stock firmly against my shoulder. When he emerged on the other side of the tree, his wings dropped and his tail feathers rose to form a perfect arch, and the small silver bead was trained on his head. But at fifty yards he was just out of range.

My gaze was fixed on that magnificent creature as he scanned the forest for a phantom, a lone siren in the hush of dawn, whose notes he found irresistible. He relaxed his feathers and stood stock-still, scanning the woods. My anxiety rose along with his impatience as I sat there, balled up among the doghobble. It was a riveting showdown. Nature had summoned in him a powerful drive to breed, and in me, the drive to hunt; the atmosphere was charged as those two forces of nature waited for destiny to split the difference. He drove his head forward with another gobble. Then, for some reason, known only to turkeys but off limits to Man's logic, he casually turned toward the opposite ridge.

My finger lay heavy on the trigger as my last chance of taking him faded away. I thought of my box call, lying in the leaves beside me. It was my only hope of keeping his attention. Without thinking, I rested the gun barrel on my drawn-up knees and reached for the call with my right hand. I sent the note of a single, awkward yelp through the woods and watched him stop and raise his head in aggravated recognition. His wings were laid tightly against his side, and his tail feathers were stacked neatly behind him; he stood tall and proud for a moment before turning in the direction of the opposite ridge. When he disappeared I reached for the call again and sent a short, excited series of yelps through the woods. He gobbled immediately, but never returned.

The cove seemed empty without his presence. A breeze moved through the forest, carrying away the dampness of early morning. I laid the gun in the leaves beside me and picked up the old box call to examine it. It bore Ben Lee's signature on the bottom. That call, like me, was a veteran of the springtime tradition of disappointment and frustration, which we call *hunting turkeys*. In the hands of a skilled user, the call sings. Such a temperamental tool is appropriate for an endeavor as dignified as turkey hunting. I slid the old call into my coat pocket, then stood up, stretched, and leaned over to pick up my gun.

The air felt cool on my face as I pulled the bandanna down around my neck. I did not feel defeated. That morning I found the thing that all of us who venture afield are seeking—the spirit of the land. ✍

TEN WAS THE DEAL
John Faris Jr.

AS I STOOD CHEST DEEP IN THE DAMP HOLE ANTICIPATING THE NEXT SHOT, THE MEMORY OF THE MAN WHO HAD DUG MY GRAVE FLOWED AS SWIFTLY THROUGH MY SUBCONSCIOUS AS THE SMALL RIVER THAT WAS RUNNING IN FRONT OF ME NOW.

It all began in this watery wilderness a year ago late last winter.

The Switch Bush Swamp, as I called it, was perhaps my favorite duck hunting spot throughout my teenage years. It belonged to Jack Whitaker. Mr. Whitaker owned about three hundred acres up on the Princeton Road, about six miles from our house on the edge of Laurens, a small town in upstate South Carolina. Jack was a big farmer, a good friend of my granddad, and he had a passion for high-blooded Black Angus cows.

The bulk of Jack's cattle farm was U-shaped. Princeton Road followed a ridge almost the entire length of the U. The whole farm sloped gradually away from the road, down a huge pasture all the way to Rabon Creek and a large swamp at the open end of the U.

You could ride up Princeton Road in the fall and winter at daybreak or dusk and look way down that pasture as you circled the ridge. If you knew what to look for, you could see big ducks, mallards and blacks, rising from or landing in this waterfowl paradise.

Jack Whitaker was obsessed with the thought that someone might accidentally shoot one of his prize black beauties. He never allowed anyone to hunt his bottoms. No one, that is, but me. In the 1930s when land was cheap but money was tight, Granddad had helped Jack buy part of the land that made up Jack's farm. Now that I could legally drive, at fourteen years of age in 1959, Granddad had taken me with him to meet Jack. He introduced me. After a thorough set of instructions from both men on the dos and don'ts of hunting near cows, I finally received the go-ahead from Mr. Jack to hunt his swamp and surrounding bottomland.

While there were more ducks in some of the other rivers, this one was my favorite spot. No one but me ever messed with those ducks for the five or six years that I hunted there. I never heard another shot or saw evidence that another person had ever walked that way. I had the place to myself.

As the long, sloping pasture entered the swamp, Rabon Creek made a large curve—high ground on the inside and large swamp on the outside of that curve. The ducks loved this area. It was wide open, and I guess they felt safe landing here. I would go to this spot morning after morning, stand at the edge of the hardwoods and watch dozens of mallards circle out over the swamp, hook back over the river, and light in this bend.

Near the big wide curve there was not a bit of cover anywhere to hide in, and the tallest vegetation was no more than a foot high. I had spent several late winter mornings with snow on the ground, watching, but I had no luck getting a shot. With no cover I could never get close enough. The later the season got, the more big ducks poured into that one spot. Finally, the season closed, and I had not ever gotten a shot at those particular ducks.

All through February and March I thought about how to set upon those ducks that used the curve. By April I had a grand plan in mind. What I needed was a pit dug at ground level within twenty yards of the edge of the river. I could get down in it and not be visible from above the ground and the foot-tall swamp grasses. I had read about pit blinds for goose hunting, but I had never seen one before. The image I had from what I had read was a hole about three feet by six feet, deep enough to stand in. What I needed was a grave!

In the small town where I lived you knew just about everyone and what they did for a living.

Big Henry worked for Kennedy Mortuary. He dug all the graves for all the funerals in town. Kennedy Mortuary owned no machine for this job, so Big Henry, working alone, would dig them with pick and shovel. Henry got his name honestly. He was big. The biggest man black or white in town—and for that matter, the biggest man that I had ever seen anywhere. I knew Henry well. Besides digging graves, Henry had the best pack of rabbit dogs in upper South Carolina. My dad paid for all the food and occasional trips to the vet, Henry kept the dogs, and we all hunted together: Henry, his three young boys, my granddad, Dad, and me.

One day while I was helping Big Henry and his boys put up the dozen or so short-legged beagles and feed them, I confided in Henry. I needed him to dig me a grave in Jack Whitaker's bottoms, preferably before fall came around. I hurriedly told him my plan. As we fed the dogs, Big Henry listened and smiled. He said he got ten dollars to dig a grave. "I don't 'spect yo daddy gonna pay no ten dollars for me to dig a grave for you to shoot ducks out of."

I told him I didn't believe Daddy needed to know about the grave. I would help Big Henry all summer at the cemetery, if he would dig the grave for me. I knew he hated fussing with the folding wooden chairs and wreaths of flowers. Henry was a dirt-moving man. Putting the chairs in neat rows and unloading and arranging the flowers were not his favorite parts of the job.

As we finished feeding the dogs I made my pitch. I'd help with ten funerals, one dollar credit for each funeral. Then he'd dig me one grave before duck season. A fair deal, I emphasized. Big Henry thought about this as we walked back to his two-story house with the chickens running in and out from under the full-length front porch.

At last he said yes, but I had to put the chairs out, take them up afterwards, and put the flowers on the grave at ten funerals before he would start digging. As an afterthought Henry said he thought we'd better keep this arrangement to ourselves. He was not too sure what Dad would say about him digging me a grave. I assured him I would not be telling a soul.

I spent all summer worrying that not enough folks were going to die. Ten funerals was a lot of dead people for our little town, and I was racing the calendar. I kept close tabs on the obituaries in *The Advertiser*, as our local paper was named. The papers were sold for five cents on the street corners of the square every Wednesday.

By late August I was a nervous wreck. Only six people had died all summer. However, September turned out to be a bonanza. Three funerals in three weeks! I was probably the only person in town who was so happy and relieved, secretly of course. Being an eternal optimist as all hunters are, I had, for several weeks leading up to September, been very busy building a big wooden box to put down into the grave Big Henry and I were going to dig.

I had gotten two old oak pallets from the glass plant where my dad and granddad worked. This glass bottle and jar manufacturing plant used four-foot by four-foot oak pallets to stack the crates of bottles on. These pallets were scrap and ended up in all types of projects around the county—hog pens, rabbit gums, and just plain firewood. These two pallets I cut to size to be the floor of my duck blind. Next, I built up the sides and ends to about five feet high. Finally, I constructed folding doors that hinged at the top. They would cover up the entire box when closed.

On several occasions my dad, returning home after work, asked what it was I was building in the backyard. I said it was going to be a duck blind. My dad looked at it the way dads always do when viewing young boys' summertime building projects—glad I was home and doing something constructive, but doubtful of the final outcome.

I got the duck blind completed, and after many dry runs in the backyard to insure that

it was neither too shallow nor too deep, I took the whole thing apart, numbering each part as I went. After all, when the time came I would have to get the whole affair across Rabon Creek piece by piece and put it back together again.

On September 20th, a Friday afternoon, as I was placing the flowers on top of the ninth fresh mound of dirt, and Henry was loading his tools into the mortuary's old Chevrolet truck, he said, "What about tomorrow?"

"But I have one more grave to do. Ten was the deal," I said.

"It's been dry for two weeks, and the river ought to be low. We better go now, and you can do the tenth grave some time later," Big Henry said.

"What time you want to leave?" I said.

"I'll pick you up at your house at 6:30 in the morning. You bring us some sandwiches, and I'll get us some drinks," Henry said.

I'm convinced God made September Saturdays just for young boys. A sort of payback for piano lessons, family reunions, and trips to the dentist. This one was a honey—cool, crisp, and clear. Four peanut butter and grape jelly sandwiches in a brown paper sack, nails, hammer, saw, and the knocked-down duck blind were ready when the long-bed Chevrolet one-ton truck pulled into our yard.

Big Henry and I loaded and started up Princeton Road. I undid the barbed wire gap at the top of the pasture to let Henry drive through. I carefully replaced the gap. I was well tutored on the proper hunter's etiquette of not climbing fences, but rolling under, making double sure all gates were refastened, and not running the farmer's cows. We kept to the very edge of the tree line and eased the old truck down the pasture toward Rabon Creek.

Big Henry, like all country folks who spend a lot of time outdoors, had picked a good day.

The river, about twenty yards wide, was down to knee-deep, and the ground had dried out, so we were able to pull to within a few yards of the big curve. As Henry looked across the river, I pointed out where I thought the pit should be. We unloaded Henry's tools. One square-face shovel, one mattock, and one long, coarse file. Henry took off his heavy shoes, tied the laces together, hung them around his neck, rolled up his pants legs, and waded across. I followed and began to make the first of many trips across, carrying pieces of the knocked-down blind.

When I got across, Henry had put his shoes back on—no socks—and was sharpening his shovel with that big file. He laid the shovel face down over a sycamore log and stroked the coarse file across the bottom edge of his shovel a few times, always pushing the file, never dragging it back. After a dozen strokes Henry held the shovel up, and the morning sun glinted off the sharp, fresh edge.

"How big you want the hole?" Henry asked.

"I've never seen you dig but one size," I said, "so I built the blind to fit—you know, three feet by seven feet, but let's make this one only five feet deep. That's as deep as I made the blind 'cause I can't shoot out of anything deeper."

Henry picked up the shovel, cleared away the grass, and started to dig. I had watched Big Henry do this most of the summer, but I still was amazed at his strength. I was pretty strong for my age and had had to dig holes for one reason or another around the yard at home. Even my best efforts would result in standing on the shovel, pushing about a fourth of it into the ground, bending it back, and actually only moving about a double handful of dirt. It was hard work and slow going.

This was not how Big Henry usually used a shovel. When Henry put the shovel into the ground, it went down until his foot rested on the top of the earth. Every shovelful was the same shape—wide as the shovel, long as the shovel, and ten inches thick. They never

varied. It was something else to see, and I never got tired of watching. The sides were perfectly straight, the corners square, and the bottom level. No machine could have done it so precisely.

By the time I had all the lumber across, Henry was knee-deep in the hole. Shirt off, pant legs still rolled up, Henry was moving dirt—steady, no talking, no breaks—just moving dirt.

By ten o'clock I told Henry to hold up. He was getting pretty deep, and I was afraid he might be going for a regular-size grave. Henry climbed out, and I climbed in. It was the first time I had ever been in a grave, and I felt a little funny down there. I knew I'd have trouble getting out if Henry had not been there. Sides straight and slick as glass. I shouldered an imaginary gun and swung left to right. With nothing in the grave to stand on, I would not have been able to shoot lower than three feet above the rim. The pallets that made up the floor were half a foot thick, so I knew we were about right. I told Henry we were deep enough.

Two hours later we had most of the blind reassembled down in the grave. We sat on the fresh earth mound and ate our lunch. When we finished our Cokes we both turned the heavy, light green six-and-a-half ounce bottles over and looked at the name of the city and state molded into the bottoms. Both had an LGW, the symbol for Laurens Glass Works, pressed in the center, showing that they had been made right there in our town. As was traditional, we bet each other that our bottle had been made for a bottling plant farthest away from our town. In addition to the LGW on the bottom, the name of the town where the bottle was going was also spelled out in the glass.

Granddad and Dad had taught me many hunts ago that nothing was going to happen until 7 a.m.

The one farther away won the bet, and the loser bought the Cokes next time. My bottle read Asheville, North Carolina, and Big Henry's was Greenville, South Carolina. He laughed and said he had never been to Asheville, North Carolina, but he 'spec'd it was farther than Greenville, where his sister lived. Looking at the bottom of his bottle one more time, he said, "Seems like most of my bottles been no further than I have." Getting up, he said, "Burning daylight. Let's get the rest of your duck blind down in the hole."

We fastened the sides, and then finally we put on the top. I was grateful everything fit with only a few minor adjustments. I helped scatter the dirt all around the blind, closed up the two doors to keep the rain out some, and we waded back across Rabon Creek. It was 3 p.m.

When we got on the other side we loaded the tools. As Henry and I sat on the tailgate of the truck and put our shoes on, we both looked across the clear two-foot-deep river and commented that the blind just might work. Henry

suggested that after a rain or two to settle the dirt I might scatter some swamp grass around the blind. About halfway up the pasture I took one last look out the rear window. I was pretty pleased with myself. I could hardly see where we had been.

September and the first two weeks of October passed with no thought of ducks. It was dove season, and I hunted with Dad and Granddad every Saturday. In late October I checked on the blind and did as Henry had suggested. I scattered some swamp grass, now turning brown after the frost and planted some low bushes on the side of the blind away from the river to help break up the outline.

Duck season would not begin until Thanksgiving, but on several occasions I was at the wood line. I was excited to see the early-flying summer ducks, which we called wood ducks, light within two dozen yards of the blind.

Since hunting season had opened I had not worked a funeral, and I was feeling a little guilty. Henry had not said anything, and I knew he wouldn't. He would understand. I would get that last funeral done just as soon as hunting season wrapped up.

Opening day of duck season I hunted with Granddad and Dad at Buzzard's Roost, probably the best duck hunting place in our county and also the best kept secret. The following two Saturdays we shot at Burton Pond and below McPherson's bridge. All these were wonderful duck hunting spots that were regulars on our early season list. When the Saturday before Christmas came, Dad and Granddad had been invited to hunt the Brick Yard ponds owned by Greenwood Mills. Since I was not invited to this most prestigious event, I planned my first trip of the season to the new blind in Jack Whitaker's bottoms.

It was cold but clear as a bell when I pulled off Princeton Road and parked. I had an old M1 ammo bag that came from the Army/Navy store. I put it over my shoulder, dropped in a box of Peter's high brass No. 4's, took the Browning A5 12-gauge that had been a gift from my dad six years before, and headed down the pasture. The moon was only two days into new. It was still pretty dark, so I walked out in the pasture farther from the tree line than I would have had it been daylight. I timed my trip so I would arrive at the blind at 6:45 a.m. The first ducks would fly at 7 o'clock sharp, just as the little birds began to make their morning sounds. Fifteen minutes would be all the time I needed to get the doors off the blind, fix a few bushes around the edges for added cover, and load up.

Granddad and Dad had taught me many hunts ago that nothing was going to happen until 7 a.m. You would only lose the warmth from walking to your blind if you had to stand around in the dark with nothing to do but wait on the ducks.

When I got to the river the water was up some, and I waded slowly across. The water as it pushed against my boots bulged up on the upriver side and came to within an inch or so of my hip boot tops. I knew it would get shallower as I approached the inside of the curve, so a few extra careful minutes in the deepest part was a small price to pay for warm, dry feet.

I cut it a little close and barely had the two pieces of the top off and stowed against the back wall of the blind when a pair of summer ducks swished overhead only ten feet above the blind. The pink of the eastern sky lit the far bank. The towhees and cardinals began their morning caroling, and soft quacks of a small group of big ducks could be heard coming from downriver.

In our part of the county, all the big ducks roosted on Greenwood Lake and would come from downriver. The summer ducks roosted in the flooded timber along the small creeks and would come from upriver most of the time. Because it is hilly in our part of the country, you can always hear ducks before you can see them. Having heard their approach, I now saw the mallards' light-colored breasts glowing in the darkened sky as the sun struck them even before it was completely clear of the horizon.

There were six of them, and they passed over pretty high. I was a little worried as they passed over. I caught a glimpse of them as they banked. I kept my head still, but cut my eyes as far as possible. I had learned long ago that you can't kill a duck until it is within thirty to forty yards, and it won't ever get that close if you keep twisting your neck and head and showing your white face. Keeping still, as hard as that was, was the only way.

The image I had from what I had read was a hole about three feet by six feet, deep enough to stand in. What I needed was a grave!

The half dozen had their wings cupped now. They were losing altitude quickly. I thought they were going to come straight in when, at the last minute and a little out of range, they pulled up and headed out over the pasture, talking to each other about whatever ducks talk about when they are flying forty-five miles an hour and trying to decide where to have breakfast.

I held my breath. At last one must have said *this looks like the right place.* They dipped their wings, banked sharply, and never took another wing beat. They were cupped up, sailing in with the winter sun showcasing the tan tummies, yellow beaks, iridescent green heads, and bright orange feet. At fifty yards out, they banked slightly to line up with the curve and passed the blind, ten feet off the water and thirty yards out. They looked as if they were frozen in time, and my first shot was behind. They backpedaled at my first shot, and I caught up with two big green heads with the second and third shots. Both colorful males fell with a satisfying splash and quickly drifted into a big brush top against the far bank.

Within ten minutes a single mallard hen came in, much lower this time. Without much reconnaissance she lit upriver about sixty yards. After looking around, making sure all was as she had left it the evening before, she noisily straightened her feathers and sailed on the current down into the curve. She purposely swam to the inside of the curve where there was very little current and began nibbling at the grass on the river's edge. A few minutes passed, and I watched her not fifteen yards away. I could hear her snapping her bill together as she stripped seeds from the heads of the long yellow grass.

Long before I heard or saw them, she tuned up and began calling to her friends that were approaching from downriver. As a pair of mallards appeared over the tree line, the gray hen convinced them that no look-see was necessary, and they locked up. I shot the right hand female two feet off the water and the big drake about two wing beats into his climb out. The Judas hen, with much protest, flew out without damage except to her reputation.

I scurried out of the blind, ran down the bank, got ahead of the last two ducks and waded out midway to catch them as they floated by. I returned to the blind and put the doors back in place, put a few bushes over the top, and reentered Rabon Creek. I collected the first two ducks and headed home.

I was pleased with myself. My plan had come together, and the work Big Henry and I had done was going to pay off for a long time to come. I determined to take Big Henry two of the nice mallards as soon as I had them cleaned and dressed. As I walked up the long pasture I thought how much Big Henry and his family would like those ducks. They ate a lot of rabbits, and the ducks would make a fine Christmas dinner. I must confess, though, I also wanted to brag some on how well the idea had actually worked. I wasn't too sure Big Henry ever really thought much of the idea.

When I got home I cleaned all four ducks, picked out the two biggest and headed over to where Big Henry lived. When I turned onto Madden Station Road, there were several cars in addition to the mortuary truck parked in front of the house. A white wreath was hanging on the screen door. When I stepped onto the porch a large lady dressed all in white opened the front door.

When she saw me she said, "Why, ain't you Miz Harriett's boy?"

I said I was, and that I came to bring these ducks, as I offered the shallow glass pan.

She took the pan and said, "News sure travels fast. Henry was killed by that drunk only last night, and already half the town has showed up." She left me standing there on the porch and disappeared back into the house. She said over her shoulder that she would see Miz Harriett's dish would be returned, for sure.

I stood there not knowing what else to say or do, and then I turned and slowly walked down the wide, wooden steps. A car full of women was just pulling up. Another car was coming up the dirt drive. Halfway across the yard I thought about the rabbit dogs, so I turned and went around back where the large, chicken-wire dog pen was. As soon as I turned the corner of the house I could see Henry's boys, my Saturday hunting companions, sitting near the dog pen on the tailboard of an old grain drill. The two youngest were crying. Ramsey, the oldest, was just staring at the ground. He only looked up after I had stood there in silence for a full five minutes.

"He's gone," said Ramsey.

"I'm very sorry," I said.

"Momma says I got to be the man of the house and look after things now. I might have to quit school," Ramsey said.

I wondered to myself exactly how my thirteen-and-a-half-year-old friend was supposed to be this replacement with less than twelve hours' notice, but instead I asked, "Dogs and chickens been fed?"

We both looked over at the fifteen nearly identical black and tan faces lined up inside the chicken wire. "No, but it's past feeding time. Look at 'em. They know he's gone too."

It was true. Instead of jumping on the wire insistently and barking to be let out, the little beagles just sat there, heads cocked in varying poses of questioning.

"Come on," I said, "Let's get started. I'll do the chickens, y'all feed the dogs."

Ramsey got the two little ones up and going to help mix the Jim Dandy dog food with water. I poured up a number ten galvanized bucket full of Spartan Mills scratch feed.

As I walked across that broom-brushed yard, scattering the feed to the ever hungry chickens, I grew very sad. Henry really was gone. His death came quickly, unexpected and unwanted. There was no long illness, no getting used to the idea. He was stabbed while trying to break up a knife fight on Back Street.

I was glad I was alone as the warm, salty moisture dropped off my chin. My Southern raising would not have allowed me to wipe my eyes and perhaps show that I was crying. That men don't cry is taught from age three. "Now, now, don't cry. Big boys don't cry" is repeated often and regularly by dads and uncles. So I slowly walked away from the boys, scattering the chicken's breakfast. I let the tears for my big friend and his boys fall among the wheat and cracked corn.

Later that day I learned that Henry's funeral was to be held late Sunday afternoon. After church on Sunday I went to Moriah Baptist Church. The small graveyard was a typical country church cemetery.

There were a few 150-year-old red cedars at the perimeter, and simple scattered tombstones, some so old they were just big field rocks turned long side up. In front of some of the tombstones were a few turned-over containers of long dead, hand-picked flowers. The grass was kept cut, there just wasn't much of it. Red clay was showing through a lot of the thin native grass, and even on a good day it was a sad place.

It wasn't a good day. A few days before Christmas and it had started out clear and cold. Now a heavy cloud cover laden with moisture had blown in with a fifteen-mile-per-hour northeast wind, and it felt much colder than it really was. The clouds were unusually low, and it looked and felt like it would start sleeting at any time.

In the graveyard in back of the small church there was a man sitting on a big, borrowed, yellow machine digging the grave. The little man on the machine was having a hard time getting it right, and it was taking a long time. The hole was too big. There were ragged claw marks from the scoop on the edges and walls. The corners were broken off and had crumbled into the bottom. Unlike the near perfect hand dug graves I had seen Henry labor over, this was the worst grave I had ever seen. Standing at a safe distance, I watched awhile until he finished. It was late, and he was in a hurry. The funeral would begin in an hour.

As he got off, I walked up to him and asked if I could help him arrange the chairs and flowers. He said sure. He said he was new at this, and they should have sent someone to help him. While the man got the machine parked away from the grave and stored his tools, I began arranging everything. When I finished, the folding wooden chairs were set up in straight rows, and the flowers were properly arranged. When I had it all ready, the man looked at it and said, "Not bad, you were a lot of help. Here's a dollar for your trouble."

"No," I told him, "but thank you." And as I turned to go and the sleet began to fall, my thought was *after all, ten was the deal.*

PADDLING

John Lane

M. Jill Jones

Gerald Thurmond

LOOKING FOR WILDNESS IN A DAMAGED SOUTHERN LANDSCAPE

John Lane

MIXING PLEASURE WITH CURIOSITY, I LIGHT OUT ON A SUNDAY MORNING IN LATE OC-
TOBER TO PADDLE A THREE-MILE STRETCH OF FAIRFOREST CREEK JUST OUTSIDE THE CITY
LIMITS OF SPARTANBURG.

Four of us will put in on South Liberty Street in
Arkwright, an old mill village, and take out a
few hours downstream on 295-Bypass. This will
be urban boating at its best. Fairforest Creek
is not a wilderness: it drains most of Spartanburg's south-side industrial zones—small-time
machine shops, distribution plants, even a large
petroleum tank farm. Fairforest Creek is not
blue-ribbon water; it's a working-class creek.
The South Carolina Department of Health and
Environmental Control (DHEC) classifies it as
"impaired," a word a nature writer friend once
pointed out tells us little about a stream, but
loads about our relationship with it.

In spite of the less-than-pristine nature of the
creek, I've convinced my companions, G.R.

Davis, his teenage son Phillip, and Gerald
Thurmond, that a morning on the water—any
water—is worth it. Paddling pleasure is not
hard to come by once the boat's in the current,
even on the Fairforest, where the water's low as
a result of a record dry fall that many are quick
to blame on climate change.

Pleasure aside, my curiosity about this area is
easier to explain and appreciate. As we load
the boats, I tell my friends that what I'm really
interested in is claiming what may be "a first
descent" through the territory of ReGenesis, a
Spartanburg organization that is a national post-
er child for environmental justice and cleanup.
ReGenesis's focus includes an EPA-cited brown-
field and two Superfund sites—what founder

and local environmental activist Harold Mitchell called "the Devil's Triangle" when he brought attention to this industrial neighborhood in the late 1990s. Arkwright, primarily a low-income African-American community, has fought for almost a decade now to clean up the horrors of an abandoned fertilizer factory, an old textile mill leaking chemicals, and a thirty-acre city dump full of industrial and medical wastes.

I've e-mailed Mitchell to warn him that if he gets reports of a fleet of old canoes headed southeast into terra incognito, it's us. A graduate of Spartanburg High School, Mitchell studied business administration in college and worked as a promoter of black gospel music in the Washington, D.C., area before returning to Spartanburg in 1991 and coming down with an illness doctors could not diagnose. Soon after, his father died from a mysterious ailment as well. Years of investigation led Mitchell to conclude that the illnesses could be linked to the environment of the small black neighborhood he grew up in. The ReGenesis project was formed to address this question. Its story, and the story of its founder, is so compelling that in 2002 the EPA gave Mitchell its National Citizens Involvement Award, known informally as the "Erin Brockovich award." Like Ms. Brockovich, a California environmental crusader whose life story was made into a movie, Mitchell has turned a hidden toxic nightmare into a crusade for a livable community.

Gerald, G.R., and Phillip don't know the story of Harold Mitchell and ReGenesis, though they live just up the hill in the middle-class neighborhood called Duncan Park. I lived in Arkwright for a year in the early 1960s, when the village was still mostly white mill workers. I was seven years old when my mother moved us there, and I have a few clear memories: eating figs off a tree in our backyard which sloped down to Fairforest Creek, and watching my uncles shoot rats spotlighted at the nearby dump.

When we turn down a street near where I lived, the creek is at the bottom of the hill. "It's so quiet here," Gerald says.

At 9:45 a.m. we unload the boats from G.R.'s green pickup next to the old mill site, now vacant land covered with bricks, small saplings, and volunteer brush. By the middle 1990s this property had become overrun with drugs and prostitution, and the only alternative seemed to be to clear it out and start anew, Mitchell had told me once on a visit to the site. A few houses and families had stayed, but mostly the vision was one of "renewal," a word used to describe the leveling of the African-American community farther north on Liberty Street in the 1970s. One can only hope we have learned a great deal more about renewal since then.

We drag the boats through busted bottles, old wire, and loose trash to put in at a small but bold tributary running out from under the old mill outflow pipe, rusted and unused for decades. Behind us, on the hilltop, several huge piles of old wood loom from the teardown of the mill. ReGenesis now owns the property, and timber is stored at the back of the site in hopes it can be reused to build a project headquarters or an ecology center someday. DHEC has approved a huge bonfire, a controlled burn, for later in the year to get rid of the ruined timber. Lumber with paint has been painstakingly sorted from the raw wood to make sure ReGenesis doesn't add more toxic waste to the air and water of Arkwright.

Soon there are three canoes and a small kayak mirrored on the creek's dark surface, a flotilla that almost overwhelms the narrow waters of the silted-in Arkwright millpond. Gerald and young Phillip head downstream, while I paddle alongside G.R. a little ways upstream against current and under a bridge. I want to commune for a moment with the epicenter of Arkwright, one of the most complex strands of my place-based DNA. There are probably layers of toxic industrial chemicals trapped below me in the millpond sediment, but I prefer to focus on what's around me. I fix on some of Spartanburg's old granite curbstones, now pressed into service to keep the shore from washing out under the bridge. I point them out to G.R., noting that they are an adaptive re-use of a local resource, having changed from quarry stone to curbstone, to riprap, to historic curiosity in one hundred years.

G.R., a nature photographer when not teaching physiology at Wofford College, is more interested in the way the early morning light bounces off the greasy surface of the water and settles on the bottom of the concrete bridge in swirling patterns. As G.R. gets his camera out, I'm reminded there is beauty all around us in the world, in spite of what we do to extinguish it.

We head downstream to catch up with Gerald and Phillip. There's a large kudzu field on river left, and the eroded, littered slope of the mill site on our right. Gerald is already birding. Sociology professor by day, writer and naturalist by evening, his binoculars are out, his passion for the natural world in full display. We've only been on the water five minutes, but by sight and call Gerald's already identified a number of species. He's left the ugliness of Arkwright behind. He repeats the names, and I write them down—eastern phoebe, song sparrow, white-throated sparrow, great blue heron, American crow, blue jay, kinglet, rufous-sided towhee, belted kingfisher, and mallard. "The mallard is the only duck that quacks," Gerald says. I tell him he sounds a little too much like a science teacher, but I write that fact down anyway. For a moment Gerald's ornithological prowess helps me focus on the wildness along this otherwise ugly dike, this endless tunnel of kudzu.

As we round another bend, the strong odor of sewage envelops us. I decide it's coming from a tributary entering the millpond on our left. This small creek, unnamed on our topographic map, starts only a few hundred yards off of Spartanburg's Main Street, parallels Liberty Street, and empties here amidst the tires and kudzu. In its short two-mile run it drains some of the poorest areas of the Southside—government housing, shotgun shacks that have somehow survived into the twenty-first century, mean streets, and vacant lots of abandoned needles and malt liquor cans. This morning there's no denying that the elements often associated with what academics and government pundits call "environmental justice" all drain into Fairforest Creek.

Around another bend, the creek looks dead, a fur coat of green algae hiding everything just below the surface—railroad ties, an old shopping cart, a city of Spartanburg plastic garbage can, a quarter panel of aluminum siding. "Gerald can have the birds. I'll keep the fish list today," G.R. jokes, knowing there probably are no fish in this stretch of creek.

Old tires are everywhere. Downstream the half-circles of four rubber radials sunk upright in sediment look like a headless river monster in the glare. As a horizon comes into sight where the creek drops eight feet over a concrete dam, four wood ducks shoot overhead like cruise missiles.

"Oh, look!" I say. "We've already had our 'wood duck moment.'"

Nobody understands my nature joke, so as we beach our boats to figure out a way around the dam I explain that a few years ago in an environmental literature class I'd asked my students to come up with a master list of the elements every nature essay has to contain. "At least one profound wood duck moment," one smart-ass student suggested after reading Annie Dillard's *Pilgrim at Tinker Creek* and Franklin Burroughs' *The River Home*.

Smart-ass or not, my student was right on. There's something about the flight of wood ducks overhead that seems to fit our idea of nature so much better than the slow, ghostly dance of blue-green algae on a twisted shopping cart thrown off a south Spartanburg bridge years before. A heavily impacted urban creek like the Fairforest has about as much in common with the literary Tinker Creek as a wolf does with a pit bull chained to a trailer.

This struggle of wild and tame, raw and baked, green and paved is prevalent in nature writing, and not until recently did urban nature become a protagonist. As I drag my boat through the kudzu and broken bottles to portage the dam, I notice native river birch and box elder reaching for sun out over what remains of a silted pond. "See, there's wildness here," I say to Gerald. "Isn't it strange that just upstream from a government-certified toxic wasteland I'm pulled toward dreams of wilderness and wild restoration?" Gerald brings up historian William Cronon, who would dismiss my hopes of wilderness as the myth of some untransformed landscape that exists somewhere else, but I'm unwilling to give up on birch and elder. Surely what's wild can creep upward through the poor Southside to the inner reaches of the city.

When we clear the dam, we leave Arkwright proper behind. From our topo we can see what lies ahead is wooded country with no houses, maybe one thousand acres or more of raw land, much of it a one-hundred-year flood zone. Renew or restore? With Arkwright's history behind us, and the vision of a "regenesis" clouding our ideas of wilderness restoration for this floodplain, we get back into our boats and head downstream, bumping over a few exposed rocks and the rubble of construction debris.

It's afternoon now, and we're strung out along a quarter-mile of shallow water, paddling in four boats, setting our own pace. Phillip leads the way, his youthful spirit of adventure pushing him downstream in front of us old farts. I watch the western shore, looking for signs of the mysterious city dump the EPA rediscovered in Arkwright's back reaches. I know it's somewhere in the woods, but all I see is trees. I don't want to paddle past a Superfund site and not see it.

"You don't have to find the dump," G.R. says. "The whole creek's a landfill." All the way downstream he's been picking up the brightly-colored bottoms of a hundred broken bottles. He has found them washed up on sandbars, a prospector along the creek's trashy shore. When I ask him what he plans to do with the bounty of glass, he doesn't know.

"It looks like somebody threw every plastic bag in Spartanburg County in this creek," Gerald says, catching up, pointing at the debris along the high waterline in the river birches fifteen feet above us.

"They look like prayer flags when the wind blows a little," G.R. says, paddling his black canoe forward toward more broken bottles.

I look downstream. There's beauty to be seen in garbage, even here, a mile or so below the old mill site and crumbling dam. The creek valley is not a wilderness, but it's not rural either. There's no patchwork of farm fields and sleepy homesteads with wood smoke drifting from chimneys. It's nothing but a flat expanse of creek bottom, just like thousands of others in the urban and suburban South, grown up for forty years in invasive privet, kudzu, and spindly South Carolina hardwood.

"What would this landscape mean to a developer?" I ask Gerald as we rest on a sandbar. "Do developers ever worry over the idea of development the way we worry over the idea of wilderness?"

"I don't think developers sit around and think about what anything means," Gerald says. "They don't do self-critiques or soul-searching when it comes to buying property. They run the numbers."

Back in my canoe, I hear 295-Bypass a few hundred yards downstream. Gerald quickly falls a little behind, birding along an opening in the power line that follows the creek all the way, hoping to prolong his day on the creek as long as possible.

G.R. has stopped at a place where a small clear stream feeding Fairforest Creek comes in from the east. I stop too and ask about Phillip, who has disappeared ahead of us. G.R. says not to worry—Phillip is probably already at the take-out. He's won the race; now he has to wait a few more minutes

> This struggle of wild and tame, raw and baked, green and paved is prevalent in nature writing, and not until recently did urban nature become a protagonist.

while the old guys catch up. I get out of my canoe to stretch my legs.

We haven't seen one human track on the shore, though Gerald points out an interstate highway of deer prints when he lands on the sandbar. "I hope Mr. Mitchell knows this qualifies as a major urban deer sanctuary," he says. "They probably hide in here and go out and eat people's yards in Duncan Park at night."

As we float, I think about how ReGenesis is an environmental coalition that doesn't address the traditional environmental issues that mostly interest me—species diversity, wilderness, habitat destruction. In the "EJ" movement, environmental concerns are often relegated to funding paved trails and "green space" when the money rolls in after cleanup—things people can use. It's not often the funding goes into preserving wilderness. Years ago at a town meeting, when I suggested more passive green space for Spartanburg, the mayor asked, "But how will we afford to mow it?"

I tell Gerald we should go to City Hall and file our own vision for this place. "I'd like to see at least a hundred acres of this big Fairforest Creek floodplain cleaned up and left wooded," I say. "They should leave at least a hundred-foot riparian buffer along the creek."

At my feet, the season's last yellow jackets work the sandbar. In a clear, shallow pool I watch a school of tiny fish feeding. These are the hopeful signs I've been watching for all along the way. There is plenty of life here, a few miles downstream from Arkwright, where one bold creek feeds another. It's mostly small or fragile life, overlooked or undervalued by those who occasionally take notice.

I lose focus for a moment, thinking how I can't wait to get home to take a shower. Then I focus again, first at the new life earning a living at my feet, and then at the distance we've traveled. In just a few miles we've floated through the footprint of the industrial revolution. Some of it is foul—mill waste, factory pollution, trash—the remnants of human exploitation. Other stretches are more hopeful.

What will become of abused places like Arkwright and Fairforest Creek? Like Harold Mitchell's African-American ancestors only a few generations ago, wild nature lacks a voice, and it often lacks the justice that comes along with counting. While we walk away at the take-out, leaving Arkwright and the creek behind, somehow these fish and yellow jackets and turtles and deer survive in spite of what we've done to make life harder for those most vulnerable.

Nature creates resilient systems, even the systems we humans call community. I look into the bottom of G.R.'s canoe and wish I could see every hand that once held the bottles he's collected there. Nothing's left now but fragments, some buffed smooth, others still sharp and jagged. G.R. empties his canoe, gathers his treasure to take home. His challenge is to make something from all those pieces. Mine is to see Arkwright, my old territory, in a new light. People live here. So do native plants and wild, resilient animals. We're all just passing through. 🖂

DROUGHT ENDING AT LAKE HARTWELL

M. Jill Jones

THE TREES STILL DRIP FROM THE EARLY MORNING RAIN AS I CARRY MY PADDLE AND LIFE-VEST DOWN TO THE DOCK.

It is Sunday of Memorial Day weekend when the lake is usually teeming with vacationers, but as I survey the big water from the end of my cove, I seem to have the place to myself.

The sky is still heavy with clouds, but I decide I will not be afraid that rain will somehow melt me. Leaving my uncertainties at the dock, I slide the long red blade of my kayak into the dark green water and push off into the great envelope of misty stillness between lake and clouds.

The cove's edge is a semi-circle of aluminum-roofed docks harboring motorboats, jet skis, sailing skiffs, and stacks of floats and lounge chairs—all still and waiting for holiday sun. But at least the water toys are there and the docks are floating now. Last summer, the coves were dry and littered with stranded and deserted docks. Even public boat ramps on deep water were inaccessible, the drought of several years having brought the lake down twenty-four feet from full pond.

There is such peace in a gentle paddle across the great expanse of flat water that is Lake Hartwell, but this day's peace is magnified by the presence of rain filling the lake again. Across the water someone is putting in a boat at Jarrett Ramp, and I realize I am finally paddling over a submerged peninsula on which I had recently walked. Just weeks ago, we joked about walking over to Georgia on this spit of land. It almost became too true to be funny.

But the spring rains have now converted the dry shoals and their plant life into prime underwater real estate for the fish to reestablish their hatcheries. The shallows teem with young bass and bluegill bream, shadows of their larger parents gliding deeper below. Fishermen quietly troll over the once-exposed area, not minding the holiday rain at all. I join in the recovery celebration by feeding treats to the fingerlings from my bag of old bread.

Hearing owls calling to each other, I paddle toward the sound to a large island of hardwoods near the main channel. The rain begins to cease, and I notice a new tree line has planted itself about a foot in front of the old one in the mica-flecked, red clay shore. So even though the Corps of Engineers report the lake four feet down, it is really only three feet down if we accept the new edge.

A motorboat roars through the main channel,

> Just weeks ago, we joked about walking over to Georgia on this spit of land. It almost became too true to be funny.

pulling me out of my reverie just in time to use the swells from its wake to push me back toward the cove. Three does grazing at the forest's edge eye me between bites of foliage, then sprint back into the woods between two lakeside homes. The lake is awakening from its sleepy, rainy morning. A breeze ripples the water from time to time but not enough to challenge my boat. Waterbugs skim about in a synchronized ballet. Swallows engage in aerial acrobatics, gathering insects to feed their young in red-clay nests under the dock-roof eaves. And the muffled stories and laughter of a family having breakfast on a screened porch carry across the water and let me know the vacationers are, in fact, still there.

As another light rain begins to pin-prick the water's surface, I ease up to the dock, climb the ladder, and pull in my boat. I imagine the vacationers inside their lakeside real estate investments, turning on the morning news to get the latest unsettling report on the current financial drought. And I want to call to them, "Why wait for the sun? Come on outside where it's raining hope."

Be...outdoors!

M. Lee Saw

THE OLD MAN AND THE RIVER
Gerald Thurmond

PUT IN: A LAUNCHING PLACE; THE SITE WHERE A CANOE IS PUT IN THE WATER TO BEGIN A JOURNEY.

My people are not river people, and I was anything but a river rat growing up. I'm from South Texas, a region of the country so dry, where water is so scarce, that if a dusty wash had water in it even part of the year, we gave it a name and called it a creek. It's not that my part of the state had no real rivers, just that it had very few. There was one northwest of San Antonio in the Texas Hill Country called the Medina, where my family went when I was a small boy. For three dollars the goat rancher who owned the land would let you drive your car down a rutted dirt road to the river to camp and swim. Upstream from where we set up our tents, the Medina suddenly emerged from underground, its headwaters coming out of the rocky, desiccated hills of stunted live oaks, cedar, and cacti, an extraordinarily clear, deep, wide, bubbling spring. The water was so cold I could bear to swim in it only a few minutes at a time even on the hottest, South Texas summer

days. For a boy like me, raised in revivalism and Baptist fundamentalism, the spring and river seemed to be like some kind of Old Testament miracle, instead of the natural product of porous limestone hills and rain.

From its headwaters, the Medina ran through pools and small rapids until it braided into several small streams a half mile below where we camped. Huge cypress trees lined its banks there, wild turkeys roosted at night high in their limbs, and multitudes of sunfish swam in the streams' pools for a boy to catch. Going to the Medina must have imprinted on me some vague sense of the beauty and wonder of running water. But canoeing wasn't something that I, or anybody that I knew, had ever experienced.

It might have stayed that way if I hadn't gotten my first teaching job at little St. Andrews College in Laurenburg, North Carolina. The college surrounded a small, figure-eight-shaped lake with a narrow passage under a concrete bridge that linked the two wider parts of the water. My office had a plate-glass window that looked out on the lake. One day I noticed that a student had left one of the college's aluminum canoes pulled up on the grass. I took my bag lunch, walked out of the building, got in the canoe, and awkwardly shoved off, allowing the boat to drift around in the middle of the lake—a fine escape for a young man burdened with a heavy teaching load of new classes. But when I tried to paddle the canoe through the narrow space under the bridge to the other part of the lake, I repeatedly collided with the concrete supports under the bridge, making the old metal boat ring like a giant pinball machine.

Embarrassed by my lack of skill, I bought *Canoeing* by the American Red Cross and studied it. By the time I moved to Spartanburg two years later to teach at Wofford College, I understood the basics of paddling. By going on whitewater trips to the Nantahala River in North Carolina with college groups led by Wofford psychology professor John Pilley, I, along with a couple of generations of Wofford students and faculty, sharpened my paddling skills. I could keep a steady course, hold my boat in place in a standing wave, dodge through rocks, and use the currents to ferry my boat back and forth across the river. Occasionally I would even experience the ultimate in canoeists' bliss, something that the best paddlers feel most of the time. Then the boat seemed to become an extension of my body, and I was completely absorbed in its movement. Rather than struggling against the river, I could instinctively use its force to go where I wanted to go in an effortless dance with the water.

Unlike many of Pilley's paddlers, I didn't go on to become a skilled whitewater kayaker. A little whitewater was fine, but I also wanted to listen to the birds, to find animals and identify plants, something that was impossible on big water. Looking at a South Carolina map, I found the nearby Tyger and Enoree, two rivers that seemed to be what I was looking for.

I also stumbled upon a book, Gene Able and Jack Horan's 1986 edition of *Paddling South Carolina: A Guide to Palmetto State River Trails*, which describes a sixty-two-mile trail on the Tyger that goes through four counties and has fifteen miles of mild whitewater, most of that on the North and South Tyger. From there the Tyger becomes a swift stream that flows into the Sumter National Forest and finally disappears into the Broad River. The Tyger River trail ends at a boat launch on the Broad below the Highway 34 bridge.

A little farther south is the Enoree River. Its trail length is about the same as the Tyger's, and it runs through the same four counties. The Enoree doesn't have as much whitewater as the Tyger, but it is a narrower stream and, because of that, requires more skillful dodging of fallen trees and limbs and more portaging of canoes around log jams. The Enoree passes by the little town of Whitmire, South Carolina. Farther down, like the Tyger, it too merges with the Broad River and ends at the same boat launch.

From my years of reading river stories and nature essays, I came to both rivers with certain expectations. First, on my river trips, I should encounter some obstacles that would test me and help me discover essential truths about my life. Second, although nature should be harsh at times, overall it should be good, understandable, healing, and spiritually consoling. And third, most important, on at least one of my river adventures, I should encounter a river sage, probably an old man, who would reveal the river's secret lore to me and initiate me into its brotherhood.

∗   ∗   ∗

J-stroke. A basic stroke in canoeing with a movement like a J. The stroke propels the canoe forward while correcting for sideways drift.

My first trip on the Tyger occurred on a gray, overcast, November day in 1986. I loaded an old, battered Blue Hole Canoe I had borrowed from Wofford on top of my Nissan truck. The canoe was faded black, deeply dented on both its bow and stern, and had several fiberglass patches on its bottom, all the products of twenty years of inept paddling by Pilley's novice canoeists. I had put several of the scrapes and dings on the boat myself.

I drove from Spartanburg,through Union, South Carolina, to the Highway 176 bridge on the Tyger. I went slowly over the bridge to catch a glimpse up and down the river. It rippled below me, shallow, muddy-brown water swirling around broken-off and half-submerged trees and branches. I had come to the river alone. Friends had warned me that I shouldn't paddle that way. What would happen if I got hurt or was thrown from the canoe, they asked? I figured that the pleasures of solitude trumped the risks. Still, the sight of the river made me nervous.

I turned around and drove back to a gravel road next to the bridge on my left that led to a circular parking area and, nearby, to a small, concrete boat launch. I parked my truck, unloaded the boat, sorted my gear, and then dragged the canoe to the river. The area was littered with beer cans and bottles. Plastic bags clung to the branches of the bushes and small trees. A heavy, putrid stench blew in from the riverbank. My first thought was that someone had drowned and been washed up. After a little searching in the bushes beside the boat launch, I found the hooves and offal of a butchered deer.

After I checked and rechecked to make sure I had loaded in the canoe my bag lunch, two canteens, life-jacket, extra paddle, binoculars, and a shoulder bag containing my journal as well as a field guide to birds and a guide to plants, Able and Horan's river-trail book, a small knife, flashlight, compass, and a map of the Sumter National Forest, I pushed off into the current.

The boat felt unsteady under me, and my first paddle strokes were clumsy and inefficient. I bumped around some debris in the river and scraped through the shallows. The whole landscape seemed shaded-dreary: low clouds, drizzling sky, leafless trees, brown water. I began to obsess about whether I had left my

car lights on or locked the truck after I put my wallet under the seat. I knew it was foolish, but finally I could stand it no longer. I paddled over to the bank, pulled the boat ashore, and started running back upstream to my truck.

Along the way I heard an odd puttering sound coming from downstream. I glanced back to see two johnboats, each of them loaded with two men dressed in camouflage and holding rifles. I crouched in the bushes so they wouldn't see me—why I did this I didn't know. I have nothing against good hunters or hunting as a sport—and watched as they went upstream. Then I hurried to my car. I found everything in order, just as I knew it would be, and then walked quickly back to the canoe and pushed off into the current. After a few hundred yards, the boat felt more stable, and my j-stroke began to feel more natural and automatic, although all the fallen limbs and shallow water still made paddling a little difficult.

I came to a small island in the middle of the river and noticed smoke rising from it. Curious, I beached my boat at its downstream end and walked up. At the island's widest part, among the black willows and small cottonwood trees, was a recently abandoned campsite strewn with paper and empty tin cans and two small campfires still burning. I gathered handfuls of wet sand and dumped it on the fires, made sure they were completely out by grinding the coals with my boot heel, and then gathered up the trash. Because the fires were not burned down, and because the men's johnboats were the only boats I saw on the river, the campsite had to be theirs. It seemed that my instincts about the men in the motorboats had been right, and that the fallen trees and shallow water that made canoeing the river difficult for me were helpful because they prevented the men and

By the time I reached Gordon Bridge, twelve miles downstream, where my wife picked me up, I felt that the Tyger could be my new river home.

their motorboats from going farther downstream.

Below the island, the river narrowed. I began to see parts of the Tyger that would become very familiar to me over the years: a place where the river, overhung with willows, broke into three streams around a small island; other islands covered with the remnants of goldenrod, bloomed-out composites and fall asters; long sandbars perfect for lunch breaks and fishing; high, mountain-laurel covered bluffs; and steep, north-facing hillsides. I flushed wood ducks, saw deer moving through the forest, heard the staccato calls of kingfishers, and saw signs of otter and beaver.

Along with the beauties of the river, I also encountered its hazards. Tree falls and piles of washed up limbs and tree trunks, called strainers by canoeists, are the chief danger on rivers like the Tyger, especially if there is a good water flow. When I came to one, I paddled to hold the boat in position until I could find a place near the riverbanks where I could squeeze my boat through or an opening below the branches where I could push under.

If the river was completely blocked by a strainer, I looked for a low bank to pull the canoe around it, but I was rarely that lucky, since they occurred most often where the river narrowed and the banks were high. Usually I had to paddle my canoe parallel to the fallen tree and, letting the current hold the boat in place, gingerly crawl out on the largest tree branches or trunk while holding the bow rope. While I straddled the rope or balanced standing up, I would pull the boat over the strainer to the downstream side, and then carefully get back in.

When a strainer consisted of three or more trees washed together, they sometimes were covered with what appeared to be solid heaps of broken limbs, sticks, and other debris. I discovered the hard way that I had to take special care with these. One of the first times I tried to cross one on the Tyger, the sticks had given way under my weight. I had crashed through up to my waist, saving myself from going all the way to

the water only by grabbing one of the fallen trees' branches. If I fell under a strainer or flipped my canoe in one, I knew I could become entangled underwater in the branches and drown.

Multiple strainers could change a river trip from a pleasant adventure into a frustrating, dangerous chore, as I would learn in future trips. But on my first paddle down the Tyger, I was fortunate and had only couple of strainers to get over. Toward the end of the trip, I rounded one of the bends in the river and noticed something odd ahead. It was the twisted hull of an aluminum canoe sticking out of a large pile of broken trees, a clear warning of the river's power.

All the way down the Tyger, there were red-shouldered hawks and other birds calling and rich hillsides and islands, and I knew that this promised many more kinds of interesting birds and multitudes of beautiful blooming flowers and shrubs in the spring, summer, and early fall. By the time I reached Gordon Bridge, twelve miles downstream, where my wife picked me up, I felt that the Tyger could be my new river home.

❋   ❋   ❋

River crest: The highest water level as it passes through a part in a river; the culminating wave of water in a flood.

Not all my paddles on the river were on flat water. I decided that a canoe trip that started with the Tyger's rapids would make a good river adventure for Nathan, my son from my first marriage. I also believed that, somehow, a three-day river trip would help me to find a way across all the misunderstandings and hurt that had come between us since his mother and I had divorced and I had remarried. The river, as it turned out, had other plans.

My idea for the canoe trip came from an earlier paddle I took mid-March with my poet friend, John, his photographer-buddy, Mark, and a local sandwich shop owner named Gary. We had driven to a put-in just below where the North and South Tyger merge to become the main branch of the Tyger River in Spartanburg County. As we carried our boats the three hundred yards down to the river, we met three young men and a short, heavy-set young woman and her small, silent child. The men were drinking beer beside the river. One of the men kindly offered me a beer, crushed his empty can in his hand, and then threw it on the ground, saying that this was just the beginning, and that last year they had made a pile of beer cans several feet high.

John and Mark paddled solo, while Gary took the bow of my old Blue Hole canoe. Gary hadn't done much canoeing, and he was a gunnels grabber, which is someone who grabs the sides of the boat when he hits a big rapid or loses his balance. It's a natural reflex, but also a sure way to flip a boat in whitewater. After we had stopped to scout a rapid, Gary had pushed the canoe off sideways into a chute of fast water. The boat tipped upstream, Gary grabbed the gunnels, and over we went for a long, frigid swim. We paddled the rest of the river well and negotiated the ten-foot drop of the last, most difficult set of rapids perfectly, but Gary was cold and miserable. Despite my bad luck, I was impressed by this part of the river, and certain Nathan would enjoy paddling it. I also knew he wouldn't mind a swim if it came to that.

Nathan and his friend James, both sixteen at the time, met me at my house. They couldn't have looked more different: Nathan was blond and broad-shouldered, James brunette and skinny, and the more experienced outdoorsman of the two. They were better than brothers, because they got along so well.

We drove out to the S 231 bridge over the North Tyger. The old, easy path leading down to the put in now had a trailer and a no-trespassing sign next to it. We had to drag our canoes under the bridge, through a thick growth of poison ivy, to launch them. It was seven in the evening by the time we started paddling down the river. Barn swallows circled under the bridge as a light rain began to fall. I wasn't worried about

the rain or the late start. By that time I had been canoeing the Tyger River for twelve years and thought I could handle anything the river gave me.

The boys were paddling tandem in the old black boat while I paddled my green, seventeen-foot Olde Towne Tripper named Mary, a used canoe I had gotten for three hundred dollars.

The boat had announced her name to me one day several years before on a twenty-mile canoe trip in August. I had paddled alone out of the mouth of the Tyger, crossed the line where the Tyger's brown water meets the green water of the Broad, and headed downstream toward Henderson's Island and the boat launch below Highway 34. Once I reached the wide expanse of the Broad, I seemed to be standing still. The day was cloudless and very hot, and, to make matters worse, I was paddling into a strong headwind. I had to work hard just to keep the boat tracking straight. That's when the canoe spoke to me. *I'm Mary*, she said. I waited for her to say something more, but she didn't. "Well," I responded, "what else would a canoe have to say to someone?" Then I realized how crazy that sounded. I pulled out my canteen, took a deep drink of water, poured a good portion of the rest on my head, adjusted my broad-brimmed hat, and started paddling harder down the river.

Speed was no problem on the North Fork of the Tyger. The water was fast. The boys went through Nancy Thomas Shoals, running it center of river right and then cutting left to make a nice three-foot drop, while I managed to scrape my boat over it. I told myself Mary was a longer boat, and heavy with all our gear and food. We paddled through some smaller rapids and did some rock dodging through Harrison Shoals.

By then it was 8:15 p.m., and I was worried about getting caught on the river at dark. The boys found a nice place beyond a river bend, where a rock jutted out into the water forming a deep pool, a perfect spot for swimming and fishing. There was a shady, flat area three

feet above the river for the tent, and a steep ridge beyond that. We pulled our boats next to the rock, and I tied them to some black willow trees, then I set up our tent while the boys cooked dinner. As I did this, I noticed some lightning to the north. The sky turned dark, and the light rain that had come and gone while we paddled quickly became a downpour, with loud thunder and streaks of lightning. I thought it was only a stray summer thundershower. Rain hadn't been in the weather forecast. We waited for it to stop so we could do some fishing, but it continued. Finally we gave up and crawled into our tent.

The storm made a heavy, powerful drumming on the tent's rain fly. Despite my ground cloth, the water started leaking from the corners of the tent and its walls became saturated. The three of us were forced to crowd our sleeping bags together in the tent's center to remain dry.

A little after midnight I woke up. I could hear the canoes sharply knocking together in the river over the sounds of the storm. To

check on them, I pulled myself out of the tent and beamed the flashlight toward the river. Through the heavy rain I could barely make out the canoes a few feet from me. I was relieved to see that that they were still tied to the trees and that, while the river was moving fast, it hadn't come over its bank. As a precaution, when I got back into the tent, I woke the boys and pointed out to them how to unzip the tent door in case we needed to get out in a hurry.

I fell into a light sleep until about 1:30, when for some reason I awoke. I noticed that one of the corners of the tent looked odd. When I touched it I found that it was floating. I shook the boys awake and told them we had to get out now.

After we were out of the tent, we began gathering up our gear. In that black night we could see only what the flashlights illuminated at our feet. At first I thought the water around the tent was from the rain. Then the water began to rise, at first slowly, and then fast. When the river crested and the flood came, it wasn't from the riverside, as I expected, but began as a wave across the bend in the river. In just a few minutes the water rose up to our waists. We had grabbed the stove, food and fishing poles and thrown them up the hill. Now we came back to catch floating gear. I tried to pull my tent out of the ground, but couldn't. By that time it was two-thirds under water.

We carried the most valuable of our gear and left the rest. James led the way up the ridge. I didn't have shoes. Nathan didn't have shorts under his poncho, but all of us had managed to hold on to our flashlights. At the top of the hill we came to a logging road. The rain began to let up. Taking a guess at directions, we followed the dirt road to a highway access road. That led us to county road 231 and eventually my old truck.

We got back to my house at 3 a.m., cleaned up, and got some sleep. The next morning James's father, Geoff, and the boys and I returned to the river. We found the tent wadded up and tangled in some brush on the riverbank, about thirty feet from where I had set it up, its poles twisted and broken and everything in it sodden and covered with mud. Mary was downriver, bent around a tree, one side ripped, gunnels broken, and most of the thwarts gone. The black boat was nowhere in sight. The boys finally found it about one hundred yards farther downstream on top of a pile of broken trees and limbs, its rope gone, but otherwise unharmed. There was a dead sunfish on the ground and another wedged up in a tree near it. Three box turtles that had somehow survived the flood were on their backs, caught in the debris. We pulled the turtles free and put them on dry land.

After two trips carrying mostly ruined gear up the ridge to my truck at the logging road, I pulled Mary over to a tree, chained her there, and left a note on her saying I would return. The boys paddled the Blue Hole down the flood-swollen river to the next bridge, where we loaded it on my truck.

Late that afternoon I took Nathan to an overnight birthday party at a hotel. I was exhausted. It was hard to say goodbye to him, because I

had felt for a little while on the trip that we were a family again.

I couldn't bring myself to go back for Mary for several weeks. When I did, she was gone.

❋   ❋   ❋

Back paddle: A paddling stroke moving from stern to bow. In a stream, it is used to slow the boat, hold a boat in place while the canoeist decides how to negotiate a difficult passage or, in a weak flow, to move the canoe backwards.

It was clear after I had paddled the Tyger several times that the river wasn't going to live up to my literary expectations. While the Tyger had given me obstacles galore to overcome, I couldn't say that it had helped me discover any essential truths about myself that marriage, children, divorce, financial problems, remarriage, and losing and getting jobs hadn't. The nature of the stream was disappointing as well. The flood had revealed a river that seemed more random than understandable, more potentially deadly than spiritually consoling.

I still believed I might find my river sage. Of course, the slob hunters and the young men beginning their stack of beer cans clearly didn't qualify, and I had met few other people on the Tyger. I decided that maybe I had been concentrating on the wrong place, that on another stream I might meet more people, maybe among them my wise man, and that he would explain the river's secret significance.

I first canoed the Enoree a year after I began paddling the Tyger. The more often I went, the longer my paddling trips became. One of my longest Enoree paddles was with a man in his late thirties named Raymond who, at the time, was a social worker in child protective services with my wife. Perhaps only the police and people working in emergency rooms saw more of life's ugliness and pain than these social workers. The river was a needed escape for Raymond.

I had arranged to meet him at the gas station in Cross Anchor on May 20th.

I was broke, the usual outcome of a divorce, and, in addition to my teaching jobs, was working nights loading and driving delivery trucks at the *Herald-Journal* newspaper. I had had only two hours' sleep the previous couple of nights. Because I was exhausted, I was an hour late getting to Cross Anchor, but Raymond was still waiting for me. To tell the truth, I was a little disappointed. The reasonable part of me just wanted to go home and sleep. But, like Raymond, I also hoped that a river trip would help me escape my problems, at least for a couple of days.

Raymond followed my truck to road S-45, Keitt's Bridge, on the Enoree. I loaded my canoe on the top of Raymond's truck, threw my gear in the back, and then parked my truck off the road. When I got into his truck, I suggested we go get something to eat. Raymond drove into Whitmire to a hotel/diner. After lunch I assumed we were going to launch our boats near the town, which would have made for an easy, two-day, fifteen-mile paddle down to the bridge. Instead, Raymond drove all the way back to the Highway 56 bridge. Now we were looking at thirty-eight miles of river. "What the hell," I thought. "At least the crazy part of me wanted this."

It was 3:30 by the time we got Raymond's boat down to the river and he loaded all his gear. I launched my boat at the old Musgrove Mill site to catch some mild rapids while Raymond put in below the whitewater. I was happy to see Raymond being a little cautious. It's not that Raymond was a bad canoeist. His problem was that he was an equipment junkie, cramming multiple items of different kinds of gear into every possible nook and cranny of his boat until there was only a small area for him to sit. That makes for an overloaded, hard-to-carry, difficult-to-steer canoe. On a previous trip on the Tyger, I'd had to jump into the river to help Raymond pull his gear and water-filled boat, now weighing hundreds of pounds, out of a strainer after he had capsized. I didn't want to repeat that experience.

The weather had turned unusually hot for a spring day, but the river was not quiet. Yellow-throated warblers were singing in the forests, and Louisiana waterthrushes called from the riverbanks and entering creeks. Our plan was to paddle slowly down the river for a few hours until we came across a good campsite on a sandbar, but because the river was up, all our usual campsites were underwater. By 7:30 we had become desperate. We finally gave up and paddled over to a steep bank, tied our canoes to some trees there, scrambled up the muddy slope, and set up our tents on high ground next to a large pine tree.

Despite the warm night, Raymond used his shovel to dig a pit and built a big fire. I couldn't stand to come within twenty feet of it, but I enjoyed the fine meal he cooked on his big, two-burner gas stove. I slept until 8 the next morning, the best sleep I'd had in a week. As we ate breakfast, a turkey gobbled from somewhere on the other river bank. Raymond searched in his gear, pulled out a turkey call box (of course he had one) and worked it, and got the turkey to gobble in response. We got a late start paddling because it took us an hour to carry all of Raymond's gear to the river and carefully lower it down the slippery bank to his canoe and load it.

After we had been canoeing for a couple of hours, Raymond began worrying about the time. It was sixteen miles to Whitmire, he said. If we didn't make it there by noon we would be in big trouble. We paddled by Whitmire a few minutes before noon. Making Whitmire mollified Raymond's concern with time for a while, and I was able to persuade him to pull our boats onto a small sandbar downriver from the town for lunch. Raymond fished while I took a short nap. We didn't get back on the river until 1:45.

If Raymond had known what was ahead of us, he wouldn't have agreed to stop. Although we were just ten miles from Brazzleman's Bridge, we had six strainers downstream to climb over, and ten or more tree falls to squeeze our boats through. I was following Raymond's boat to what looked like an opening in one of the tree falls when his canoe became stuck in a tangle of branches. I tried to back paddle, but I had allowed my boat to get too close to his and the current was too strong, so I steered my boat under the bole of the tree and an arching limb where I thought there might be just enough room for my boat to pass under. The trunk of the tree caught my paddling arm and held me there while the canoe's bow slipped under the limb a few feet downstream and lodged.

I was in a precarious position, certain I would capsize. I started to panic, imagining myself tangled and drowning in underwater limbs, when a surprising calm came over me. "O.K.," I said, "you can get yourself out of this." Holding on to the tree trunk, I managed to brace my knees against the sides of the canoe and, using my lower body, pulled the boat free from the limb and even with me. Then I bent low, my face almost touching the bottom of the canoe, and, grabbing limbs, propelled the boat under the tree and out the other side.

In another logjam I lost a contact lens when a branch whipped into my eye. Despite our struggles, I enjoyed this part of the stream. Birds were particularly abundant along the banks there, including the lemon-yellow prothonotary warbler, a bird I consider the presiding spirit of Southern swamps and meandering rivers.

Again Raymond became worried about the time. If we didn't make it to Brazzleman's Bridge by 5, he warned, dark would surely catch us on the river. I was glad Raymond was doing all the worrying for us. That meant I didn't have to do it. At ten minutes to 5 we came to the bridge.

As we approached Brazzleman's, I noticed a couple of old men fishing. Maybe one of them, I thought, could be the river sage I had been looking for. I put off Raymond's concerns about getting down the river, paddled over to the old men, and got out of my canoe. One of the men ignored me, but the other smiled. He was listening to a University of South Carolina baseball game on his radio with the volume turned up very high. I soon discovered why. He was almost deaf. "Nice day," I said, practically yelling. "Nope, not such a long way," he replied. After we had a shouting conversation about fishing, different kinds of fish and bait, and the many

years he had come to this spot to fish, the old man fixed me with one milky blue eye. "There's something I need to ask you," he said. "What's the name of this river anyhow?"

The Enoree below Brazzleman's Bridge slowed down—in some places it was barely flowing—but it was much clearer of fallen trees. We had only a five-and-a-half-mile paddle to my truck. I knew we would make it by dark and allowed my boat to drift for a while to enjoy the river. At 7:30 we arrived at Keitt's Bridge. Loading the canoes and all of Raymond's gear in my truck, driving to Highway 56, and reloading it on Raymond's vehicle, took a long time. I made it home at 11. In just one hour I had to be back at my job at the *Herald-Journal*.

*   *   *

Eddy: An area of slack water or where the water is moving much slower than the river as a whole or moving in a reverse direction from the main flow. An eddy is formed by rocks or other obstructions.

My last trip on the Tyger was with my son Nathan, thirteen years after I had first canoed that river and a year after we had been caught in the flood. It was the middle of October, a cool fall day. I taught my morning classes and then drove home to meet him. As usual he was late. We didn't launch our boats at the Highway 176 bridge until 4:15 p.m. Nathan paddled a fine little river kayak I had borrowed from the college while I canoed in the battered, old Blue Hole.

About five miles downstream from the bridge was an area Able and Horan's river guide called one of the prettiest spots on the Tyger. Once I saw the place I knew why. I started calling it my Beauty Spot. There the river made a sharp bend. On the left side was a low area that had abundant wild flowers: spring beauties, butterweed, early buttercup in spring, and a great variety of yellow composites and asters in the fall. An immense laurel oak towered over the other trees thirty yards down the river, and a beautiful shagbark hickory grew beside a lovely small pond. On the other side of the river, before the low area, was a north-facing slope. Jack in the pulpit, dogtooth violets, bloodroot, foamflower, sweet shrub, and large hop hornbeam trees grew there. At the bottom of the slope next to the river I had found a medium-sized beech tree with "Alvin Brown 1936" carved on it.

Across from the lower bank rose a thirty-foot bluff, where mountain laurel and a wild azalea, called pinkster, bloomed. The bluff had a narrow, nice flat area perfect for camping above the river where I had often set up my tent. Someone had made a fire ring and a neatly stacked pile of firewood nearby. Below the bluff was a large limestone rock that projected out into the river, creating a deep, swirling eddy perfect for swimming or fishing. Depending on what the water level had been, the big sandbar at my Beauty Spot, where I always beached and tied my canoe, was either on the low or bluff side of the river.

Nathan and I started paddling too late to make it to my Beauty Spot in time to camp there. I had to settle for a site on the left side of the river, where the Tyger went around a small island. It turned out to be a good place. We put up our tent about twenty yards from the river on a high bank and built a small fire on a long sandbar. That night Nathan talked about his boredom with school and his problems with girls. I didn't know what to say and so I listened. Whatever had once divided us didn't seem to be there anymore.

The next morning it was misting and overcast. I let Nathan sleep late. We finally started paddling at 11. While I hadn't been able to camp in my Beauty Spot, I planned to explore it once again with Nathan.

In less than an hour, we arrived there. At first I didn't recognize—didn't want to recognize—it. The low area that had had all the wildflowers was an ugly tangle of broken limbs, rutted mud and stumps. It had been clear cut. The bluff side of the river now had large, no-trespassing signs on it.

*   *   *

Take out: A place where the boat is pulled from the river: journey's end.

Nathan and I canoed in silence out to the Broad River and on toward Henderson Island to the take out below the Highway 34 bridge. On the Broad, Nathan paddled far ahead of me in the faster kayak. I could follow his progress in the distance by the flashing of his double-bladed paddle in the sunlight. Finally he stopped and waited for me above Henderson Island. Despite the beauty of the place and the fun of paddling the rapids around the island, my heart wasn't in the trip anymore. Because of what had happened to my Beauty Spot, I decided that I never wanted to paddle the Tyger again. That didn't mean I would stop canoeing. There were other rivers and places: the Chattooga, the Enoree, the Pacolet, Lawson's Fork Creek, the Black, the salt marshes and tidal creeks of Edisto Island, and Lake Craig at Croft State Park that wouldn't remind me of what had been lost.

I came away from the Tyger and Enoree with something. Over fifteen years of paddling had taught me that rivers aren't concerned with your well-being. They don't teach you great truths about yourself, and they don't heal your relations with those you love, or console you. Time, and the rest of life, does that. But rivers teach important things, river things, such as that the quickest way to get from one point to another isn't always a straight line. The deepest water is on the outside, not the closer inside of the river bend. In swift water, always aim for the base of the "V" the water flow makes between rocks and follow the current. Use your imagination and avoid rigid plans. A take out and journey's end, and put in and beginning, can be almost anywhere on a river, or even the same place. That's the beauty and freedom of a canoe. And finally, and most importantly, be still, pay attention, and allow yourself to drift sometimes.

*   *   *

I haven't canoed on the Tyger for almost nine years. I figure that's enough time for some of the wounds to heal, and I'm preparing to go back. I won't on this paddling trip bring with me all the romantic notions I first brought to the river, but I'm sure to find an old man there, one who, if not wise, is wiser. It will be me. 🖎

HIKING/RUNNING/JOGGING

Ned Barrett
Heather Magruder
Gerald Teaster
Missy Nicholson

IF I EVER WAS MYSELF
Ned Barrett

"IF I EVER WAS MYSELF, IT WASN'T THAT NIGHT." —Wilco, "Handshake Drugs"

One day I sat in on a college classroom that hosted Joyce Carol Oates, the remarkably prolific writer, whose work I admire. My friend Sam had received a grant to bring Miss Oates to town, and he had invited me to the class. I wasn't the only person invited of course. There were many others, and they held the class in a large meeting room, the students themselves sitting around a long table, with Miss Oates at one end, and me at the other.

A small woman, thin, with glasses and a soft-spoken manner, she talked about writing, her life, her life as a writer. At some point in the conversation, she mentioned being younger and being able to "run 26.2 miles" without feeling the pain of it. She sounded like a runner to me, but since she is the author of an acclaimed book about boxing, I figured she just knows things.

Later, though, in response to a question about how she occupies the time when she not teaching or writing or traveling, she gave an answer that could easily have been mine: "I run," she said. "In fact, I feel most human when I run."

So do I—I've said many times over the past twenty-five years how running even a half hour makes me feel better every time just for having done it. I've talked about the incredible high I feel, running alone in the woods for an hour or two; I rant, practically, so stoned from endorphins. My face aches from the grin.

As the class time continued, I kept thinking about running with her, about asking her afterwards if she wanted to go for a run. I figured she had some other engagement, or would think I was maybe just a little weird for asking, or, just maybe, she'd say, "Sure. My shoes are in the car."

Throughout the class, she had done as any

good teacher does—made eye contact with just about everyone in the room, including me. I always appreciate a good teacher, and she was inspiring and forthright in her discussion. She hates writing a novel, she said, because it takes too much time and commitment, and the pain she feels when writing one—the pain of trying to get it right on such a large scale (I think it was here she used the 26.2 line)—that pain has become almost more than she can endure. She researches, and researches. And, I thought, *she feels most human when she runs.*

I had, of course, every reason to hang out afterwards to get a word with her. This was my friend Sam's class, and I had come with his wife, Margaret, who was a colleague of mine. I hadn't asked any questions, feeling it was the students, and not I, that had been granted this opportunity. She had made eye contact with me more than once, so she knew I had been there throughout. I even had a tie on.

So I waited my turn. Even if she didn't go running with me, it was an entrée into a longer conversation, especially to the human-feeling aspect of running, of sweating, of aching, of feeling muscle and bone. When at last the class had finished thanking her and commenting on something or other, I stepped up to her and did the same. "Thank you for coming, that was truly inspirational. I just wondered if you might have time to go for a run."

She nearly collapsed into herself, stepping away slightly, and murmuring, "No, um, no, it's very hot down here," meaning the South, I reckon. She turned to the door, where the department chair was waiting to move her on to her next gig.

I felt terrible. I had seen her read before, and knew she was shy and reserved. But I had scared her, I think. Someone said that she's not used to Southern hospitality, where inviting someone onto your porch for a glass of lemonade isn't uncommon. She's a Yankee, and the invitation led her to close up like an apartment door; I could almost hear the locks clicking closed down the jamb.

But I have a hard time with that, since my Southern-ness is suspect; I've never liked being lumped in as anything—a man, a West Virginian, a hippy, whatever. I just thought that if someone had come up to me after a class, I would have at least talked about running in some way. I thought it a little rude of her not to acknowledge that, or maybe she was, moving to a how's-the-weather kind of comment that maybe makes it feel uncomfortable. At any rate, I stopped blaming myself, understanding that at least I had a great story to tell.

*   *   *

The Mountain Bridge Wilderness protects a dramatic section of the Blue Ridge Escarpment, a major geological feature that runs from Georgia along the border between North Carolina and South Carolina and into Virginia. The escarpment, sometimes called the Blue Wall, formed when the African plate began to separate from the North American plate 220 million years ago. At that point, along the edge of the Blue Ridge Mountains, the North American plate snapped back and up into a formation called a rift-flank uplift. About ninety million years ago, during the Cretaceous period, when warming led to a rise in sea level, waves crashed against the rift-flank uplift, and the subsequent erosion moved it farther inland. When the Earth cooled and the ice caps reformed, drawing sea level about nine hundred feet lower, the Blue Ridge Escarpment became an inland land feature. Hiking and running in the Mountain Bridge Wilderness offers an opportunity to admire the fissures created by that geological turmoil. Ever since the Appalachian Mountains upheaved in a major continental collision 330 million years ago, they have been eroding. The ruggedness of the terrain shows the continued action of the erosion, as I cross many fields of large boulders,

> I like to be out in it, the heat, the cold, the rain, the snow, exposed to what's there, where I am, at the moment, to challenge, I'll say, my humanity ...

fairly recently part of the cliffs that hang over head. Streams cut down through the rock over time, leaving deep gorges and slashing gaps.

When I go to the Mountain Bridge, I don't look for easy runs. First, there aren't any, and besides, I want the ruggedness, the difficulty, the stripping down of worldly cares to a point where I teeter on the edge of being okay and not being okay. With very few and generally memorable exceptions, all my long and hard runs have a rough time or two, where I question whether I can go on, where I feel leaden, weakened. I want to be reduced nearly to tears, giving me the feeling that my survival could depend on me putting one step in front of the other. Though I know I'm not far from the rest of the world by distance, I want to get far from the safety of sidewalks and awnings.

The fourteen-mile run doesn't allow for any warm up. A hundred yards or so up the Jones Gap Trail, Rim of the Gap trail turns to the left and begins its ascent. About half a mile beyond that junction, Pinnacle Pass trail turns left down the Gap and actually begins to descend, crossing several rock gardens.

Running through Pinnacle's rock gardens, even downhill, is difficult, as knee-high blocky boulders create mazes of narrow trail. Much of the trail passes over the blocky granite that loosed the smaller rocks. A slip here will stretch muscles, and bash shins. Leaving blood on the trail reminds me of the visceral contact I seek, a breaking down by pressure and stress, transforming me through the experience to a new mineral content. Assuring your step is crucial.

I pick a line, and try to connect moves like a dancer. Light feet, with a flat fall and a slow rise, never tentative or I'll fall, never out of control, sometimes on the rocks and sometimes on the dirt. Be careful, though, because it's easy to go into oxygen debt from running while holding your breath. I remember to breathe.

The trail turns to packed dirt and ascends sharply, climbing hard to the ridge. I focus on the friction of feet on trail, setting them straight and strong, maximizing the tread. The first time I ran this trail, twenty minutes into the three-and-a-half-hour run I thought I would have to turn around, that I wouldn't be able to make the climb, already so deep was I in distress.

It's okay to walk; though I move fast, I never hurry. As the trail climbs, I turn around to get glimpses of what I've been climbing for. The opposite ridge of the Gap, equally sharp, rises just as steeply as this one. At what seems like the top, the trail switches back; a wintertime view of the surrounding mountains gives you a chance to stop, and drink some water, and catch your breath. This rough spot of the run is over, though there may be others.

I'm anxious to hit the ridge where I can open up my stride, lengthening muscles tight from the steep climb. The trail continues to climb slightly, packed dirt of a well constructed trail. This part of the woods is park-like, with large hardwood trees and not a whole lot of under-brush. I often wonder what these woods looked like four hundred years ago, two hundred years ago, fifty years ago. Now I see a healthy forest, with trees of varying calipers, tulip poplar saplings with huge leaves competing with the tall beeches, branches climbing to feed from the sun. At the top of the climb, or almost at the top, the trail turns sharply right to a rock outcropping, with a chain strung between two trees warning of the exposure.

From the little outcropping I look down the Gap into the Piedmont, ridges rolling back into the haze, and up the Gap, at cliffs exposed among the tree canopy. The trail here continues a gradual climb to the peak of Little Pinnacle Mountain. At the peak, covered in trees and offering no distant views, the trail turns left and crosses a wide draw. The woods here, while not old growth, have been left alone enough that I can imagine what the woods may have looked like when hunted by the Cherokee, or traversed by Bartram. The open understory trees—rhododendron thick in the seat of the draw and dogwoods scattered across the slope—bloom throughout the spring, not showy but woven within the land-scape. I hone my focus to small things, bloom-ing in patches.

This part of the Blue Ridge is home to more than four hundred plant species, and more species of trees than all of Europe. This wealth alone marks the reasons for preserving the area, which was a coup of the Naturaland Trust, a nonprofit conservation organization located in Greenville. Beginning in 1972, the Naturaland Trust worked with landholders, most of whom readily understood the reasons for preserving their properties, and sold or donated their land to the Trust and the state of South Carolina. A collection of federal and state agencies then pieced together the various properties, and by 1980, the Mountain Bridge Wilderness, connecting and protecting the Table Rock and Poinsett Reservoir watersheds, was complete.

Crossing the shoulder of the draw, the trail turns onto an old road bed. Here I can really run; I ratchet down the pace, following con-tours among the tall trees and open forest. My stomach settles. After a mile and a half, I reach the John Sloan trail, which climbs up and over the ridge to the Rim of the Gap trail.

The Rim of the Gap trail narrows, wedged in by rhododendron and mountain laurel and sassafras. Though high above its fall, this part of the watershed is governed by the Middle Saluda River as well. The Rim of the Gap trail is very wet; water seeps and falls down the rock faces, creating naturally cool areas. There, the sweat chills on your body. In late winter, chunks of ice sit at the bottom of these cliffs, thick like wet snow.

The trail hugs the wall; rhododendrons make a kind of guardrail on the other side. Nonethe-less, I wouldn't want to fall as I pick my way quickly along the trail. My focus is down, on the soggy leaf-strewn path, with rocks and roots to high-step over, picking up and putting down my feet very quickly. The changes in moisture—running along a relatively dry trail and then suddenly hitting water sliding down

rocks—force your attention away from the views, or the flowers. It's the body's turn, not the eyes. I'll stop if I want to look at the mossy rocks, or catch that glimpse between the trees up the Gap.

I stop and take a picture of the mossy rocks, small pink flowers barely visible from even six feet above. Small things attract my eye when I'm focused so closely on the trail. My periph-ery jumps and shines. On this trail you'll fall if you're not watching where you're going. For two miles I climb up and down ladders, many times using hands and feet to descend and as-cend steep, rocky, narrow passages. One, called Weight Watchers Rock, seems almost a joke, a tight square made by a falling rock. The yellow slash of paint that marks the trail cuts the square in half. My claustrophobia kicks in, and I get ner-vous passing through it, but pass through it I do.

I pass another waterfall. Each of the ten or so on this section of the Rim of the Gap trail gets

After the second such waterfall, the trail climbs through the woods to the junction with the lollipop loop of the Frank Scoggins trail, about six miles and over an hour and a half into the run. I climb up and to the right, past a significant chestnut stump, jagged and broad, about the only thing left of the American chestnut, wiped out by an Asian blight within forty years at the turn of the twentieth century.

Not far from here, in Oconee County, Joe James is trying to revive the American chestnut. Dr. James, a retired orthopedist, has been crossing American chestnut specimens with a blight-resistant Chinese chestnut. The continued crossings result in trapping the blight-resistant qualities in the trees with stronger American chestnut features. The project is a perfect blend of science and romanticism, the kind I love.

Ahead on the right, the Coldspring Connector drops steeply to Coldspring Branch. The creek runs shallow, narrow, and rocky, with water pooling where the trail crosses it. The crossing requires a sudden shift in footfall, putting my feet down much more quickly, in short bursts to maintain my footing as I hop among the rocks. The trail turns back, then climbs steep stairs for a short distance to the junction with the Coldspring Branch trail. I turn left, climbing the old roadbed around the contours to the ridge.

I turn right; the Bill Kimball trail climbs slightly, following the ridge line through tall straight hickories and oaks, the terrain dropping off both sides of the nut strewn trail. The winter views must be spectacular here. In the summer heat, the leaf cover keeps the breeze cool. The trail is soft; I lengthen my stride again, stretching hamstrings that have been grinding through two-and-a-half hours of steep climbs and descents. The trail begins to wind slightly downhill, not enough to engage the quadriceps. I hesitate to let myself roll too fast, but appreciate the shift in muscle tasks.

Now the trail turns sharply downhill, hugging the bottom edges of the cliffs, the long stone

progressively more tumbling. Here, up the gap, the water cascades, and I wonder about its fall to the Middle Saluda. About eight hundred feet below, less than half a mile on the map, the Middle Saluda gains steam, having been joined by Coldspring Branch and plenty of other unnamed streams. This section of the river is early in its trip to the ocean, young, maybe, top of the watershed fresh, wild, and cold. You can hear it in its rumble, which pervades the quiet of the trail, though many times you can't make it out among the brush.

Twice here at the western end of the Rim of the Gap trail the path turns steeply up, switching back to the top of the falls I just passed a quarter mile before. The pitch leaves me breathless; I even walk slowly, taking the opportunity to follow the water in its fall. The view down Jones Gap is sometimes hazy and doesn't photograph well, but I know it's there. I imprint the view the same as my body imprints the ruggedness of the trail.

faces of El Lieutenant, so called for its resemblance to El Capitan in the Yosemite Valley. The trail continues its sharp descent, and I pick up four more views of the marvelous rock face.

The great value of the Mountain Bridge Wilderness lies in its geological and biological uniqueness. El Lieutenant is granitic gneiss, a metamorphic rock formed in this case from the original igneous granite buried under miles of rock and earth that formed here 450 million years ago. As the surrounding rock eroded, the harder granitic gneiss was revealed, leaving this formation and the nearby Caesars Head and Table Rock. The rock rolls upward from the trail, smooth and rounded, rising some three hundred feet above.

Here the trail drops suddenly, very steeply. The pace slows to meet the force of gravity. Each step requires a stopping action and my quads, already raked from the intense climbs of the previous ten miles, are challenged again by terrain. Pressure and heat transform those muscles to jelly, I think, and falling is not out of the question. I balance, and try to find the rhythm I had over the rock gardens earlier in the run. Just as suddenly the terrain flattens, and I hear the rumble of the headwaters of the Middle Saluda.

Here the river is untamed, rolling down the bed in cascades and roils. The run becomes almost casual, loping, quads untangling. For the rest of the run, the trail follows the Middle Saluda through Jones Gap. Farther downstream, the Middle Saluda will join with the other two branches to form the Saluda River. Its journey becomes much more complicated here, and even on the other branches, courts will determine the fate of the river.

American Rivers, a conservation organization dedicated to the protection and restoration of the country's waterways, recently named the Saluda one of the top ten most endangered rivers in America. The effects of development, damming, and its flow through the urbanized parts of Greenville County have resulted in the heavily impacted flow into Lake Greenwood

downstream. The river provides drinking water for over five hundred thousand residents of the Upstate, according to American Rivers, and the as-yet unregulated phosphorous pollution resulting from the nine wastewater treatment plants located on it endanger wildlife and human beings as well. The phosphorous feeds algae in the river, and the resulting blooms deplete oxygen levels and destroy habitat and property values.

Flowing through one of the most sprawling urban environments in the country, the Saluda's troubles belie the otherwise clear, protected trout stream that is the Middle Saluda. Here near the headwaters of the first river designated "wild and scenic" under the state's Scenic Rivers program, the downstream troubles are distant and almost inconceivable.

I fall with the river, running slightly downhill for the rest of the run. The Jones Gap trail, a road bed cut through the gap by Solomon Jones in the 1840s, follows the river among the American beech, Eastern hemlock, and tulip poplars that surround it. It is rocky and traversed by small streams along its length. The rocks make for more dancing, light feet, trying to maintain a pace after the battering of the previous miles. The fall of river and trail is easier here, not tumultuous cascades, but consistent, with a few steep drops where the fault lines have slipped.

In the winter, I often have these trails to myself, it seems. In the summertime, the closer I get to the trailhead the more people I see. Many are off for longer adventures, but most sport clean white sneakers, carry store-bought water in throw-away bottles, and have that pudginess of untested ramblers. In the summer, I'm completely drenched in sweat, my clothes, hat, socks dripping; I practically slosh in my shoes. I wonder what they make of me, grinning, often bloody, always dirty, carrying little in the way of gear, running down the trail toward the comfortable cars they have just left. My energy level is high despite the depletion, having been stripped down through erosion of physical output, changed by the pressure and stress of difficult terrain and quick pace. Do they guess at the changes?

* * *

I've always had a fascination with the local, I think, and with the small. I laugh that the first pictures I took on an adventure to Mount Mitchell were of a butterfly on a rock in the trail. I have several pictures that include my shoe, which I slide in to show how tiny the flowers peeking through the rocks are, or how thick the blanket of blooms really is. It's part of these runs, to be focused on the small parts in front of me, aware of the wholeness of where I am, unimpeded by work, and hustle, and the baggage we all carry with us daily.

When I run, I wear a water-filled bladder in a fanny pack, a system I bought a little over fifteen years ago. I have a hand-held water bottle I carry in a sling of sorts, a usual accessory for trail runners. I wear light-weight clothing and depend on layers for warmth on colder days. In deep winter, I might carry a rain jacket rolled up and tucked under the bungee cords on the fanny pack. I wear all high-tech materials that pass perspiration away from my body to evaporate, a key component of wilderness travel in any weather. I almost always wear a baseball hat. When I find a pair of running shoes I like, I stick with them, buying new pairs of the same model as the old ones wear out. Over twenty-five years of running I've pared down the gear I use to a narrow variety of items entirely chosen because they don't get in the way.

For most of those twenty-five years, I've done a long run at least once a week. The length, the pace, the fitness level, the location, and, to a certain extent, the motivation change, but for some reason—I think the love of habits—I run long on the weekend. I like to run fast, I like to be fit enough to respond, "You bet," when asked to go for a long run or bike ride or hike or climb, I like to be outside, I like to scare myself, I like to be in the weather, I like to bare my soul deep in the woods, I like to feel my body function when I don't trust my mind. I've run in New Hampshire when it was 25 below; I've run in Arizona when it was 108. I prefer to run in the mountains and on trails now, but I loved the rolling dirt roads of Virginia, the Philadelphia streets, and the high peaks in Colorado. I've run a couple hundred races, including one in Alaska. I've run everywhere I've visited, including the streets of Beijing.

I like to be out in it, the heat, the cold, the rain, the snow, exposed to what's there, where I am, at the moment, to challenge, I'll say, my humanity, what others might call God, what I say is worshipful of the world around me. There in the woods of the Mountain Bridge Wilderness, like Joyce Carol Oates, I feel most human, I am, perhaps, myself. 🏔

NEW WAY HOME
Heather Magruder

ON MY FIRST WALK THROUGH THE WOODS IN THE PIEDMONT OF SOUTH CAROLINA, I LEARNED THAT MAPS WEREN'T MUCH USE IF YOU STRAYED FROM THE DESIGNATED TRAIL.

I'd grown up thousands of miles away and had been used to wandering all over hills, maps rarely needed. When I tried the same technique on Paris Mountain, I quickly found myself squinting up, shading my eyes against the oak- and hickory-filtered sun seeking a sense of direction and finding, instead, trees for what looked like miles. I managed to scramble back to the trail and then to my bike, which I rode just about everywhere, not having discovered the rule about it not being cool to own a bike with tiny wheels, a bike that folded in half for easy carriage on a bus or train.

The year was 1981 and I'd recently shed my school uniform—grey skirt, white socks, black shoes, blazer, and tie—and moved away from the craggy landscape of my childhood, the west coast of Scotland. My dad had earned a

promotion and was eager to navigate his new workplace in this land of opportunity. I, on the other hand, had no idea how I would navigate the crowded hallways, lockers, or lunchroom of an American public high school. I'd come from single-file lines and rigid rules during the week and from weekend walks across the bare Scottish hills, which I'd been navigating since as far back as I could remember. Our headmistress belted out instructions for the uniformed time at school. At first my grandfather, Papa, and then just a map and my eyes led the way across my weekend landscape.

When I was four and five and six, I'd taken Papa's hand and walked through Douglas Park to the base of the hill we called the Muddy Mountain. From its foot, I could see the sheep dotting the hillside, the paths they'd made, the bracken around which we'd walk. I could see my destination. An indicator stood at the top, pointing out Arran and other western isles across the Firth of Clyde. On one such walk, when I was six, Papa turned inland, suggesting we walk farther instead of turning for home as we usually did, and letting me lead the way. I navigated us across the moor on the flat top of the hill and then down the other side, finding a new way home.

Later on, whether at the Muddy Mountain or on larger hills—the Corbetts and Munros as they are called there—I'd stand at their feet and see every inch of where I'd tread. I'd mark my way around knee-high bracken or low-slung gorse and heather or through soggy moorland grasses and over rock. I could point my way over miles and then step across the land, every move clear. Maps were necessary only on the occasional long walk over multiple hills to keep my orientation. For the most part, though, bar the odd closing in of cloud cover, I

made my way without ever fearing I'd get lost. In this new country, I had no such confidence. The rules of school and friends in this new land, of who was crowned homecoming queen and who got to talk to her and why that might matter, I had no idea how to uncover. Even the land itself was hidden. Pine and hemlock, hickory and oak lined the hills, preventing a view of the actual rock and dirt that held things. I thought this first looking at Paris Mountain, then going for a Sunday drive with my dad past other hills in the Piedmont.

When I began to navigate my way into the terrain of my first American friendship, I also began my discovery of the land. I was fourteen when Jeff, who lived around the corner and was a year ahead of me at school, took me on my first real hillwalk, called a "hike" here, at Table Rock State Park. The map at the trailhead offered multiple choices, from a simple loop that wound along a small creek, to the one that led to the top. This was the one we took, marching into the woods and soon finding ourselves hiking blind to our location except for the slashes of paint on trees, blazes that told us we were on the right path. The trail rose and curved quickly up and away from the creek. A small burn in my calves was all that told me that something had changed. Even in the woods on the trail, with feet on the mountain, the land still felt hidden for me. In the middle of the hike, I could see only one curve of trail up ahead and one curve behind. Side to side, trees blocked any potentially clear view. I could see neither destination nor origin. I was meant to trust the blazes and keep going. On that first hike I trusted Jeff, who trusted the blazes.

We stepped on and up, farther from the water, deeper into the trees, at last rounding a curve and coming upon huge boulders rising from the land. In the gap between the rocks, with each hand on solid granite on either side of me, I found my first sense of safety. These were a treasure, hidden by the trees, and uncovered on the trail.

Jeff and I pressed on, around curve after curve, quads and calves beginning to shout their testament to our progress as we marked our first hour on this terrain. Soon after, the trail yawned out onto a huge outcropping, Governor's Rock. From there, I saw hundreds of miles in one direction, the final hump of the mountain on which I stood blocking views of the other side. From Governor's Rock I felt my first real connection with this new land. There, I had the first inkling that it might be okay to stand in a location from which I couldn't see where I'd begun. Governor's Rock held no indicator like the ones on top of so many Scottish hills, orienting walkers to their place in the world. Return trips with maps and compass were necessary in order for me to orient myself to what I saw when my boots were on that rock.

From Governor's Rock we hiked on, stopping at open rocky spaces on the top of the mountain, each one offering tree-topped hills, sprawling valleys, lakes that comprised this new land, each one allowing me to uncover a context for this country I was meant to call home.

I was hooked. From then on, I sought new walks in the woods, travelling up and down trails on which only the footfalls of others and the occasional blaze on a tree, sometimes in dire need of fresh paint, told me I wasn't completely lost. From eight a.m. to three p.m., I staggered through the halls of high school, still mostly blinded by the forest of students. On weekends, or, when the days grew longer, I dashed straight out of the school parking lot, anxious to find myself moving forward, eager for a path on which a blaze showed the way. At fourteen and fifteen and sixteen, uprooted from the land where I'd begun, I found solace on those paths on which, after a few minutes, I could see neither where I'd begun nor where I would end.

Since I didn't have to plot my own course on those trails, I learned to pay attention to the small, discovering between each curve bright orange mushrooms nestled at the bases of trees, delicate ferns rolling away into the deeper woods, plants and flowers whose names I soon learned: walking fern, lady's slipper, bloodroot, sweet white trillium. I found these on trails that wove over Table Rock and around Caesars Head and across Sassafras Mountain. And in not so very much time at all, no matter how ill-used the trail or how faded the blazes, I found these to be the clearest markings in my life, teaching me that if I could trust and keep moving forward, the clear view would open up for me in the right time, showing me new ways to find home. 🖎

> For the most part, though, bar the odd closing in of cloud cover, I made my way without ever fearing I'd get lost.

THE GREAT JOCASSEE DEATH MARCH
Gerald Teaster

IT SEEMED LIKE A GREAT IDEA AT THE TIME. AND IT WAS A FINE EXPERIENCE LOOKING BACK ON IT AND HAVING LIVED TO TELL ABOUT IT.

It started as a casual conversation about hiking and backpacking with my two sons, Raymond and James, and Raymond's wife, Arlene. We had been on several hikes together and one short overnight backpacking hike on the Appalachian Trail. They were looking for something more challenging.

I should have known that something requiring great exertion would spring from all of this. Most of our family amusements turned into endurance contests of one sort or another. Both Raymond and James have long had a favorite saying: "Anything worth doing is worth overdoing."

They were physically up to almost anything we planned. James had recently returned from a two-year Peace Corps tour in equatorial Africa which had involved, among other

things, a twenty-mile hike into the Congo where he had been held overnight by Communist soldiers, then freed in a deal that involved trading a pair of combat boots. Raymond and Arlene, meanwhile, ran in races to keep themselves in top condition.

I, on the other hand, an Eagle Scout as a teen and a former dedicated hiker, camper, and hunter, had put on some weight. It did not seem like much—only about two pounds a year. However, over the thirty years or so since my teens, this added up to sixty extra pounds. As this was a fifty percent increase over my high school weight, it seemed to me to be a *small* handicap.

We came up with a plan for a three-day trek on something called the Foothills Trail around Lake Jocassee. James, an architect by education, holds to the school that if you plan a thing too much the spontaneity is lost. But Raymond, a chemical engineer by education, planned every move. He had a trail guide and numerous topographic maps. We should have had a clue from Raymond's book. It described the nineteen-mile stretch of trail that we were to go on as "severe." Our hike was to end with a 1,200-foot vertical climb up Whitewater Falls, which the book described as the highest falls east of the Mississippi.

To add to the experience, we chose to make our hike "non-returnable." Raymond and Arlene hired a boat guide service to take us up to the end of Lake Jocassee and let us out on the trail. After a false start with a dead boat battery, we had a beautiful trip across the lake and were let off on a deserted part of the trail. The boat pulled away and there we were. It would be nineteen miles of "severe" hiking between us and civilization. There were no roads or houses that we would pass on the trail.

We put on our packs. Mine weighed right at fifty pounds on the bathroom scales back at Raymond's house, but it felt much heavier there in the woods. I had a clue it was going to feel even heavier when I realized I was sinking into the soft ground just standing still. I had received considerable verbal abuse about my pack's contents while we were packing. I had brought a number of canned items that I remembered fondly from the camping trips when I was a teen. I also had a quantity of Snickers and hot chocolate packs. It had been my experience in my youth that you could not have too many Snickers or too much hot chocolate. I certainly did not remember the stuff being too heavy back then.

Raymond's trail guide said there was a beautiful view of a swinging bridge "only" a half mile up the trail, so we set off in the opposite direction. We found out later that there is no "only" distance of any length on the trail. The trail was basically level on the way

to the bridge and at one place we saw five or six deer in one group. After viewing the bridge we turned around and started back to where we were supposed to start in the first place. Our "only one-half mile" each way had turned into one hour of lost time and we were late in starting the real hike.

This time we were on our original route and the trail immediately got steep. Within a half hour, we established the order of march for the entire hike: James and Arlene leading way ahead, Raymond hanging back so that he could hear my death rattle, and me far behind.

They stopped somewhere on the slope and waited for me to catch up. I arrived gasping for air and they later described me as "flinging off my pack like a madman." After a while, I had enough oxygen to begin normal speech and reassured them that I wasn't having a heart attack. James volunteered to carry some of my stuff, and I graciously agreed. I really believe that he only volunteered because he thought that carrying my stuff would be easier than carrying my corpse—which he feared.

With my pack ten pounds lighter, we set off again. The going was still slow for me but at least I realized that cardiac arrest was not imminent.

At one of the early stops, Raymond pulled out one of his topographic maps to find out how far away our intended camp site was. James immediately held his hands over his ears, hollered "Don't tell me! You'll spoil the surprise!" After Raymond put his maps away, James accused him of being a "right-brained" hiker.

James, an architect by education, holds to the school that if you plan a thing too much the spontaneity is lost.

We had a campsite in mind that was about five miles from where we started, but we were not making very good time. It was starting to get dark, and I was about to collapse. We found a campsite that had been used quite a bit, and Raymond and I convinced each other that it was the site we had planned on. We pitched our tents, had an early supper, and went to bed.

We had planned to get a very early start and be on the trail by about 7 o'clock. As things worked out, we were finally packed up and on our way by about 9:30. Even though the trail was steep, we thought, *this is still not too bad*. It wasn't long before we got into our places—James and Arlene far ahead, Raymond close enough to hear my gasping and cursing, and me bringing up the rear.

We had gone about two hours when we came to the real campsite—where we thought we had been last night. It meant that we were a half day off schedule. James and Arlene pressed on, redoubling their efforts to make up for lost time. Raymond was still holding back, but now less from concern about my plight than from difficulty in keeping up with "The Hikers from Hell" as he now started to refer to James and Arlene.

Every so often they would stop, and I would finally catch up—wheezing, sweating, and cursing. James looked at Raymond and said, "Do you remember that documentary we saw about Eskimos abandoning their old people on an ice floe when they can't keep up? Do you think we can find some ice?"

The two "Hikers from Hell" took off again and we were on our way. If anything, the trail got steeper. There were sections with steps cut out for an almost vertical climb. Much of this part of the trail was too steep for even for a horse.

Finally, we came to the Horsepasture River, where we stopped for lunch. My feet hurt, so I soaked them in the cold water. Here, we saw the first people we had seen in the last twenty-four hours. It was a family that had put their boat ashore from Lake Jocassee and were walking along the river. They observed us from the footbridge over the river in the same way they might watch animals in the zoo eat their lunch.

Since we were far behind our schedule, we had to press on. Our new plan was to make up for lost time and get to the campsite where we had planned to be for the second night. James, being far ahead, came upon a beautiful campsite beside a little creek. The campsite had everything—wood, water, flat land, and a beautiful view. But it was three miles short of where we were supposed to camp. I saw him say something to Raymond, and then they hustled us off. They did everything but blindfold me and lead me past it. They told me later they were afraid if I had time to settle into the campsite they might have trouble getting me back on the trail. They could have been right.

We were strung out over a distance when we started to smell a musty odor. A short distance ahead, very plainly visible in the soft dirt, was a bear footprint, fresh that day. A few minutes later we realized that we were all walking in a tight little huddle and not spread out nearly as much as before. Finally, after what seemed like a million miles, we came to where we were supposed to camp. We had a very nice supper and went to bed early. It was barely dark.

* * *

The next day we got on the trail early. Our packs were much lighter, and we were getting into the rhythm of it. After an hour or so, we began meeting people on the trail coming from the Whitewater Falls area. Just before we came to the trail to the falls, we came to a road and a parking lot. It was designated something like "Bad Creek Viewing Area." It came to me in a clear vision that the road must lead out to civilization. We had left one of the cars at the parking lot at Whitewater Falls so that we would have a way to get back. It struck me that the others could stop by this area later and pick me up and that I could avoid the climb up Whitewater, which appeared to go straight up. So I wimped out and told them that I would just wait on them there. Without too much argument they all agreed. I think they were glad not to be faced with the prospect of carrying my remains.

Looking around to find a place to wait, I saw a beautiful green area of grass under some trees. The grass was thick as a carpet. I took off my pack and lay down on the grass in the sunshine. I was so tired that it took me a while to figure out why the grass was so green and thick—it had been fertilized with a considerable quantity of cow manure. By the time I smelled it, the damage had been done, so I just lay there and took a little nap.

Lying there in the odoriferous grass, I thought about how this hike had not happened exactly as I had planned. I realized that the imagined hiker in my mind was going to be the seventeen-year-old Eagle Scout from my youth. The hiker that actually showed up was a middle-aged man who was thirty years older and sixty pounds heavier than the imaginary scout. Still, even with all the difficulty, it was great fun. The truth of another one of my sons' sayings also came to mind: "What does not kill you makes you stronger." 🖎

I AM NATURE GIRL

By Missy Nicholson

WHEN MOST PEOPLE DREAM OF BEING A SUPERHERO OR HAVING SUPER POWERS, I THINK THEY IMAGINE THEY CAN FLY, OR THEY CAN MOVE OBJECTS WITH THEIR MINDS, OR MAYBE THEY CAN EVEN SHAPE-SHIFT. FOR ME, MY SUPER-ALTER-EGO HAS ALWAYS BEEN NATURE GIRL.

In real life, I'm a chubby, forty-two-year-old CPA turned stay-at-home mom who spends her days washing clothes, working with the PTA, and sitting in school car lines. But in my mind, I'm a granola-eating, mountain-climbing, Teva-wearing Adventuress who's out to conquer the world.

This past spring I decided it was time to do something about this dream. I planned to officially become an "Outdoorswoman." I would transform myself by hiking everywhere I could within a fifty-mile radius. By the end of the summer, I figured I might even be one of those cool people that shop at Outfitters and look like they belong there (well, minus the athletic build and the tan—I'm sensitive to the sun).

I enlisted the help of my good friend Traci for several reasons: she likes the outdoors, she's easy to talk to, and she knows CPR in case I have a heart attack trying to realize my dream. We decided that since I was incredibly out of shape, we should start small.

And small it was. Our first hiking challenge: Reedy River Falls Park in Greenville. Hey—don't laugh! Rome wasn't built in a day. We parked at the Greenville Zoo and began our fearless trek across miles and miles of asphalted trails in a quest to build endurance. We followed the Reedy Riverwalk from Cleveland Park to Reedy River Falls. My hiking skills were put to the test when I had to force my jiggly quads to make it all the way to the top of the steps at the Overlook Grill so I could use the public restroom. The view from up there was breathtaking—the water flowed freely over the falls, the grass was green, and the mulch beds sprouted gorgeous flowers. It was a Greenville spring at its best! All sorts of folks walked the paths, played Frisbee with their dogs, and lay on blankets reading and writing. For just a few minutes, I fit in there. It didn't matter that I was trying to act like that hike up those stairs hadn't completely exhausted my supply of oxygen. While panting, I tried to breathe in the sweet-smelling air (gotta love those West End restaurants) and relish my role as Nature Girl Wannabe. I was one step closer to realizing my dream.

We started back toward the zoo and finished our hour-long trek by lunching on peanut butter sandwiches on a bench next to the river. And as we listened to the zoo monkeys howling (I swear we might as well have been trail-side in the Costa Rican jungles), I tried to quiet my mind and just "own" that little piece of nature for a bit. Sweaty and exhilarated, we giddily planned our next hike: Paris Mountain State Park.

It took several weeks and proper alignment of the planets to enable our hectic schedules to come together so we could make our next outing. In the intervening days, I took the initiative to really dig in and learn more about hiking … not by actually hiking, mind you, but just by Googling stuff on the internet and watching nature shows on the Discovery Channel. I decided it was time for me to get organized. I needed the proper gear. I needed maps. I needed granola.

I rifled through my closet and found some old boots and a small Vera Bradley backpack (think how cute I looked on the trail with my Java Blue small pack with coordinating sunglass holder). I then headed for the mecca of all outdoors shops: the Wal-Mart sporting goods section. I even went to the one in Travelers Rest because it's closer to the mountains, and well, just because when I'm driving on Highway 25 I *feel* like I'm healthy and outdoorsy.

I bought a whistle/compass combo (I have no idea how to use a compass, but I figured

I surely needed one). I bought an emergency poncho and a small first aid kit. I bought granola bars (chocolate chip—yeah, baby!). I was now ready to begin the next phase of training.

We arrived on Paris Mountain on a beautiful spring day in April, promptly showing our ignorance by being totally unaware that we had to pay admission. After scrounging around in the floorboards for a few minutes, we found enough quarters to get past the guards. We parked at Buckhorn Gate Trailhead, eager to start the day. I had my Java Blue backpack loaded with all kinds of necessities: tweezers for pulling out ticks, splinters, or those pesky chin hairs; a can of pepper spray for possible unpleasant encounters (Traci wondered if we could hit a snake in the eyes if necessary); and my insurance card and driver's license in case I became the main story on the 6 o'clock news and had to be rescued off the side of the mountain by one of those hunky, uniformed guys that hang out of helicopters on a rope (I wish … Wait, did I just say that out loud?).

We hiked about twenty feet from the minivan to the trailhead to take a look at the maps. We had been outside now for about three minutes, so naturally we were beginning to feel a little hungry. Traci whipped out a bag of Chex Mix, and we munched on that while congratulating ourselves on getting this far. While eating, I noticed a sign that explained the rules of outdoor potty breaks. You may not relieve yourself near any water source. If you have to #2, you must either dig a "cat-hole" six to eight inches deep and bury it or be prepared to "Pack It Out." Under no circumstances are you supposed to leave TP on the trail. I felt sorry for the poor hiking fool who might be unprepared to deal with that!

This past spring I decided it was time to do something about this dream. I planned to officially become an "Outdoorswoman."

Right then, a woman sprinted by us, coming up the hill from the Sulphur Springs Trail and immediately running down Brissy Ridge. My jaw dropped open and a little piece of Chex Mix fell onto my chin. This woman—SHE was Nature Girl. She was everything I wanted to be and more! She moved like the wind, and she wore all the right hiking clothes and shoes. She even had this cool belt strapped around her waist with two big water bottles hanging from each hip. She looked just like a gunslinger from the old West. All this AND she was at least 15 years older than me. So, as I was standing there in my black velour sweatpants with my Java Blue backpack, munching on Chex Mix, I had an epiphany: I, too, could become Nature Girl. All I needed was one of those awesome water belts!

We started down Brissy Ridge with high hopes of taking that trail to Pipsissewa so we could see the reservoir. The day was a bit hazy, but we still had a fabulous view of the surrounding countryside. After thirty minutes or so we were really working up a sweat. We chugged some water, pacing ourselves a bit so we were sure to have enough for the entire hike (we're experienced hikers, you know). When we began to feel a little hunger pang again, Traci whipped out a bag of Official Trail Mix (it said so on the bag). We had almost finished the bag when I noticed the expiration date—May 20, 2005. *Whoa*, I thought. *That was four years ago!* I began to wonder about the Chex Mix we ate earlier— was it old too? Maybe it was my imagination, but suddenly my stomach started to rumble and groan.

We kept on trekking, sloshing in some muddy trail parts, noticing the new growth of pretty spring plants alongside the trail, and meeting an assortment of hikers in all shapes and sizes. As we rounded a bend in the path, my stomach growled loudly in protest. I wondered if there was a public restroom here like at Reedy River. Where were the cute restaurants and asphalted trails when you need them? Sweat broke out on my brow as I looked at the map and realized we had been walking almost an hour, and we were only halfway through. We had hiked about a mile on Brissy Ridge and then about another

mile down Pipsissewa (an "out and back" trail). So we had close to another hour of hiking to get back to the trailhead, and I knew I couldn't make it that long without a potty break. At that point, I tried to decide if Traci and I were good enough friends to share what was about to become a memorable experience.

It wasn't long before I became desperate. I frantically scanned the surrounding woods for an appropriate place to potty, trying to follow those rules from the trailhead. Traci stood guard as I wandered off the trail in search of a tree with a width larger than my hips. I couldn't help but think of the Stephen King novel *The Girl Who Loved Tom Gordon*. Nine-year-old Trisha McFarland got lost for eight days when she stepped off the trail to take a potty break. Would that happen to me, too? Would swarms of mosquitoes also descend to feast on my flesh? Would a hideous creature stalk me in this deep dark forest?

I finally found a good spot. It was far enough from the trail not to be seen, close enough for me to still hear Traci, and it was nowhere near water. So I was at least obeying the water rule. Now what was the other rule? Oh, yeah, you must either "Pack It Out" or bury it in a cat-hole (TP wasn't an issue since I didn't have any, although I briefly looked at the compass and wondered if I might actually find a use for *it*). I gazed at my cute Java Blue backpack and immediately decided that I would NOT be packing it out. That only left me with one choice— dig a cat-hole. Good thing I brought a shovel … NOT! I found a stick strong enough to allow me to carve out a nice hole in the ground. I'm pretty sure it wasn't six inches deep, but desperate times call for desperate measures.

Traci yelled to remind me not to use just any leaf for cleanup. I was suddenly regretting not listening to my dad when I was twelve years old and he showed me how to identify certain poisonous plants. What was that saying? "Leaves of three, leave them be." Or was it "Leaves of three, friend of thee"? *Maybe I should just look for a four-leaf clover.* When I returned to the path, Traci tried her best not to laugh while offering me the rest of her outdated Official Trail Mix.

We continued on without further incident, even stopping one time to give directions to a mountain biker. After two hours or so of hiking, we finished—we successfully hiked about four miles on the Brissy Ridge and Pipsissewa Trails. We were sweaty, thirsty, and of course, hungry—but we did it! We celebrated by driving back to the park center. We sat in rocking chairs on the covered porch, enjoyed our peanut butter sandwiches, and began to think "where next?" Out there on the trail in the midst of bugs, stale trail mix, and cat-holes, we caught hiking fever. The only cure: more hiking.

I was riding high that day. I felt great. The blood was singing through my veins. I was alive! Of course, by the next morning, I was sure that I must have run smack into a truck on that trail and blocked it from my memory. I was so sore I could barely fall out of the bed. I discovered exactly how many muscles you use hiking—*all* of them! I hobbled around for several days popping ibuprofen like candy and walking stooped over like that Tim Conway character from the Carol Burnett Show. You know—that old guy with the wild white hair who shuffled along, stooped over, moaning and mumbling to himself. Well, that was me, only I was mumbling "ohmybackohmykneesohmy-feet" until my body returned to normal.

Apparently the pain of hiking is as easy to forget as the pain of childbirth because it wasn't long before I was back to planning another hike. For our next trip we kicked it up a notch, planning to tackle Raven Cliff Falls at Caesars Head State Park. In the days leading up to this momentous hike, I gathered additional supplies I was sure to need: a "Life is Good" shirt that has one of those cute stick figures hiking on the front, a small shovel with a six-inch blade, and a pack of travel Charmin wipes. I also acquired a hiking guidebook combed from the numerous volumes found in the Carolinas section at Barnes & Noble. And my Dad made me a walking stick from the woods in our backyard.

I even ventured into a *real* outfitters shop in Greenville. Even though the bearded fellow working there totally knew I was a Nature Girl poser, he introduced me to the wonders of pricey but sweat-free wool socks (who knew?) and never once rolled his eyes when I asked stupid questions like "is it true that I should run from a bear in a zigzag line?"

A couple of days before our hike, a news report relayed that an actual bear had been seen in the vicinity (somewhere within the surrounding three states). That whole zigzag line question was now very relevant. I headed to Mast General Store, where I noticed that you could buy a bell to wear that tinkles when you walk and warns the bear that you're coming. I wasn't so sure about that—not that I wanted to surprise a bear, but I certainly didn't want to give him a head start on an attack either. Then someone told me that if I did happen to encounter a bear on the trail, all I really had to worry about was outrunning my hiking partner. Since Traci's a softball and volleyball coach, a physical education teacher, and weighs about thirty pounds less than I do, I thought my chances of outrunning her were not very good. But then my husband showed me a few self-defense moves, and I began to plot how I could take out one of Traci's legs and leave *her* on the trail for the bear. I started to feel less worried. Hey, that's what friends are for!

I also decided that if I was going to survive this four-mile "moderate" hike to the Raven Cliff Falls Suspension Bridge, I better get in shape. I started walking at least forty-five minutes daily, even occasionally mustering the energy for a short run. It was hard to fit this exercise into an already hectic schedule, but after that Paris Mountain hike and the pain afterwards, I wanted to be better prepared. Nature Girl could not die from exhaustion while hiking—or worse—she could not *quit*. As my weight dropped and my energy increased, my excitement over the coming hike soared.

The day of our hike, the skies were a cloudless, brilliant blue. We followed the Gum Gap Trail to Naturaland Trust. On the way out to the falls, the trail wound up and down many times, like a corkscrew. The path was glorious in some places, smelling mossy and loaded with mountain laurel. And in other places, all I could concentrate on was putting one foot in front of the other and silently wondering why anyone would voluntarily subject themselves to such physical exertion.

As we got closer to the falls, the hill steepened—we climbed and climbed. At last, we descended steps built into the hill and reached the top of the falls with the river snaking right beside us. It was absolutely beautiful. There were no other hikers around. It was cooler and calmer than the rest of the trail—a spiritual retreat. Unfortunately, I couldn't completely enjoy the beauty. I was only too aware that every step I had taken down to the falls would be a step up on the way back later.

The path continued to a bridge that crossed the expanse of the falls at the top. It swayed slightly as we walked over it. I sucked in my fear, peered over the rope railing and peeked down the waterfalls … what a long ride down that would be! At the other end of the bridge, the path was completely different. It looked like a barely cut swath through a rainforest—the guidebook labeled it "strenuous," but the path's name was even worse: Dismal Trail. I wondered if this trail had served as inspiration to Michael Crichton when he was penning *Congo*. That was enough for me to decide that continuing farther was out of the question. We backtracked a little and found a big rock jutting out into the water. We sat and ate our peanut butter sandwiches, watching the water flow past us and topple over the falls. The only noise was the sound of the moving water and a few birds.

And as I sat there, I began to understand a few larger truths about hiking. Yes, it's important to have the cute t-shirt and backpack. Yes, we can overcome bad potty experiences while hiking. No, you most certainly should *not* run from a bear (unless you've taken out

the legs of your hiking buddy). But right then, I mainly understood what true beauty was. I could easily envision what the Garden of Eden must have been like. It's hard for me to imagine someone experiencing the unspoiled beauty of the Upstate's many nature trails and parks without communing in some way with God and without wanting to work toward keeping these areas pristine and protected.

All too soon our watches reminded us that we had to trek back to reality—the school car line awaited. The hike back was hard, harder than I had imagined. I had to stop twice on the way back up those steps to catch my breath. And I knew without a doubt that even though I was in better shape physically, I was going to be hunched over like Tim Conway the next morning.

As we neared the end and got to the part of the trail that is a steep gravel service road leading up to Highway 276, I began to hallucinate. I imagined a Disney shuttle was waiting to ferry me to the top and dump me in some cute gift shop loaded with Nature Girl merchandise. I could clearly see a whole rack of "Nature Girl Water Bottle Gun Belts" on display and hear that great whistling song from "The Good, the Bad and the Ugly" playing in the background. When I finally made it to the top on my own and my vision cleared, I paused to catch my breath and look back down the trail. I couldn't help but smile and think *I came, I hiked, and I conquered*.

Hiking will be a part of my life forever now. The entire Mountain Bridge Wilderness area, Table Rock State Park, and miles of trails at Paris Mountain are just a few of the many close by just waiting for me to conquer them. And even though I never seem to hike as much as I want, I am constantly dreaming about my next adventure.

Where to next, Nature Girl? 🍃

BIKING

Skip Eisiminger

Jim Magruder

T. Craig Murphy

DOUBLE THE UNICYCLE, HALF THE CAR: AN HOMAGE TO THE BICYCLE IN FOUR PARTS

Skip Eisiminger

"WHEN I SEE AN ADULT ON A BICYCLE, I DO NOT DESPAIR FOR THE FUTURE OF THE HUMAN RACE."
—H.G. Wells

I.

If either of my Depression-era parents had a bicycle, I never heard about it, but their recreational shortfall ultimately translated into my gain. Parents are odd in that respect: many are convinced that what their kids need most is what they never had, yet to hear their stories about growing up, you'd think they had very full lives. Mother, in fact, had a pony named "Tony," and Dad built a "car" from a wrecked chassis and a Model-T engine. He drove it perched on a soap box. The absence of bicycles in their lives may have had something to do with the negative press that bicycles were receiving around the turn of the century when cars started nudging bikes off the road. One anonymous critic of the two-wheeler wrote,

"Man is a locomotive machine of Nature's own making, not to be improved by the addition of any cranks or wheels of mortal invention." By that logic, this critic should have been writing with his finger in the sand. Imagine, if you will, the furry parental critics of the first bipedalians: "Don't climb this tree again unless you're walking on the four feet that Mother Nature gave you!"

Without ever having the opportunity to ride a true bicycle, the Romantic poet John Keats (1795-1821) dismissed the newest extension of human legs as the latest "Nothing of the Day." Since he had the pedal-less, brake-less Velocipede (1818) in mind, I'd have to agree with him, for this device was little more than a scooter with a seat requiring "fast feet" and a flat road.

I'm not sure which would have been worse: pushing the thing uphill or dragging one's feet going down. A truer bicycle that the rider propelled by shuffling two pedals forward and back didn't come along until 1839, but neither this fifty-pounder nor the famous "penny-farthings" that followed had a sprocket-and-chain drive. That clever innovation, which would turn the bicycle into the most efficient mechanism known to man for converting his energy into forward motion, would have to wait until 1885. Tensioned-spoked wheels and pneumatic tires would follow in short order. Prostate-friendly saddles, however, would have to wait about a century to make their first appearance.

Keats's contemporary William Wordsworth (1770-1850) is reported to have logged 150,000 miles walking about the British Isles. Just think what he and sister Dorothy could have seen in tandem on the "cycle tracks" that H. G. Wells forecast in 1896 for *Utopia*. In 1926, Christopher Morley was more effusive than accurate when he observed, "The bicycle, the bicycle surely should always be the vehicle of novelists and poets … the bicycle sets [the writer] free. He sees it all afresh; nothing, nothing has ever been written yet: the entire white paper of the world is clean for his special portrait of all hunger, all joy, and all vexation." Alack, there's no evidence that Eliot, Faulkner, O'Neill, or any of their esteemed contemporaries inked their "white paper of the world" after a bike ride. I'm not saying it couldn't happen, it just didn't; but Morley got one thing right: biking and what it reveals to the cyclist is both a joy and a vexation.

II.

In 1947 when I was six, my father taught me to ride a two-wheeler on Mozart Street in Heidelberg, Germany. I don't recall if "training wheels" had been invented yet, but I know I never had the luxury of that four-wheel interim between a two- and a three-wheeler. At any rate, the rubble of war had long been carted away from the street before our family arrived with the allied army of occupation. Though the area streets were unevenly cobbled, the tooth-chipping experience of riding a two-wheeler in Germany was, nevertheless, liberating even if I was forbidden to ride on or cross the streets where the streetcars traveled. The prospect of getting my tires in one of their steel-and-stone grooves and then meeting the wheels designed to ride therein still gives me the willies. Yet, with all the restrictions that my parents placed on their son, my bike projected me into nature in a way that made and still makes my nervous system tingle with trepidation and pleasure. I wasn't one of them, but more than one cyclist had her first orgasm coasting down a hill at a speed calibrated for the right vibrating frequency.

One outing when my whole body was set *un*pleasantly aquiver occurred when I collided with a girl on her bike. I was about ten at the time, and Alice was a year or two older, but she was a better baseball player than I was, so I always felt intimidated. One evening after supper before a sitter arrived, I was riding down the street in front of our house in Falls Church, Virginia, and up ahead, I saw Alice headed directly for me. Neither one of us "chickened out," and in a flash, the adage about the middle of the road being a dangerous place was proven true. Lying with my head against the curb, drifting in and out of consciousness, I saw my father racing down the street to pick me up and carry me home. After Mother got some ice on my face, Dad drove me to the dispensary at Ft. Myers where a doctor put four stitches in my nose. My parents' evening out was cancelled, and Dad's best suit had to be sent to the cleaners. The next morning, I received a stern lecture on yielding the right of way, especially to women who outweighed me and threw a sharply breaking curve ball. My new front wheel was paid for out of my savings.

Over the next thirty years, I had more than my share of bike accidents, and three of my bikes were stolen—one right off the front porch! Accidents and thefts, however, have not always been a bad thing for me because most of the time I've been able to upgrade after the dust has settled. A few years ago as I was riding home from work, a small white Pontiac drove through a yield sign and struck me from the rear, rolling me over the handlebars, off the road, and onto the concrete apron of Kelly's BP Station. I'll never forget looking back and seeing that wedge of steel knifing into my rear wheel. My new helmet, however, a gift from my son, saved me from a concussion, but it did not dampen my ire. I leapt to my feet, rushed over to the passenger-side window of the car that had hit me and grabbed the driver by the front of his shirt. Luckily for me, he had the courtesy to stop. At this odd angle I wanted nothing so much as to reconfigure his nose, but then I noticed he was crying, and the fight went out of me. Since there were three witnesses to the accident at Kelly's, the seventeen-year-old's insurance company did not hesitate to settle for enough to buy me a new Cannondale. The frame on the old Cannondale had been slightly bent, and even though I thought it was still rideable with a new rear wheel, the claims adjuster declared it totaled. I didn't argue, and suddenly I had two Cannondales. Five years after the accident, both of them are still on the road.

One other memorable accident occurred shortly after my old Raleigh ten-speed was stolen off the porch. A colleague of mine told me I could have his 1950s-era Schwinn if I just wanted some wheels under me. Ever protective of my green image and a little short of spending money, I leapt at the offer. About the third week that I rode this rusting piece of rebar with its ruby-studded mud flaps, fenders, and teardrop fuselage (what was that about?), I was pumping up the longest hill on my short commute. But because "Rebar" had only one gear, I had to stand on the pedals to get over the crest of the hill. Suddenly half of the handlebar broke off in my right hand, and I rolled off onto the pavement. Not that I had much choice in the matter, but rolling to the right as I had done when the car hit me probably saved my life because there was traffic on the left.

I'm not positive, but I suspect that the unfortunate experiences described above have contributed to my own form of road rage. I'll never

forget being chased by a German shepherd up a long country hill—had it been downhill, I'm confident I could have outrun him. Finally the hill and the dog were too much, and I braked to a stop. Dancing about on the shoulder, trying to keep the bicycle between me and the snarling dog, I watched out of the corner of one eye as the dog's owner casually made his way across his broad lawn. Said the esteemed landowner, "Randy done had his shots."

"So I should let him bite me?" I inquired.

As I rode off, I yelled over my shoulder, "Buy a leash!"

When I'm calm, I realize that dogs are territorial by nature and are just doing their job when they chase a cyclist who drifts too close to their master's property. What really steams me though are the drivers who make a right turn immediately after passing a cyclist. Instead of pulling in behind the lead vehicle and waiting a few seconds, the driver accelerates and then makes a quick right turn causing the cyclist to brake hard or worse. After this happened to me once, my mountain bike and I went off road to chase the rude young driver in Spandex. I cut across a mortician's lawn just in time to see the culprit parking her car near the gym. As she was walking to the front door, I shot down a grassy embankment and screamed, "Are you crazy? You almost killed me back there!" She acted like she didn't know what I was talking about and went blithely into the gym. I thought about keying her car, but I knew that parking lot had security cameras, and I didn't have a key in my bike shorts.

I think the angriest I ever got on a bike was the time I was pulling up a long hill in a Clemson suburban neighborhood when a Chevrolet station wagon went laboring by. In the back of this leviathan were two boys about twelve. Seconds later, a string of firecrackers flew out of the rear window and started exploding over a span of about fifteen seconds directly in my path. Only some wildly improvised maneuvering on my part kept them from exploding under my wheels. When the fireworks ceased, I yelled some expletives at the thirty-something driver, who surely was their "boys-will-be-boys" mother. She had to have heard me and the firecrackers, but she drove blissfully on. Over the next twenty minutes, I tried my best to locate the car without luck. Several garages had their doors closed, and I imagine the three jokers were snickering behind one of those as I cruised by looking for a clue. I've often wondered what I would have done if I had caught them. I suspect I'd be like the dog that catches the eighteen-wheeler it's been chasing, bites into a rubber mud flap, and wonders, "What now?"

As a rule, I tell my wife about my biking adventures, but fortunately the great majority of my rides are not much to talk about. Frequently, though, I have a choice piece of hardware, a coin, or some clothing that I've found to give her, but she's seldom as impressed as I am. After years of riding, I still can't get over all the stuff that's lying about on America's curbed highways. I once did a tally during a ten-mile ride and found nine significant pieces of automotive hardware per mile!

Ingrid just yawned at my statistical report, but there was a day when she was not so indifferent. For about twenty years, she rode her Libella to school and work in Germany, where she grew up, until a back operation forced her to give up the benign practice. Before she had a bike of her own, she rode her father's while he was in a French POW camp, with her right leg under the cross bar to reach the far pedal. That hunched and twisted posture may be the source of her back problems, but right after the war, few families could afford bikes properly sized for kids, and Ingrid's was no exception. Her mother had a bike as well, but it was in such frequent use that Ingrid seldom had a chance to ride it. When she did, she turned the saddle's nose down and used it as a back rest as she cruised through Wolsdorf, the small village on the outskirts of Helmstedt where the family lived out the war. I don't have any photographs of this, but often Mutti, Ingrid's mother, would place Ingrid's brother in a front seat, Ingrid in a seat over the rear wheel, and then pedal the five miles to Helmstedt, the nearest town of any size, to barter for food or medicine. Along the way, all three kept their

eyes peeled for any allied aircraft, such as the American Mustang that had strafed their backyard garden in 1944. Picking apples, Uncle Willi had ignored the air-raid siren, and it had almost cost him his life.

My favorite stories involving my wife and her bicycle are set after the family moved to Helmstedt and Ingrid had been given a bike of her own on Christmas of 1953. Now in her early teens, she was a forward on the Helmstedt Sport Club (HSV) field hockey team. Half of the games were played on the hilltop sporting fields above her home, but the rest, of course, were played out of town. To attend these matches, the girls were expected to supply their own food and transportation. Usually this meant fifteen girls, many in long skirts and high heels, riding their bikes as far as thirty miles to play a ninety-minute game that consists mostly of running after a ball with a crooked stick. Win or lose, they still had to ride home—often, since this was northern Germany, in the rain.

These young athletes, most of whom were too young to have a boyfriend, remind me of Gloria Steinem's observation that "a woman without a man is a fish without a bicycle." These very capable "fish" were as strong as their mothers who had picked up the pieces after the war and helped Germany rise to her economic feet. Stoic as their mothers had been in the bomb shelters, they rarely thought of themselves as deprived. Ingrid's mother and many like her remind me of a joke photograph (circa 1890) showing a woman wheeling her bike out the front door and telling her feckless husband, "Sew on your own buttons; I'm going for a ride." Thus feminism was born.

Turn-of-the-twentieth-century promoters of the bicycle hoped that their technology would take men and women "away from the gambling rooms and rum shops," as David Herlihy writes, "out into God's light and sunshine." While the first home my wife and I made was hardly a "rum shop," I did worry that our children would receive too little exposure to "God's light and sunshine." So in short order, Santa started delivering a steady supply of

tricycles, Big Wheels, scooters, and "banana-seat" bicycles with "ape-hanger" handlebars. Our son Shane took to anything with wheels on it like a bird to a headwind. When he was thirteen, he was riding "centuries" with a couple of fellows who worked for a local Michelin plant and had ridden professionally back home in France. By the time Shane had finished high school, he wanted to ride across the country with a friend of his. I'm afraid I had filled his head with my own dreams of riding across Europe, but most of these phantoms had dissolved with the sun's rising. When Shane told us he wanted to ride to California to visit his aunt and uncle in Oakland and then fly home, I worried that he'd fall in love with the place and wouldn't come back. So the next time we rode together, I pointed out how nice it was to ride with a tailwind. I suggested that he if flew to California and *then* rode home, he'd be more likely to have a favorable wind since most of South Carolina's weather comes out of the west. As soon as we turned into a stiff headwind, I think he convinced himself, and he soon persuaded his buddy Mike that "west to east" made eminent sense.

A few weeks later, Ingrid and I drove the boys and their camping gear to the Atlanta airport and wished them Godspeed and a good trip. Four months, fifteen flats (mostly in the desert), and four thousand miles of "wheel estate" later (they'd followed the "blue highways" for the most part), Shane rode his bike up our driveway. That night, unable to sleep in his bed, he got up and pitched his tent in the backyard where he slept for close to twenty-four hours.

The amazing thing was that he wasn't burned out on bikes. The next summer, he flew to Portland, Oregon, and rode all the way down the coast to San Diego. And when he finished college, he and Mike rode from South Carolina to Maine. That last trip was the most difficult because I knew that this time he wasn't coming back. I rode about five miles out of town with the lads to the crest of a big hill. There I gave them a hug, but the words just wouldn't come to my lips. I stood there and watched as they coasted away and then climbed the next hill, waving most of the way. I blotted my eyes on my sleeve and rode back home alone. I had known this day was coming from the moment he learned that if he just kept his speed up, he could maintain his equilibrium without me. It's a curious paradox, but support and freedom are what parents must supply in carefully calibrated doses if their sons are to survive independently. As for the rider, sufficient forward motion is essential, for as Newton stated, "A body in motion tends to remain in motion." And while rest occasionally is welcome, stasis is death.

Daughters are another matter altogether. Suspicious of their vulnerabilities, most parents tend to play them a little closer to the chest. Support and freedom are still important, but the timing and dosages are different. Our daughter, Anja, "The Rider," was a natural, learning to ride her German two-wheeler, "Little Red," the first time she tried. Like her mother, she also got up on water skis the first time she tried, while I did my best to assimilate the contents of Lake Hartwell through every orifice in my body. If there had been some other girls her age who had wanted to ride farther than the corner grocery, we might have considered letting her ride the distances her brother had ridden. Women, however, have always had more to lose than men, and we were not going take the risk of sending her off looking "sweet upon the seat of a bicycle built for two," one, or any other number. Occasionally, the two of us would ride a ten-miler together, but more often our excursions involved a friend of hers, a bag of Fritos, and cruising over to the President's Park.

III.

Like me and the Segway, Mark Twain discovered the bike too late in life to fully appreciate it. Said Twain, "Get a bicycle. You will not regret it. If you live." Now I've loved and taught Twain for thirty years, but if I thought I was taking an inordinate risk when cycling, I wouldn't have helped teach our three grandsons to ride. Despite what you may be thinking, I'm not one of those grandfathers who put the *loco* in *parentis*. It's true that

about a thousand American cyclists die each year in accidents, but that's out of a population of three hundred million. Risk is surely involved, but then everything that's not shrink-wrapped and floating in formaldehyde has a risk. Take the friend of mine who broke his leg walking his dog around the block; he suffered a torsion fracture in the right fibula when he stepped on a stone and slipped. And then there's my maternal grandmother: she died in her sleep at an age younger than I am now.

Of course, the risks that exist should be recognized and minimized: there are small planes now equipped with parachutes to permit the plane with its passengers to float to earth should the engine die. Already 177 people owe their lives to this innovation. Since parachutes and air bags are impractical for cyclists, here are some realistic ways to improve your odds of returning whole from a bike trip.

First, buy yourself the largest mirror you can locate and bolt it to the left side of your handlebar. When I ride in traffic, I probably spend as much time looking behind as I do in front.

Second, when you see in your mirror a car approaching, especially if it's crowding your lane, wiggle your front wheel as if you were spastic or drunk. In my experience, eighty percent of the time motorists will give you a wider berth after they perceive your "unsteadiness."

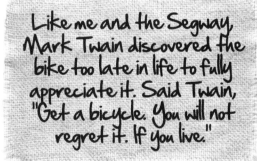

Like me and the Segway, Mark Twain discovered the bike too late in life to fully appreciate it. Said Twain, "Get a bicycle. You will not regret it. If you live."

Third, wear a helmet even if studies show that motorists give cyclists less room when they're wearing a "skid lid." The wheel-wiggle more than compensates for the helmet.

Fourth, while you're buying a mirror, buy a bell. Schwinn makes one that will clear a herd of cattle from a railroad crossing in five seconds. But there's an added benefit: I frequently use my bell to say "hello" to the pedestrians I pass. Most adults smile and wave because it sounds like the Good Humor man from their "Happy Days." As for children, the Pied Piper had no flute; he had a bell made by Schwinn.

Fifth, ride in the country, not the city. Urban biking has been described by one Clemson pre-med student as "hyperventilating in a bath of exotic hydrocarbons." Unless you're comfortable riding in a gas mask, stick to the back roads. One of my retirement goals is to buy a pickup so I can throw my bike in the back and drive into the country rather than buck the traffic getting out of town.

Sixth, expect the worst of motorists because, for one thing, they often do not see you! They may appear to be looking directly at you, but they're looking through and beyond. They're like the quarterback, so focused on a wide receiver he never sees the blitzing linebacker. Of course often the motorists *do* see you, as when a car speeds up to pass and then brakes hard to make a right turn right in front of you! It's the acceleration and the glance to the right that says, "I've seen you, but I'm in a terrible hurry, and you're just riding a bike." As I said, expect the worst; the last thing anyone wants to be is dead right.

Seventh, ride single file if you're in a group. I have an otherwise rational friend who used to insist on his God-given, constitutional right to drive down the center of the road if he was riding with someone else. I was secretly glad when he moved out of town before I had to stuff his giblets into a body bag.

Eighth, when riding in a group, you're more likely to get in a tangle with a fellow rider than a car. Someone described the *Tour de France* as "a traveling traffic jam," to which I say, "Who needs it?" Competition for the great majority of bike riders just spoils the fun and increases the chances of turning a *salto mortale*.

Ninth, don't hesitate to break the law if the traffic situation demands it. I traded in a road bike for a mountain bike for just this reason—not to jump stumps, but to go off road if a car cuts me too close. With the bigger brakes and fatter tires I have now, I can ride though sand or jump curbs and not fall or blow a tire. Riding onto the shoulder is not against the law, but within the city limits of Clemson where I usually ride, I often find myself using the sidewalks when a wheel wiggle fails or if I just have a bad feeling about a situation. I try not to do this downtown because the fines there start at $1000, and the cops are on bikes! I understand the reasons for the law's strictness: in New York City one year, cyclists killed three pedestrians in crosswalks. Still I'd rather pay a $1000 fine for jumping a curb than be pasted across some unforgiving pavement by an eighteen-wheeler.

Tenth, learn to balance your aggressions with your vulnerabilities, and you'll live to ride another day. So buy a canister of pepper spray for the dogs that chase you, and remember to take your cell phone in case you have a flat. If you can't find that equilibrium, try a stationary bike.

Safety concerns aside, one of the best reasons to ride a bike is the opportunity to muse the obscure. I'm thinking country roads now, not six-lane, urban arteries with or without bike lanes. Those painted four-inch-wide lines have never stopped a car from crossing into a bike lane, so the city is not the place to cogitate or meditate unless you're thinking about what that driver ahead of you is going to do at the light that just turned yellow. No, I'm thinking especially of the times when Shane and I would take a twenty- or thirty-mile ride in the piedmont of South Carolina, stopping every now and then to pee or get a soda. Riding with a companion can create a rapport that didn't exist before the ride began far faster than beer or bourbon can. It's a lot like tossing a ball back and forth. The ball, like the bike, makes humans (especially men) less self-conscious and thus more comfortable speaking from the heart. I think it has to do with focusing some of one's attention on balancing the bike or catching the ball. The attention paid elsewhere is attention not on oneself. If riding a bike or catching a ball is not something you're comfortable with, try tossing a Frisbee, building a tree house, or taking a walk together.

When Shane was much younger, I bought a bike seat that placed him behind me, *à la* Lucy's younger brother, Rerun, in *Peanuts*. It was the only child seat available at the time. We both hated it, though at age two he never said so, but I knew what he was thinking. Then out of the blue *Zeitgeist*, my German in-laws sent us a wicker bike seat that placed the child in front of the driver, not behind. Suddenly I had my rider between my arms, in my line of vision, and close enough that we could have a conversation regardless of the wind speed.

When our three grandsons came along, I searched high and low for a bike seat that could be bolted between the rider's saddle and the handlebars. If one existed in the U.S., Germany, or the nether world of eBay, I could not find one, so I built one. I took Ingrid's saddle from Libella, stripped off some of the hardware needed to fasten it to a seat post, added two long bolts and a piece of hard rubber of my own devising, and *voilà*, I was in business. When the boys' legs grew to where they could reach the front spokes, I added a footrest complete with toe straps to keep their busy little feet in one place. Long before that, however, I added two bells to my already crowded handlebar. As I instructed Edgar, Sterling, and Spencer, the smallest bell was to be rung whenever a squirrel or dog appeared, the middle bell was for humans, and the mighty Schwinn was reserved for vehicles or herds of cattle. The boys loved the bell system because it gave them a sense that they were doing something for our mutual safety. It also gave us a lot to talk about! According to the boys' parents, who sometimes rode with us, the boys never opened up at home quite the way they did on the bike, which naturally pleased me and made them jealous.

IV.

I'll close now with three stories drawn from a half century of cycling to suggest the range of experiences open to cyclists. On no other vehicle, and that includes my Lazy-Boy recliner, could I have had these encounters with the world.

The first happened about two miles from where I'm writing on a Saturday afternoon. I was on the way home in heavy traffic when I swerved to miss another possum "born dead on the side of the road," as we say in South Carolina. Being a mite squeamish when it comes to the dead, I averted my eyes, but my ears picked up a faint squealing. When the traffic cleared, I circled back and discovered three pink pups perhaps a day old in the shambles of their mother. Two of their siblings lay dead beside her. Across the road was a tavern where I found a plastic cup large enough to accommodate the survivors. With one hand on the handlebar and another holding the cup to my chest, I rode off supposing myself a vet ambulance minus the siren. At home, Ingrid tried feeding our guests some milk, but cow's milk from an eye dropper is apparently no substitute for a possum's teat. We called the animal shelter, but it was closed on the weekend. What to do? Finally, I decided that rather than have them starve on my watch, I'd end their squealing misery. So I struck all three a sharp blow with a spade, placed them in a common grave, and begged a mother's forgiveness.

The second tale took place on a Saturday morning in August when Ingrid and I were minding our grandson Spencer. Once he'd reached forty pounds, I realized that I needed something other than the seat that bolted to the crossbar, so I bought a tandem trailer. This ingenious device, which attaches to the seat post, gives my two-wheeler a third wheel, a wheel that the passenger can propel if he has a mind to, but Spencer usually coasted.

After a six-mile trip to the DAR's Ft. Rutledge monument that we refer to as the "Pirates' Castle," we headed home having slain all the "bad guys." About halfway to our destination, I noticed that Spencer's singing (he often sings when he's riding) had stopped, but I didn't think much about it except, "He must be tiring because he sure is not peddling." A car then pulled up beside us, and what appeared to be three Indian graduate students slowly passed us waving, smiling, and pointing at Spencer. In my mirror, I could see that he was unimpressed by our well-wishers, but his helmet visor covered his face, so I just smiled and waved back. Lots of folks look and wave. Then I noticed that the Indian driver made two U-turns, passed us again, and stopped a few yards before us. Fortunately there was no traffic. As we reached the students' car, I pulled over to see why they had stopped. Said a sari-clad young lady in impeccable British English, "Excuse me, sir, but your little boy, he is asleep." And he was until he woke with a sheepish grin on his face.

At the end of the experiential spectrum is the following tale: about five miles north of where we live, S.C. 93 parallels the railroad tracks used by Amtrak's Southern Crescent, which runs daily between New Orleans and Washington. One quicksilver morning in early spring before the church traffic cluttered "my road," I found myself gaining on the tail end of the Crescent. The sleek passenger train had apparently made an unaccustomed stop in either Clemson or Central and was just groping along trying "to get up a head of steam" as my Grandfather Floyd used to say. As I passed the caboose, I noticed a black porter on the back "porch" smoking a cigarette. He yelled something that I didn't understand but which I took to be encouragement as I made my way toward the engine. As the pine boughs overhead blurred in a green mist, I thought, "I've never ridden so fast in my life on a flat road, but then I've never had a hundred-ton locomotive pacing me either." The truth is I never even saw the engine because the train was quite long and gaining speed faster than I'd expected. Before long, I was side by side with that rattling caboose again. The porter now had some company on his porch and all of them were cheering. This time it was unmistakable. I gave it all I had like those pale Europeans matched with Jesse Owens in the '36 Olympics, but it was no use. I sat up, took my hands off the handlebars, and waved back at my fading fan club as they headed north. Just running with "Jesse," though, had been a privilege.

MY BREAK WITH GEORGE

Jim Magruder

WHAT DOES IT TAKE TO COMPLETE A BICYCLE RACING CAREER? SEVEN *TOURS DE FRANCE?* A DOZEN EUROPEAN SPRING CLASSICS WINS? A SIX-FIGURE CHAMOIS BUTTER ENDORSE-MENT? OR, FOR AN AGING OVER-ACHIEVER LIKE ME, A $50 *PRIME* (CYCLING'S VERSION OF THE PLASTIC RABBIT AT THE DOG TRACK) AND A BREAKAWAY WITH GEORGE HINCAPIE?

The first thing to understand about bike racing is that the heroic guy cranking at the front of a line is doing twenty-five to thirty percent more work than the good-for-nothing, life-sucking leeches hiding in his draft. Guys who never take a turn at the front are called "wheel suck-ers." On the ladder of contempt wheel suckers cling a couple of rungs below Wall Street bank-ers.

The second thing to understand about bike rac-ing is that wheel suckers—who are understand-ably fresh from letting somebody else tow them around the course—win a shocking majority of races. Guys like me, who haven't a quick bone in our bodies, hate to drag a pack of wheel-sucking sprinters around the course, only to watch them

dash by in the last fifty meters to the finish line. So we tortoises of the cycling world jump at ev-ery opportunity to *break away* from the cowering hares, accelerating ahead of the pack at least far enough that the chasing wheel suckers have to put their own twitchy noses in the wind.

Breaking away was what I had planned for that Tuesday at our local club's weekly practice road race at the Donaldson Center. I crafted a plan both brilliantly simple and elegant in design: Step 1: Jump away from the field while they're not paying attention; Step 2: Latch lamprey-like onto the wheel of the first speedy-looking fool who crosses the gap. Comprehensive as it was, my plan didn't account for the possibility that George Hincapie would horn in on the action.

I know you're thinking, "Yeah, right, George Hincapie, twice U.S. National Champion, Engine #1 of the U.S. Postal/Discovery teams that powered Lance Armstrong's record-book Tour wins, European Classics winner, and international cycling star, *that* George Hincapie, showed up at your little Tuesday night club ride, and his old teammate Olympic gold medalist Viatcheslav Ekimov rode along to carry water for him!"

No, Ekimov did not show that Tuesday, or at least he didn't make it into the break.

On this particular Tuesday George came with his brother, Rich, and Bahamian neo-pro Elliot Hubbard. Greenville, South Carolina, is not exactly Boulder East, more like Lodi East, but George's brother Rich married and settled in Greenville in the mid-'90s. After the Tour, George would come to Greenville for some R&R under the radar screen. I guess Rich managed to drag him out to our club ride to give the local boys a thrill.

Not that our Tuesday night ride is your typical spin through the trailer park. For the last twenty years the Greenville Spinners Club has run this police-escorted practice road race on a rolling seven-mile loop around the Donaldson Center business park. We split into two groups, creatively named the "A Group," for experienced racers, and the "B Group," for sandbaggers and guys who like to test their limited abilities and crash.

We take our Donaldson World Championships pretty seriously. There have been Tuesdays when we've had five amateur national champions and a couple of pros in the *peloton* (a fancy French bike racing term meaning "the largest glob of cyclists who are still hanging on by their fingernails"). Ever since George himself made Greenville home, it hasn't been unheard of to see stars like Viatcheslav Ekimov and Frankie Andreu chilling at the back of the peloton. Still, the majority of us are Cat 3 and 4 yahoos. Race promoters segment amateur racers Categories 5 through 1, according to experience and skill. Category 5s ("Cat 5s") are squirrely-wheeled total beginners, Cat 1s are seasoned and scarred nearly-pros. Cat 3s are generally kamikaze youngsters on their way up or glory-days oldsters on their way out, which pretty much sums up the crowd at Donaldson most Tuesdays. So if one of the Big Guys is feeling frisky and suicidal enough to risk life, limb, and a lucrative pro contract to mix it up with the locals, he just might end up in a breakaway with a six-race-a-year Cat 3 hack like me. *My* break.

Yep, if I were a bragging man, I'd have to tell you that it was *my* attack that set the whole break in motion. But I prefer to let the record speak for itself, except when nobody notices the record and I have to bring it to their attention: "Dude, did you see me launch?"

"Yeah, McDoogle, just like a North Korean missile."

It's amazing how much of a lead you can build up on the "neutral" warm-up lap while the other guys are talking up their weekend exploits. I figure that's how Oscar Pereiro grabbed twenty-nine minutes in Stage 13 of the 2006 Tour: he paid one of the officials to tell everybody the race was neutral until the 5K marker.

Anyway, there I was, slogging solo off the front, when THE George Hincapie and a handful of locals chased me down like Republicans after an earmark. They were doing a pretty good job of pretending to look fresh. I was doing my best to keep that right lung from catching in my spokes.

We fell into rotation. When a small group of riders break the tether of the peloton, they trade turns "pulling" at the front. This usually involves forming two lines, inches apart, one advancing, one receding. The rider pulling the advancing line faces the full force of the wind for only ten to fifteen excruciating seconds—just long enough to get past the last rider who came off the advance line—before moving sideways to the receding "relief" line. A precisely executed rotating paceline is a thing of beauty, a ballet of man and machine, sweat and grease. But one weak rider can throw the rhythm of the whole group, and I was rapidly losing my groove. I managed to pull through for about thirteen miles. George was following his off-season program and was under strict orders not to let his heart rate exceed ninety beats per minute. I was anaerobic for two full laps. I thought I saw six hundred on my heart rate monitor a couple of times, but the roaring in my chest made it tricky to see, much less think. I tried to find my happy place. One thought kept me going: Do I get upgrade points for this?

Meanwhile, I could swear I heard George talking to his broker on a cell phone. "Dump that Cofidis junk and get me ten thousand shares of Discovery Communications!" Elliott Hubbard, the other pro in *my* break, was also taking a rest day. He was doing crosswords between pulls. Craig Lewis, local *wunderkind,* tossed me an "atta boy" as I feebly pulled through and immediately tucked in for shelter. George rolled through cool as, well, George. He was wearing that poker face that Lance Armstrong taught him, but I could tell I had him fazed by the way that he eased several bike widths away as he passed me in rotation. The drool hanging from my lower lip was purely for effect.

After about thirty minutes of blissful agony, I passed into an alternate universe, one where accurate steering was not highly valued. A couple of the other riders grumbled, though George kept quiet, obviously not wanting to unleash the hidden tiger within me. I was pulled back to earth by a growing fear that I would suffer Cat 5 flashbacks and take George out. How would you like to be the goofball who ruined George Hincapie's chances at next year's Paris-Roubaix or a *maillot jaune* of his own?

Each pull grew more painful and time began to elongate and quiver like heat waves over the tarmac. Finally came my turn at the front when my legs abandoned me, and I could no longer even hold pace. The rider who had just pulled off turned and glared at me like I was a six-race-a-year Cat 3 hack. I didn't see a rock around to crawl under, but it seemed like the others felt

that any nearby moving vehicle would do. Suddenly, I felt a hand on my butt, and sensed my bike gliding ahead of the line. It was the Rapture, and my Angel of Mercy had arrived! But no, a drunken loll of the head informed me that George Hincapie was gently pushing me up and off the advancing line. "Just sit in," he said in a kindly voice, as I drifted to the back. No doubt he was safer with me behind him.

I hung on in the back until the next bump in the road. As the road turned up, George stood on the pedals and exploded off the front like a shot from a bazooka. Only Elliot managed to claw his way onto George's wheel, while the others dug deep and reformed hopelessly out of reach ahead of me. Thanks to the massive lead we— and when I say "we," I mean "they"—had built, I was able to hold off the peloton for the last bit of that final lap. I rolled in alone with a smile on my face as wide as the Champs-Elysees.

Back home I bragged to my wife about My Break With George. She masterfully contained her awe. *I'll never wash these shorts again,* I thought out loud. Not yet attuned to the god-like nature of cycling pros, she nixed that pungent idea. And that's too bad: these days I could sell those shorts on eBay for enough to buy a good set of wheels, maybe a whole bike, if that salt-encrusted hand print resembled the Virgin Mary.

> Anyway, there I was, slogging solo off the front, when THE George Hincapie and a handful of locals chased me down like Republicans after an earmark.

So Lance has his seven Tour wins, and I have a couple of amateur wins, one Donaldson World Championship, and My Break with George to complete my racing career. Hey, you gotta dream big, right? Thanks for the push, George, and keep the rubber on the road.

REMEMBERING SOUTHSIDE

T. Craig Murphy

IF YOU TAKE HIGHWAY 56 TOWARD PAULINE YOU'LL SEE A BATTERED, BLUE SIGN FOR SOUTHSIDE PARK ON THE LEFT-HAND SIDE. THIS FORESTED PRESERVE BORDERS CROFT STATE PARK AND CONTAINS A NETWORK OF MOUNTAIN BIKING TRAILS ALONG FAIRFOREST CREEK.

Southside is intriguing because when I ride through those woods, it feels much larger, more remote, and wilder than it actually is. Occasionally I meet other bikers, but typically the wilderness is empty and serene when I slip through the undergrowth and follow serpentine tracks through stands of pine that smell of wintergreen and peppermint.

In high school I got lost riding one Saturday afternoon at Southside. I was with my brother and a few friends and we got turned around somewhere near the shooting range. You know you're near the shooting range when you start to feel like you're being fired upon. The sublime tranquility of the empty forest is suddenly shattered with the boom and crack of rifle fire. This is not a good place to get lost. We came to a sign that said:

"Shooting Range: Keep Out!" and we did our best to "keep out," but mostly we just didn't want to get shot. I remember getting low, hunkering down in the dry pine needles and discussing options. Eventually we reached a consensus, which was not to proceed past the "Shooting Range: Keep Out" sign. We turned back, pushing our bikes through the bush, the back tires so gummed up with sticky, red mud they were hardly spinning through the frame.

We lost the trail and continued through wisteria, laurel, and periwinkle in a direction that seemed to be away from the thundering range. When the shots were in the distance, we came up on a country road that I'd never seen. It was mostly dirt with washboard bumps. Sections of the road were rutted and washed out. We looked at each other, unsure whether we should go right or left. We reached another consensus and went right, but for no apparent reason. Off to the side of the road was a deep gully covered in thick weeds. Someone had dumped old truck tires, a rusted refrigerator, box springs, and bags of trash into the gully. This deserted country road, cutting across a remote part of Spartanburg County, was like a scene out of a Faulkner or Flannery O'Connor story. All was quiet except for the crunch of bicycle tires on grit and gravel.

Our right turn proved to be correct. Our country road fed into a paved road, then a street, and eventually we were on Highway 56. I was vaguely familiar with that section of road, so we gambled again, went right, and eventually made our way back to the parking lot late in the day. Our water bottles were empty, our shins were lacerated, poison ivy had attacked our ankles, and mosquito bites covered our arms. In the end, it turned out all right. At least nobody got shot.

The woods at Southside are dense; huge old oaks share the land with poplars, maples, beech trees, and pines. There are wild ferns growing along creek banks, and mountain laurel shrubs line some sections of trail. The soil and riding surface changes at Southside—sometimes it is sandy, when the creek floods; other times it is muddy and wet. It can be covered in leaves in the fall or bone dry during a summer drought. The trails at Southside reflect not only the season, but the weather. During August rides there is thick foliage with occasional patches of pokeweed full of dark purple berries and blossoming flowers of kudzu. Later in the year, when leaves begin to drop, the air is musty as dead leaves and branches rot back into the rich, red earth. After rain the trails taste of mildew and the soupy mud is pungent as it splatters on riders' legs and bikes.

I usually stop to rest at one section along Fairforest Creek. I look into the creek at boulders worn smooth by moving water. There is a sandy beach on the far side of the creek. I often see a blue heron standing there, looking for fish to pluck from the moving water. Where fallen trees and soggy branches clog a section of water, the creek backs up and pools. I notice evidence of beaver activity—wood chips and stumps visible downstream.

The light is dappled in the summer here with the green canopy. Sunshine filters through, but mostly all is in shadow. Brown, red, and tan rocks are covered in glistening green moss. The water babbles over the rocks, and the sound mixes with twittering songbirds and the intermittent banging of a woodpecker searching for bugs high in the trees. The moving water smells of crawfish and bream, salamanders and bullfrogs. I walk down to these rocks, passing through flowering mountain laurel, and sit on the sandy beach. I unbuckle my helmet, pull off my riding gloves and shoes, and slide my bare feet into the cool creek water.

One hot August day when I was a teenager, my friends and I had been riding pretty hard and were frustrated with the trail condition, which was wet and muddy due to recent rain. When we came down to the sandy beach on Fairforest Creek, we got off our bikes to sit by the stream. I don't remember who went first, but suddenly someone was in the creek, jumping and splashing and taunting the rest of us. It didn't take much—soon we were all in a huge pool of chest-deep orange water splashing about. For that moment we forgot about riding. The bikes got us to that spot in the forest, but that day when we all swam, the occasion was more about being boys who all grew up in the same neighborhood, whose parents and grandparents were also friends.

Several times while mountain-biking at Southside I have seen deer. One time I was coming down the power line trail, moving with the wind and savoring the speed of the descent. Only the trail before me was in focus—everything else was a chaotic blur. I gripped the handlebar and felt the downhill strain in my forearms as I came to Yakima Hill. There's a nice view at the top, so it's a good place to rest before making the technical descent. Sometimes I ride straight through, but on this day I came to a stop and stood over my bike. I looked down the ridge to the flat floodplain below, where I noticed an odd, tan patch of color against the green kudzu background. The tan patch swung his head around, displaying a huge rack of horns on a whitetail buck. He smelled me upwind and turned to run. The large rack balanced majestically on top of his head like a crown as he bounced up and out of the kudzu where he was grazing. With each lunge the kudzu swallowed his front haunches before he quickly sprang into the next leap. His neck extended and chin protruded with each jump as he headed for cover. For several seconds I stood perfectly still on top of Yakima Hill and watched that big buck bounding across the floodplain. His tawny, short-haired coat was only broken by the conspicuous white tail bobbing across the sea of green.

Another time I was deep in the forest riding steady on a flat, wooded plain. The trail meandered to the right and back to the left in a series of non-technical bends. Moss and lichen-covered vines hung from some of the mature oaks. Ferns grew in clumps in the loamy soil. It was late summer and the still air pushed against me, heavy with humidity. I was riding alone this day, and suddenly my peripheral vision filled with movement. At least four does started to run as I approached where they had been grazing. They ran in the same direction as me, on either side of the trail. Most of the herd broke off and disappeared into thicker brush, but two of them kept charging ahead. I shifted gears and pedaled harder, trying to keep up with the deer as they effortlessly, gracefully darted ahead through the thick brush. I recall hearing the crunch and rustle of their hooves digging into the groundcover of leaves. They sounded like horses galloping at a steeplechase. I pounded the crankshaft to keep up. The doe to my right veered left and came onto the section of trail just ahead of me. The veiny muscles in her rear haunches mechanically pounded the forest floor. She moved ahead of me and eventually cut off to the left, joined the other deer, and went out of sight. I kept riding.

✳   ✳   ✳

Cycling at Southside for me is more than outdoor recreation on a high-performance mountain bike. Spinning through the forest on two wheels out there exposes hints of history to the observant. My knowledge of historical facts about that section of forest is limited. I can only describe what I have seen and what I have heard, and the resultant questions that linger when I ride.

At one point a wide section of trail drops straight down to the creek. It appears wide enough to have been able to accommodate wagons or perhaps vehicles. Maybe it was a road? I speculate this because where the section of trail meets Fairforest Creek, there is evidence of an old bridge. Most of the bridge is gone, but today you can still see several support structures, pylons, and cross-beams that were used as a bridge. What was that bridge used for? Did early settlers use it to get back and forth? If so, where were they going? Was the bridge used for commercial purposes? Was there ever mining in or around the creek that would have necessitated building a bridge? Or was the bridge built by the military? The surrounding Camp Croft area was an Army Infantry Replacement Center from 1940 to 1946 for soldiers deploying to World War II.

The remains of the old bridge cross over to another vast section of wilderness. This section, now known as Croft State Natural Area, has recently been linked to Southside with the construction of a footbridge. Years ago I explored that wilderness by bike and was struck by the haunted emptiness of the woods, because at that time no trails had been developed. When I pedaled up and down paths padded with leaves, I envisioned young soldiers, not yet twenty, running with their weapons and backpacks preparing for war. I thought of tanks churning up the soil and officers orchestrating field movements that would soon be implemented on the battlefield in France, the Philippines, and North Africa. I imagined that the air would have smelled of engine oil, gasoline, gunpowder, and the sweat of young men doing manual labor outside. But when I rode there, on the other side of Fairforest Creek, across from the old washed-out bridge, the forest had erased this history. Trees had come back, and cuts in the soil had been filled in with rotten leaves and branches. Its past as a military training center, and the potential presence of unexploded shells in the ground, had kept people away; the woods are flourishing in the absence of people or development.

There's also a pile of rocks nearby that I speculate are the remains of a foundation of a building or home. The rocks are moss-covered and camouflaged, but they appear to have been selected, cut, and put together. They are roughly the same size and are in a slight clearing of otherwise dense woods. When I ride by, sometimes I imagine that pile of rocks was part of a still for a moonshine operation. During the Prohibition and later, during the Great Depression, many people in the area turned to distilling alcohol in wood-burning stills and selling it on the black market. Moonshiners preferred thickly wooded areas because the trees made it more difficult for the police and federal agents to follow the smoke and find the stills.

Or perhaps the rocks are the remains of an old settler home for a family eking out an existence farming the land and raising animals. I imagine hardworking pioneers driving mules through the woods carrying provisions. I see a woman in a bonnet churning butter, and barefoot children fetching wooden buckets of water from the nearby creek. Perhaps these were the children of John Oeland, whose family cemetery is off one of the trails at Southside. There is a wrought-iron fence around the cemetery with a low, swinging gate. The graves are covered in leaves and fallen branches. I often stop when riding that trail. I enter the graveyard and remove branches that cover where the dead lie. I dust off a headstone and read the engraving:

Sacred | To the Memory | of | JOHN OELAND | Who died | On the 8th of Feb. 1843 | Aged 72 Yrs 3 Mos and 2 Ds | As a disciple of Christ he loved | His teachings | In his walk meek and humble | As a Husband devoted | And affectionate | As a Father and Master, kind | And Indulgent | In truth the noblest work of GOD | An honest MAN

*   *   *

Pedaling around Southside as a teenager is one of the experiences that whets my appetite for discovering what might be "out there" in the wider world. Now many seasons have passed, and my bond with the land where I grew up is strengthened by the years I've lived away in Asia, Africa, and the Middle East. When I return home and ride at Southside, I'm visited by memories of biking from continents away. I enjoy the interconnectedness of my experience.

During my first journey abroad to Australia, for instance, I decided to take my mountain bike. A few days before my departure, I had gone for a particularly muddy mountain bike ride at Southside. When I had come back I had hosed off my bike and let it dry. I had started disassembling the bike to pack for Australia. My mother had suggested that I clean the bike more thoroughly as there was still a lot of mud and, she said, "it might cause problems at customs and immigration in Australia." I had shrugged it off, assuring her it would be fine. I was wrong.

After a twenty-eight hour journey I landed bleary-eyed in Cairns, Australia, with a group of twenty students. We collected our luggage and proceeded to exit. I was pulled aside by an immigration officer. "What's in the box, mate?"

"A bike," I responded.

He continued, "We need to inspect it."

All of the others in my group exited the arrivals hall; I went to a back room and unpacked the box. They handed me a bucket of soap and water and a brush. The immigration officer asked me to thoroughly clean the mud from my tires. For the next thirty minutes, while nineteen people waited for me, I scrubbed those knobby tires and rims and watched the cool liquid-red earth of Southside run through my fingers and splatter like blood in a huge white wash basin. It swirled around, and a little piece of Spartanburg ran into the drain and entered Australia.

A few years later I accepted a job in Japan and again decided to take my bike. I was heading to the mountainous Nagano prefecture, and I knew there would be good riding. I explored Matsumoto city by bike for hours each day until I got oriented. As I pedaled by Buddhist temples,

> Cycling at Southside for me is more than outdoor recreation on a high-performance mountain bike.

ancient castles, and groves of cherry trees, my mind wandered back to Southside. I thought of magnolia trees, pine forests, and a flock of wild turkeys near Fairforest Creek.

Later I lived in Kenya for several years and did a lot of mountain biking there. I read an account of a large expedition in *Mountain Bike* magazine in 2005 that claimed to be the first and only successful ride up and down Mount Kenya. Inspired, I decided to try it. I rode or carried my bike up to Shipton's Hut and then trekked on foot up to Point Lenana (elevation 16,355 feet), one of Mount Kenya's peaks, with the assistance of one porter for most of my gear. I descended back to Shipton's to sleep for the night. The next day I managed to get the bike up to 15,153 feet by carrying it on my shoulder to Simba Col, where I began my long descent of more than 10,000 feet in a day.

While I was thousands of miles from home, near the Equator in Kenya, I was amazed at how close I felt to Southside, and how I fought through the cold and exhaustion by focusing on the warmth and camaraderie of a summer ride at Southside. I felt like my Mount Kenya attempt was for my riding friends that I grew up with. I couldn't let them down, and I couldn't let the limited oxygen or the icy trail conditions deter me.

The sun was out, but it was windy and cold at Simba Col when I readied myself for a long, arduous descent of the mountain. I looked out to my destination that day—the village of Chogoria, about thirty miles away, at the end of the Gorges Valley. I stood over my bike, not unlike the countless times I've stood over my bike at the top of Yakima Hill. But now I was on much more than a hill—I was just below the summit of the second highest mountain in Africa, my lungs were heaving, my toes were numb, and adrenaline coursed through my body. I imagined verdant kudzu below me, the thick oxygenated air of Spartanburg County at nine hundred feet above sea level. It kept things in perspective. The principles and techniques for riding were the same; I just had to apply them now on a much grander stage. Several thousand feet above the tree line, I surveyed the lifeless, barren landscape—behind me were the rocky switchbacks up from Shipton's Hut; in front

of me was a vaguely defined track of loose, jagged rocks. I looked out at the equatorial sun, the thick band of rainforest where elephants roam, and the many steep, rocky miles before me. I tightened my helmet strap, clipped into my pedals, and pedaled toward Mount Kenya.

I found my rhythm and with lots of brake work and steering, my descent was underway. When I passed through a long deserted section of bamboo forest, I steered around fresh piles of elephant and buffalo dung. After a monumental day of descending, late that afternoon I arrived in the village of Chogoria, having completed the ride in three days. I rested on a wooden slab propped up with plastic soda crates. I bought snacks and water from a roadside shop made of clapboards. I sat there with a pile of gear as a crowd of curious Kenyans gathered to stare at me. Chickens scuttled about at my feet, and a young boy guided a small herd of goats down the dirt road. While I was far removed from Spartanburg, the feeling I had sitting there alone in that Kenyan village was the same as if I was sitting in the grass next to my Subaru at the Southside parking lot after a ride. I was exhausted, but with my exhaustion, this ride on Mount Kenya also stirred feelings of contentment, serenity, and home.

Spending limited time in Spartanburg over the years has given me a greater appreciation of the place and the outdoor recreation at Southside. When I'm abroad and longing for the familiarity of my roots, my thoughts return to the woods and my bike. In my mind I'm at Southside flying through the trees, descending, climbing, and steering. I envision whitetail deer bounding through a cottonwood forest, and I think of Queen Anne's lace and black-eyed Susans. I know humidity hangs low in that ancient South Carolina forest where gnats fly, flowers bloom and die, and wildlife flourishes along Fairforest Creek. Then the ride is over. From half a world away I recall pulling off dirty socks and helmet and resting in the hatchback of my station wagon. I see myself on the road, driving back to town. My bike is secured on the roof rack of my car. The windows are down and bluegrass music is on the radio. I come full circle and weave together the various worlds where I reside.

EXPLORING

Diane Milks

Ellen E. Hyatt

Peter Godfrey

D.W. Damrel

Jeanne Malmgren

Shandi Stevenson

Dawn Johnson Mitchell

MUSHROOMS OF THE MOUNTAINS

Diane Milks

DANK. PUNGENT. INSIDIOUS. I HAD USED THOSE WORDS TO DESCRIBE MUSHROOMS. IN TRUTH HOWEVER, MY KNOWLEDGE WAS LIMITED.

My exposure to the world of mushrooms consisted of slipping on them every time I tried to mow the swampy area of my backyard, rubbing up against them while weeding the mulch beds, and, during an occasional outdoor trek, encountering them in dark, murky places. So I admit I stifled a smirk when I saw "Mushrooms of the Mountains" listed as an event on the Mountain Bridge Wilderness Area park schedule. I questioned the merit of cataloguing it between "Hike the Dismal," a particularly grueling eight-mile trek, dodging superb rock outcroppings and showcasing thunderous waterfalls, and "Annual Hawk Watch," a spectacular display of majestic birds soaring along their seasonal migration route. But, willing to try something new, I signed up.

Mycology. I didn't know that word existed, much less that mushrooms were worthy of scientific study. To be precise, mycology is the study of fungi. A fungus is a non-photosynthetic organism that feeds on organic matter. Types of fungi can include yeast, molds, mildew, and mushrooms. Already my knowledge of mushrooms had expanded ten-fold, and I was no further than the bookstore, trying to decide which of the dozen or more field guides would be most appropriate for the day. These thick, weighty volumes were holding their own next to the more revered guides for birds, trees, and insects, many of which I already owned. As someone who enjoys being outdoors, with a healthy propensity for exploring new places and learning new things, I was a bit surprised. Glancing through the selections, it became clear that I had been missing a world a lot of other people seemed to know about. I began looking forward to this little adventure.

There are over ten thousand species of mushrooms in North America. I pondered that vastness during the forty-five-minute drive to Jones Gap State Park, and then along the quarter-mile nature trail from the parking area to the visitor center. Heavily forested and dominated by a rocky, tumbling river, the environment for this day of mushroom hunting was moist and shady. Lush. It certainly seemed conducive to growing mushrooms; however, the skeptic in me wondered if the draw to this particular location was more likely the obvious beauty rather than any particular fungus-growing ecosystem. Not that I minded. The prospect of a hike through these woods coupled with my interest in photography and art was already enough to satisfy me. The real question I had as I reached the park center was "What kind of people had chosen to come here today? Who were mushroom people?" An image of a biology class sprang to mind, replete with class nerds ready to dissect. With some trepidation, I slipped though the back door of a room where a group of twelve were already engaged in a lively mix of questions and storytelling.

A teacher, a student, a farmer, and a naturalist. A couple of gardeners. Bridge club ladies. Tourists. Me. And of course, our host, Roman Stanley from the Asheville Mushroom Club, who at first glance completely shattered my illusion of a spectacled professor. A jovial man with white hair and tanned skin, his knowledge of mushrooms struck me as coming simply from a life spent living and working outdoors. The array of books, pamphlets, displays, and specimens on hand seemed a testament to years of admiration and dedication. I registered Roman as an odd cross between Bill Nye the Science Guy and Andy Griffith, but clearly as a man who knew and loved his mushrooms—a "mycophile." Before embarking on our hunting excursion, his slide presentation armed us with the basic facts we would need to successfully locate and appreciate mushrooms.

A mushroom is the "fruit" grown by a fungus—much like an apple is grown by a tree. Fungi, however, are not considered plant life or animal life, although they show some relationship to both. I was surprised to learn this, which unfortunately shows my age. When I was in school, science taught us that all organisms were classified under one of two kingdoms—Plants or Animals. Fungi now claim their own kingdom. While not all fungi grow mushrooms, this rather stunning fact certainly justified the size of my field guide. The mushroom's sole purpose is housing millions of spores, which are the reproductive cells of fungi.

Spores are one of the main components of mushroom identification. A true mushroom hunter will have a spore print book on hand, and our host for the day was no exception. "Take the cap of the 'shroom off the stem and place it on white or clear paper," Roman instructed. "Put a glass plate over it. The mushroom will release its spores on the paper and you will be left with a print." The color of the spore print is used to identify the species and often can be the only clue. "Beware of the white spore print," Roman admonished. White spore prints generally describe a deadly poisonous group of mushrooms know as *Amanitas*.

Now, I was enjoying the presentation and gaining an appreciation for the unique nature of mushrooms, but my observation was that one could only be deadly if a person actually ate it. As someone who diligently plucks them out of the melted cheese of my pizza, I started to squirm in my seat a little. Listening to the other avid "shroomers" in the group, it seemed that eating mushrooms is the most rewarding aspect of the hunt. "The sponge morel is the best eating," declared one of the group. "But finding them is the big secret." This statement was followed by an exchange of personal preferences and experiences. Roman told us that a man once offered "my girlfriend's phone number if you tell me where to find the

There was a joke in there somewhere about the "morel of the story," and I found myself really beginning to like these people.

best morels." There was a joke in there somewhere about the "morel of the story," and I found myself really beginning to like these people.

We left the building and started toward the trailhead of a gentle path that would take us a half mile or so along the bank of the Middle Saluda River. Before reaching it, the "mushrooms of the mulch beds" beckoned our attention. "Boletes," Roman announced for the benefit of general identification, and then proceeded to address the clusters by the species' Latin names. He pointed out that the underside of the caps were soft pores rather than gills, an important feature in identification. These mushrooms looked familiar to me: orange-brown with thick caps growing low along the ground. As I looked closer, I noticed the second grouping was a deeper yellow color, and the mushrooms were much more uniform in shape, clearly indicating two different species.

Once along the trail, nature set out to prove just how diverse her gifts can be. One mushroom resembled a flower and was colored an amazing mint green. "A green russula," said Roman. "They're delicious." Another, identified as a stalked puffball, looked exactly like its name implied and was such a brilliant red it didn't seem real. Pure white polyporus grew in ledges along deadwood logs like ruffles on a little girl's dress. By the time I saw the bi-color boletes, transported directly

from the pages of *Alice in Wonderland* with their large red caps sporting white and yellow dots, I was completely entranced. Here among the more obvious displays of grandeur was a quiet, remarkable world, hugging the bases of those towering trees, nesting in the crooks of those rocky outcrops, running in the shadows of the flowering woodland undergrowth.

"It's a world worthy of respect," Roman reminded us. We were stopped in front of a myriad of yellow hoods, clambering up the vale of an old tree stump. "Sulphur tuft," he said, looking at the smoky color of the gills. "Deadly poisonous." He explained that the real challenge to identifying mushrooms was how much they can change as they grow. An infant mushroom can appear different in color, shape, and even in spore color than an adult of its species. "And the only way to be safe is to know which species you have."

As we looped back along the trail, I listened with new interest to tales of the most elusive mushroom finds—mushrooms whose existence depends on a very particular habitat, or a single species of wood decay. I couldn't help but relate to some of the excitement and passion shared by the others at finding a rare species or witnessing a spectacular display of the most unusual forms or textures. There was much to know and appreciate about this new world I'd been given a glimpse of.

Back at the visitor center we reflected on the success of our hunt: a dozen species of mushrooms in a spectrum of shapes and colors. I thanked Roman for such an educational morning, shook hands with the other shroomers, and came away with a satisfying feeling. Discovery. Heading back along the path to the parking lot, I spotted something I hadn't noticed on the way in and bent down for closer examination. "Well hello there. You're quite a little bolete aren't you?" I let my finger trail along the edge of the cap, upturned like a new leaf reaching for the sun, and across its smooth surface where a soft peach color melded into apricot. How exquisite. Intriguing. Alluring. 🍂

AUTUMN, AS A VERB
Ellen E. Hyatt

"I ALWAYS IMAGINED THE CLOUDS BEING MORE FIRM" IS A LINE I RECALL FROM A BIZARRO CARTOON.

Above the caption are people in a condition between people-dom and angelhood. Though trying to keep their halos in place, their wings are sinking into clouds, which appear to be at a cumulus level. I imagine the beings will soon be lost—maybe at the level of a stratus. And I think sometimes "lost" is a good place to be.

"Lost" happens to me each time I drive in Pickens County, South Carolina. Sometimes I cannot even state my location because I really do not have much of an idea where it is. I might be somewhere nearing Twin Falls, one of the waterfalls Benjamin Brooks and Tim Cook write about, reminding visitors that waterfalls are less "spectacle" and more "experience" if looked at "properly." It might be somewhere warm and apple-cinnamon homey around Six Mile; or somewhere near Birchwood Center for Arts and Folklore where past, present, and future seem to be one; or somewhere in awe in Table Rock State Park. No matter. What I do know is that I always feel better "There." In that state of being in the Upstate and outdoors, I am most definitely somewhere. That "somewhere" is a place I call "Between."

Whether toward, at, or during "Between," I feel metamorphous. In "Between," don't we have the opportunity to become less chrysalis and more emergent? We begin unswaddling all we must be when we are encased in our routine roles—roles that wrap us with titles, personas, responsibilities, awards, accomplishments, demographic profiles, others' expectations. When in Pickens, I start feeling similar to the people in the cartoon: winged, adrift— yet unbothered, neither in the weft nor the warp.

On the way to the lodge at Table Rock State Park on the second Sunday in August, for instance, I am not concerned about the "firmness" of clouds being miscalculated or—for that matter—my own miscalculations about how many miles I should have traveled after turning left (or was it right?) at the gas station with the ostrich out back behind a rusted, grid-wire fence. I reread my scribbled notes, which were based on what the young farming couple at the corner peach stand advised; what the girl at the gas station, who revised my map, said; and what the men, rocking in conversation and chairs while enjoying ice cream at Aunt Sue's, directed.

Several abbreviated notations on yellow legal paper cluttered the dash of my car and were beginning to reach the length of a receipt for a very large grocery bill or shopping spree. By all indications, I should have been on S.C. Highway 11. Checking another map, I affirm that S.C. 11 is the Cherokee Foothills Scenic Highway, although I myself could not honestly

vouch for the name of the road. Nor could I be of much help to the middle-aged couple from North Carolina who stopped to ask *me* for directions. I could, however, testify to the variety of greens in the area. I had pulled off the road yet again but this time to reflect on the leafiness, the mountainous landscape, and all which air, land, and water offer.

I handed the couple my map of the area. They figured out their route just fine, explained to me how they were getting away for a few days because the angst of building a house had overwhelmed them. We discussed how Sunday morning *here*—wherever "here" was—actually evoked a spirituality none of us would have experienced in church, if we had chosen to go. I privately wondered how differently the Ten Commandments would have turned out if Moses had been navigated to this edge of these Blue Ridge Mountains.

The couple also tried to help me with *my* directions. For a moment, I wished I could have followed them. Instead, I sat to study the arrangement in greens and reflect in the vein of Thomas E. Lovejoy, the conservation biologist. He reminds us: "It is impossible for art to improve upon nature. ... It is, however, possible to see nature with special eyes."

With "special eyes," I noticed the warm, deeply dark green of pine. The color conjures up winter holiday. There was the lighter, fresh green needles on some variety of pine whose upward direction looked like tangible hope. There was the glossy green of scarlet oak leaves, their lobes ending in bristled tips. There was green the color of eyes. Doesn't that shade always seem to summon June Christy's tune "Something Cool" and lead to a labyrinth of memories filled with passion and trouble, loss and regret?

I noticed there was no green the color of money, but there was a green richly quiet. It allows us to begin to "hear the silence," as Jack Gilbert mentions in his poem "Waiting and Finding." There was also a spangled green. A yellow-green. Green that is uniquely river birch. Leaves of river birch which, when turned by a breeze, offer a silvery underside.

Andrew Wyeth once wrote, "If a painting is good, it will be mostly memory." It was the green of hickory that brought to my memory the selecting of leaves for a scrapbook my mother helped me to make when I was around ten. It was this summery green-and-silver of hickory that reminded me that these leaves would soon turn autumn's golden-brown.

I started toward my destination for the day again, realizing that I would have missed part of the program at the Table Rock State Park lodge. It was already afternoon, that time of day "Between" morning and night, and, as I mentioned, it was August, the month "Between" a full summer and the soon-to-be-discovered autumn.

Thinking about the word "autumn," I wondered: why can't we make "autumn" a verb? After all, each of the other seasons has a verb.

Somewhere near Table Rock is where I want "to autumn" during my own autumn, whose onset is due to occur sometime between now and the approaching, inevitable winter. The mountain provides the means to know silence and our place in it. At Table Rock Mountain— who knows what might happen? I might just be "Between" enough to try out the clouds for firmness—in case at the end of my very own wintering, I land in the vicinity of the cumulus. ⬞

THE ALTERNATIVE TOURIST'S GUIDE TO CAESARS HEAD

Peter Godfrey

IT WAS STILL EARLY WHEN WE GOT UP TO CAESARS HEAD. THERE WERE ONLY TWO OTHER VEHICLES IN THE CAR PARK, PROBABLY BELONGING TO THE STAFF OF THE GIFT SHOP, AND WE HAD THE OBSERVATION PLATFORM TO OURSELVES.

From this promontory South Carolina unrolled all the way to the Atlantic, according to my guide, three hundred miles away.

Very little of it was visible as yet; shreds of cloud clung to the treetops below us and spread themselves out across the hills, breaking up the view into blotches of green and gray and white. To the southwest, a huge smooth rock rose out of the forest and the clouds. It was flat-topped, and from this distance the trees that grew on it appeared no more than moss on a boulder.

"Table Rock," my guide said. "And next to it is the stool that the Great Spirit sits on when he eats." I spotted the smaller outcrop, partly obscured by clouds.

"Kind of a cosmic picnic table," I said.

My guide blew air through his nose in that laugh that is barely an acknowledgement. "This rock we're standing on was once called the Sachem's Head," he told me. "The Chief's Head. There are stories that Indian sacrifices used to be made here." We leaned on the metal fence running around the edge of the rock promontory and looked down, through the shredding clouds swimming hundreds of feet below, to the treetops a quarter of a mile beneath them. "The fevered white imagination dreams up romances to go with all these places," Red continued. "A place like this, naturally, beautiful young virgins must have been tossed out into the air. That's what we'd do if we wuz them, ain't it?" He snuffled a seedy laugh. "And who knows?" He spun around and raised his arms in mock horror, leaning back and making slow-motion falling movements, backstroking into the sky. "Maybe it's truuuuuuue …"

My guide was known as Red because of his hair. He was big and supposedly had a temper, but I had never seen that. I'd known him for years. In real life he was an itinerant illusionist, and our paths had crossed from time to time, when he was touring his revivals of classic Houdini tricks. In London and Edinburgh he had been the observer; now I was on his turf, and I was the one doing the observing, so when I needed an interpreter, I summoned his spirit and he materialized at my elbow.

"Come see the Chief," he said, and he led me down through a cleft called The Devil's Kitchen and then along a path to a place where you can see a hook-nosed profile jutting out of the rock face. "I don't know any stories about the Chief. But, hey, this is America. Make up your own reality. My guess is he's looking across the Dismal—that's what the gorge between here and Table Rock is called—and maybe communing with the gods."

The Chief's expression was inscrutable. The face in the rock was squashed as though by the weight. His eye seemed to be closed.

"You think he's meditating?" I asked.

"Kinda looks like he's sleeping something off," Red said.

We walked back up through the trees to the lookout. The clouds were thinning out. Soon it would be worth putting a quarter in one of the pay-telescopes and sweeping the vista for detail.

Red followed my gaze. "And after the Red Man," he said, "a new people came, and with them they brought new gods. And they set up their gods on the Sachem's Head." He kowtowed to the pay-scopes on their swivel stands.

"Tiny gods they were, with massive appetites, who devoured not virgins but whole planets."

He raked the 'scope across the sky like a machine gunner.

"Now man did not stand here and pray across the Dismal to the distant gigantic gods, oh no! His gods stood here with him; and they were small and silver and when you looked into their eyes you saw the world not as man sees it but as these new gods see it: frameable, reducible, lifeless. Or if not lifeless, then devoid of spirit. These new gods watched the world, they glared across at Table Rock; for them it was Tameable Rock."

He swiveled the payscope around and pointed at its silver face. "Behold!" he exclaimed. For a moment he lapsed into a normal voice. "Look at this for a mask!" he said, patting the fat silver cheek. "Is that the face of our gods? Of our culture? Is that angelic or demonic?"

I shivered at the look the machine gave me.

"That's the face of an alien invader," Red said, and resumed his inflated delivery. "And by golly, it's our face too if we don't wake up." He held the serious pose for a few seconds and then relaxed, grinning broadly to let me know he was being extravagant.

"Join us again next week when Professor Pinko takes another look at Science and Technology," he announced, and did a little soft-shoe shuffle.

Looking at his great figure standing there with one enormous red hand gripping the silver machine and his great blue eyes shining in the light blue air, I felt buoyant. Red kept a shred of the old sixties romance alive.

"Hippy shit," I said.

"Aw, yeah, yeah," he said, ruefully, and his mood changed down several gears. He looked out toward the East, nodding pensively. "Yeah, yeah, yeah," he murmured.

I felt bad for taking the wind out of his sails. I tried to make up for it. "I like your angle, Red. I wish I had one like that myself."

"You don't have one of your own?" he snapped back. "Why, you gotta have one of them. Whatcha gonna do without a hangle?"

"I know you gotta have one," I said, "but I don't anyway. It's all just one thing after another as far as I'm concerned. Totally random. No connection, no pattern. Chaos."

Red looked at the green mountains thoughtfully and said, "Well, then, I guess you have to keep moving. Just to keep alive."

"I guess so," I agreed.

We stood and stared at the huge lumps of rock.

Tourists have a bad reputation from way back. When Dr. Johnson said about the Giants Causeway in County Antrim that it was "worth seeing, yes, but not worth going to see," he may have been the first to express a distaste for all travel that is frivolous in purpose. We share his contempt for the sightseer, rushing through countries on a tour bus, collecting snapshots. But perhaps there are others, let's call them touristers, who travel more like secular pilgrims, seeking not merely the relief from tedium that novelty provides, but something more profound. The tourister is, let's say, an archaeologist of the present. The good tourist takes pictures and notes and collects artifacts, and can later give an illustrated lecture to those who stay at home. But that is not the purpose of tourism, not for the tourister. The purpose of tourism goes further, to achieve an intensification of experience, an increased awareness of the world, a fresh sense of life, that doesn't merely refresh, but feeds the hungry spirit. This is the tourism of the hippy trail, the seeker after truth, the Grand Tour. The purposes of the tourister's tools—the camera, the sketch pad, the notebook—are to focus attention and preserve information for further consideration; like a student, the tourister is on an internal journey as well as an external one.

I, however, was just a tourist. If I was ever on a pilgrimage, I had lost my way and fallen back into serial visiting. I had come to the South more or less by chance, and I had toured it pretty intensively, at the grassroots level. Now I was spending most of my time in the Upstate of South Carolina. It wasn't that I found the Piedmont uniquely attractive or sympathetic, or anything like that—a lot about it reminded me of the South Wales of my youth; the Baptists, the blue laws, the boiled greens. Bob Jones. But it was sufficiently different to keep me interested. Novelty is like oxygen to the restless spirit. When you've seen, read, tasted everything available, you look for new material, new fuel for your motor. You take it in, it goes through a process of combustion or interpretation, and the result is a sense, at least, of movement, and therefore of direction.

And yet my tour had come to a dead standstill. All sense of progress had gone from it. At that moment, standing on Caesars Head, I was at a tourist crisis. I closed my eyes to see where I was. Nothing. I was not moving inside or out. I wasn't going anywhere. It wasn't a dark forest I was halfway through. It wasn't a crossroads I was at, either; all paths had petered out at the edge of this cliff. There was no way ahead, up, or down. Tourism had become a shallow and unrewarding thing; something had gone wrong with my equipment, and taking photographs was replacing rather than recording experiences. My compass was haywire. Direction was lost. Internal architecture finally succumbed to anarchy. My itinerary had failed me. The events of my tour, which had once seemed to be aligned, now appeared scattered, unpatterned.

I had to face the fact that I had been doing what women accuse men of all the time: refusing to buy a map. I was trying to interpret my surroundings as though they might indicate some possible course when of course they don't. Never do. Road signs are notoriously inadequate and misleading. Even if they tell you where you're going, they seldom tell you why.

But I was hungry for signs. All sorts of signs. Perhaps that's really no better than collecting snapshots. Sign-reading may be a form of sight-seeing, but America is a land full of signs, and they provide plentiful pretexts for making up stories. Some of the signs I saw were awesome—an enormous phallic thundercloud from the plane window over Washington, D.C., and bear prints in the flower beds. Some signs were puzzling—the road sign "Ped Xing" sounded to me like a Vietnamese grandfather. Some were strange in their straightforwardness, like an MG on the top of a pole outside a sports car repair shop. Others are straightforward in their strangeness, like the Gaffney Peachoid, a water tank disguised as a giant peach.

From the moment I first saw bright, red earth from the windows of the Piedmont Airlines plane stooping down over GSP, I had been reading the world around me with renewed interest. Some things I had found disturbing; there were, for example, discreet notices on vans that informed the reader that "in the event of rapture" the vehicle would be "unmanned." What kind of sinister humor was that? And the fish on the backs of cars—the empty fish, the fish with "Jesus" in it, the fish with "Darwin" and legs, the fish with "gefilte"—they seemed as pointless as Child On Board, and yet they must have some meaning to their owners. The stop signs riddled with bullet holes or plastered with paint balls—anti-government rhetoric? Even the unfamiliar company names and the slogans on the billboards had an element of mystery: Boring-Smith; Jeeter and Plaxto; KEEP THE TORCH LIT; RE-ELECT FATE THOMAS; WE DON'T PLAY NO BLACK SHEEP GAMES. I liked the folksy hand-scrawled signs that are little artworks of their own: *small engine repair, will work for food, yard sale Saturday*. And everywhere the celluloid moveable-type inspirational, punning on scripture, mordant in humor, culminating in *I am Jesus and I approve this message*, and perhaps most mysterious of all: *Jeremiah 13:4*. Not to be outdone, nature provides gigantic heraldic green kudzu animals clinging to telegraph poles and ruined kudzu castles. All of these signs gave me clues to some hidden narrative that tempted me like a will o' the wisp, a Dixie Pixie light guiding me through the labyrinth to the heart of Southness.

But on Caesars Head even the mysterious face of the Payscope Gods couldn't keep an awesome vertigo from getting to me. The high places and the dark corners defeated my reader's instinct. The enormous and empty overawed my every exposition. The abyss, it seems, is not open to interpretation.

> Road signs are notoriously inadequate and misleading. Even if they tell you where you're going, they seldom tell you why.

"You want to look in the gift shop?" Red asked. I nodded and we climbed down from the high viewing place to the low trading post.

"From the Empyrean to the Emporium," Red chuckled.

In the souvenir shop I regained my equilibrium. It was full of strange things. A gift shop is always the repository of arcane signs; it is where you find the ubiquitous bumper stickers: *I ♥ Jesus*; *God is my co-pilot*; *Don't like my driving? Call 1-800 CRYBABY*. Here, illustrated pamphlets explained regional dialects in humorous fashion. Cat hats and wall plaques and coffee mugs bore slogans plain or piquant or purposeful, although being at a holy site none of them were salacious. Wind harps hung from the walls.

I poked around with an antiquarian's interest for a while, bought some small items, satisfied my juvenile hungers. Then I went back to the high place to see if the clouds had parted.

The sun had burned away most of the mist. Red was nowhere to be seen. I just stood there for a while, not even bothering with the pay-scopes. Standing there looking out into the void, breathing deeply, felt good. Maybe I could come to light down there, somewhere. Give up my futile scavenger-hunt.

After a while I realized that Table Rock looked more like a motor scooter than a table and chair: the long green double seat, on the gray-brown engine fairing; and over there was the steering post ... 🖎

GHOSTS AND MUSHROOMS AT GLENDALE SHOALS

D. W. Damrel

EVERYONE KNOWS GLENDALE SHOALS EAST OF SPARTANBURG IS THE PLACE TO FIND THE GHOSTS—THE GHOSTS AND MUSHROOMS LURKING UNEXPECTED, BIZARRE, AND BEAUTIFUL ALONG THE SHADY, BROKEN-UP SLOPES THAT HOLD LAWSON'S FORK CREEK IN ITS PLACE AND PUSH IT DOWN INTO THE PACOLET RIVER.

This isn't the part of the creek where the kayakers go—they have to pull up at the dam that signals no passage ahead and can't follow the stream where it drops broad and thin as a veil over the top of the dam before it regathers in the shallows and rolls on like a tongue in a stone-filled mouth, gushing over boulders, whispering in a few still, broad flats, singing softly over sunken logs or joining the wind, the sad peewees, and the cicadas for a lazy summer lullaby.

The kayakers can't paddle down to the stretch of the creek that limns the old mill, where the fire left ruins and a few footings, brick-

red towers and smokestacks, abandoned like forgotten toys from some child's wondrous dreams. Here's where the old mill ruins sit doorless and windowless, letting ghosts flit in and out through them like the itinerant finches and mockingbirds, the birds always bound for somewhere else, the birds always glad for a place to rest.

You can take an easy day hike along the creek from below the dam and past the shoals—past where the kids spray-paint the rocks with the dirtiest words they know and tag about the sweetest love they can dream of—and then keep going past the old mill site until you pick up the trail alongside the water. The day you choose to go makes all the difference. The summer is always best, but the summer is such a lie in the Upstate. For every single perfect sky stretched high and beautiful over the summer trees and vines and forbs, there's always another day, a different summer's day, where it's as if a strange foreign sky that was passing overhead in the night somehow got tangled and snagged in the trees, so in the morning you find a sky trapped low and heavy over the shoals like a forsaken kite, a sky that's desperate to leave but going nowhere on its own. It's those different summer days, those days for dreaming by the creek, that are best for finding the mushrooms and ghosts.

The mushrooms are the hard part. Covered under sheaves of snub-ended tulip poplar leaves, waiting for their chance, they spring out overnight where you would swear there was nothing before. Blue inky caps, wood ears

and morels, black trumpets and apricot milks, porcinis and painted suillus, jack-o-lanterns and chickens-of-the-woods, bright, glowing on the forest floor like fairy villages or fluorescent porcelain sculptures of flame, they come and vanish overnight, so perfect to find fresh, but so sad to find shriveled and discolored a few days too late with their prime long past. You didn't want to pick them anyway, but how wonderful to

know them fresh. The trail by the creek is green and easy, mostly level, and unchallenged by the sun—if the summer has been wet, you can smell the damp, rich air as you leave your track in the mud bend to inspect the fungi growing at impossible angles from bark and branches, leaves and detritus, necromass and debris. And, of course, that's the trail where the ghosts are.

What about the ghosts? Here, and by now, they are just types, not the individuals they once were. Solomon Barrett is no longer the mill boy who went fishing in the creek and drowned, the boy who broke his mother's heart—she had already lost so much, and now this!—when they found him cool and blue a hundred yards downstream. He's any boy now, a nameless, excited bolt of rushing airy joy sweeping under the trees and along the creek, a sudden burst of an emotion that passes over you and makes you ask, *What was that?* And the quiet nameless girl who spent hours walking by the creek remembering a song—how could a girl love a man who drowned seven wives?—see her now, a perfect pillar of light in the midst of dark trees, standing motionless in the daylight, as still as if the sun and earth had both halted at once, just to let her shine in the gloom. But then you start to breathe again, and the girl is gone, and so is the ghost: you can see how the perfect sculpted light is filled with gently drifting dust that hangs and floats, and you hear the creek and the cicadas and the peewees again.

By then it is time to go back, back up the trail, and walk past the old burned mill. The way out is so different from the way in, the trail turned over and over into something else, so much longer, or so much shorter—just so different now. Take the path up to the dam, and find the kayakers, helmeted, in life-jackets, paddling and circling above the dam. Now, they can't go where you were, down with the mushrooms, down with the ghosts. But someday they will. 🖂

SPRING EPHEMERAL

Jeanne Malmgren

I AM A PILGRIM, PICKING MY WAY ALONG A MOUNTAIN TRAIL.

Some seekers, the ones who walk long, lonely roads to shrines and cathedrals, wear sandals with a coat of dust on them. Not me. My feet are clad in hiking boots, old ones caked with red clay.

I drove forty-five minutes, wasting precious fossil fuel, because my soul needs refreshment and I know I'll find it here. This chilly cove is a sacred place—if you're a lover of wildflowers, that is, and if it's early spring.

Every March I come here to Devils Fork State Park to see the Oconee bells. Like me, they're native to this corner of northwest South Carolina. In botany-speak, they are "spring ephemerals," wildflowers that bloom for a brief, rapturous time, just as the world is stirring from its winter sleep. They pop up, little miracles, from the leaf litter on the forest floor, stretching toward a weak sun as snakes emerge from hibernation and icy creeks thaw.

Oconee bells grow wild in only a very few places: one county in northeast Georgia, another one or two in western North Carolina, and here. In 1973, when Duke Power Company flooded the Jocassee Valley to make a lake for recreation and hydropower production, sixty percent of Oconee bell habitat was lost. So to see them in bloom is a privilege.

No, strike that. "Privilege" is not strong enough. To see Oconee bells in bloom is a sacrament, an act of hope in a world where tiny white flowers are easily trampled by development, where a species can disappear— just like that—without a whisper.

Each step must be chosen carefully. I'm not so young anymore. My days of hiking the Appalachian Trail with a fifty-pound backpack

are gone. In this shadowy forest a tree root, hidden by wet winter leaves, could twist an ankle. The arthritis in my knees is speaking, and I have forgotten my walking stick.

There are rewards, though. The air is sweet and restless, stirring the tops of hickories overhead. It's still too cold for most hikers, and it's a weekday, so the nature photographers with their tripods and digital light meters are not here. I'm alone, as a pilgrim must be. Only the calls of Carolina wrens bear witness to my walk.

As the trail drops gently, I hear water. It grows from a murmur to a gurgle to the pleasing music of liquid sluicing over flat boulders. Soon I see a curving ribbon of a stream—ground zero for these fragile flowers. Oconee bells are notoriously picky about where they grow, and this is their ideal habitat: a tree-shaded creek with banks of spongy humus, sheltered by an umbrella of rhododendron and mountain laurel.

The Oconee bell owes its scientific name—*Shortia galacifolia*—to Charles W. Short, a botany professor at the University of Kentucky who never saw the plant. It was discovered in 1787 by French explorer Andre Michaux, who took a single, flowerless specimen back to Paris and stored it in an herbarium there, with the cryptic notation that he had found it in "the high mountains of Carolina."

More than fifty years later, in 1839, renowned Harvard botanist Dr. Asa Gray came across the herbarium specimen and was intrigued. He searched the Blue Ridge Escarpment for years, but never located Oconee bells in the wild. He did, however, claim the honor of naming the plant: *Shortia* for his friend, Dr. Short, and *galacifolia* to signify that its foliage resembles the leaves of galax, a common mountain perennial.

Inspired by Gray, other scientists joined the fruitless search for Oconee bells, and it went on for decades. The so-called "Lost Shortia" became a sort of Holy Grail for collectors of Appalachian wildflowers.

> I'm alone, as a pilgrim must be. Only the calls of Carolina wrens bear witness to my walk.

In 1877 a teenage boy happened upon Shortia growing along the Catawba River near Marion, North Carolina. A few years later, nearly a century after Michaux's discovery, another Harvard botanist, Dr. Charles Sprague Sargent, came across a colony of Oconee bells while plant collecting at the confluence of the Horsepasture and Toxaway rivers—the area later flooded by Duke, and near where Michaux is presumed to have first glimpsed these elusive treasures.

The romantic in me thrills to this story of discovery, loss, rediscovery, and loss again—like lovers parted and reunited, over and over. I also thrill to the plant itself: a groundcover of perfectly round, deep green leaves. Each of those leaves, serrated and glossy, is the size of a silver dollar. When the sun hits them, they glow.

The flowers, though, are what make Oconee bells so endearing. Held on five-inch stalks, these little blushing debutantes hang their heads shyly, their beauty hidden from above. You have to crouch—arthritic knees be damned—to fully appreciate the loveliness of Oconee bells. Each one no bigger than a thumbnail. Fringed petals as delicate as gold leaf. They tremble in the slightest breeze.

While I walk the path, sunlight pushes through tangles of laurel limbs. I look down. At the edge of the trail, next to some clumps of Oconee bells, are trodden-over places where other pilgrims have stood to get their close-up shots. Will this endangered plant be able to spread across that hard-packed earth? Will it be trampled by the next group of admirers? Will we love Oconee bells to death? This gives a whole new meaning to the word *ephemeral*.

Overhead, hardwood trees are budding. In a week or two, they'll have young leaves on them. Not as much sunlight will reach the forest floor. The last of the Oconee bells will fade.

I sit on the ground, next to the stream, and close my eyes. The sun makes me drowsy. I can feel the breath in my throat. All around me the trees are breathing, too. Oconee bells nod in the wind.

Here, in the heart of the cathedral, a pilgrim with muddy boots has found what she was seeking. 🖎

ICE STORM REFLECTIONS
Shandi Stevenson

"EVERYONE BEGINS AS A CHILD BY LIKING WEATHER. YOU LEARN THE ART OF DISLIKING IT AS YOU GROW UP." —C.S. Lewis

My family moved to the Southeast from the mountains of western Colorado. At first, I pined for the dramatic, overwhelming landscapes of the West—for snowy peaks, brilliant skies, arresting contrasts. And every winter, especially, I longed for dazzling drifts of snow sparkling under blue skies. I felt cheated by the chilly rain, the cold, soggy mud, and the earth-toned palate of winter in the Southeast. This, I felt, was not real winter.

My first Upstate ice storm was a big one—and it did nothing to endear the southern winter to me. Like many who move to the South, I couldn't help snickering at first at the way our new community locked down at the first warning of possible freezing rain—the school closings, the stores stripped of milk and bread, the hasty cancellations. But once the first needles of ice began to rattle against the windows, and

the first deadly sheen glistened on branches and power lines, I stopped laughing at the neighbors.

As the treacherous embrace of the storm closed around us, stranding us in a cold, silent house, without heat, light, water, telephone, or any access to the world beyond our own glassy-slick and limb-littered driveway, I also realized something. One thing I had always enjoyed about winter was being able to go out and admire it, and then come in, take a hot shower, eat a hot meal in a warm, bright house, and pop into the car to drive on safely sanded roads to other warm, bright buildings. The Carolina ice storm brought the experience of winter to a new and uncomfortably intimate level. Messy, inconvenient, and intrusive, this kind of winter did not wait patiently until I was in the mood to notice or enjoy it. It interrupted my life, ready or not.

But something happened when I stepped onto our slippery and crackling country road that first morning when the sun shone again after the storm. The tinkle of the frozen twigs and the insistent patter of melting drops striking the fallen leaves filled the keen air with a strange music. Encased in immaculate sheaths of ice, the details of each blade of grass sprang out at me, like the colors in a Renaissance painting. Every gangly roadside weed was transformed into a thing of mystery, of surreal and dazzling beauty. The glitter of the sun through the trees, still shimmering silver, took my breath away.

Nothing matches that brief, magical sight, the one you have to get up in time to catch before the returning sun melts away the ice and life returns to normal. Nothing is more beautiful than the fairyland left behind by an ice storm, when the sunshine first finds it again and lights up the world, flashing like a thousand diamonds.

Somehow, the moment evoked memories of splashing in rain puddles, lying face-down to smell the grass, squeezing mud between my toes, catching snowflakes on my tongue, holding my breath on the edge of a fog-haunted forest, racing after wind-blown leaves. Memories of embracing, with the fragile wisdom of childhood, the wetness of water, the coldness of cold, the greenness of grass. Where does it go, that gift of loving every moment for its own sake, celebrating life just the way it happens?

The next thing I knew, I was running, sliding on the ice, leaping to touch the glittering branches, stamping on the frozen puddles to see the cracks shoot out around my boots. I thought myself safe from embarrassment because so few cars had ventured onto the roads, but even when, at last, a car did sidle cautiously by, I found that I did not care. I waved cheerfully to the driver, not bothering to conceal my flushed face, tangled hair, wet clothes, and mud-spattered boots. Perhaps I wanted to share something I had just learned: When the weather shuts down your life, there are only two choices. You can resent the interruption with a helpless bitterness—a bitterness that won't let you remember how you used to roll in the snow or leap laughing into mud puddles, when as a child you were in love with the experience of life. Or, you can take the enforced vacation as a much-needed reminder

to enjoy being alive. To stop, to look, to notice. To pay attention.

For me, ice storms have become a reminder that sometimes life needs to be sudden, messy, and unpredictable—that I need to experience the world around me, and not always on my own terms. It's easy to be irritated by many uniquely ice-storm hassles—the steaming piles of muddy shoes drying out in front of the kerosene heater, the canned soup heated on the woodstove, the backlog of work accumulating relentlessly on your dormant computer. But I try to remind myself that maybe ice storms are just trying to tell me to stop and enjoy something wonderful. Maybe they are saying that exploring a vanishing silver world outside is more important than the things I had planned to do today. Or that nothing is more urgent than the beauties and surprises of life that interrupt us with rough, yet seductive, insistence.

I have now lived in, and loved, upstate South Carolina for fifteen years. Our rare but dramatic ice storms have become for me a metaphor for things as various as traffic jams, delayed flights, computer problems, car trouble, unexpected visitors. When life is inconvenient, when it upsets my agenda, when it intrudes upon me, when it's not what I planned, I hope I'll remember to splash in the puddles, rather than huddling fretfully under an umbrella, and to marvel at the fleeting beauty of the storm, rather than sulking before the fire.

When I am trapped in long lines, I remind myself that there is nowhere else I can be, and nothing else I can be doing. This is not an interruption in my life—this, for the moment, is my life. I look with renewed interest at the luckless fellow human beings surrounding me, whose elusive, unknown personalities touch mine for this fleeting moment, whose tales of ambition and friendship and heartbreak I shall never know. When I am stranded in a strange airport, cast ashore with other querulous and irritable odds and ends of the traveling public, I treat myself to the unexpected hour with a favorite book. I watch the currents of humanity flow back and forth, feeling the rush and murmur of a hundred lives and a hundred extraordinary stories throbbing like a pulse all around me.

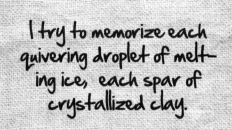

I try to memorize each quivering droplet of melting ice, each spar of crystallized clay.

And I haven't missed a morning-after ice storm walk since I first discovered the strange, secret world of our Carolina winter at its most fragile and mysterious. The same road I walked down the day before, the same row of naked trees, the same pebbly roadside puddle—all are transformed into something utterly unfamiliar. I study every detail of this strange new country as I explore a place no one has ever seen before—a place no one will see again. I try to memorize each quivering droplet of melting ice, each spar of crystallized clay. I know this melting world—like life itself—will vanish before I can notice half its wonders.

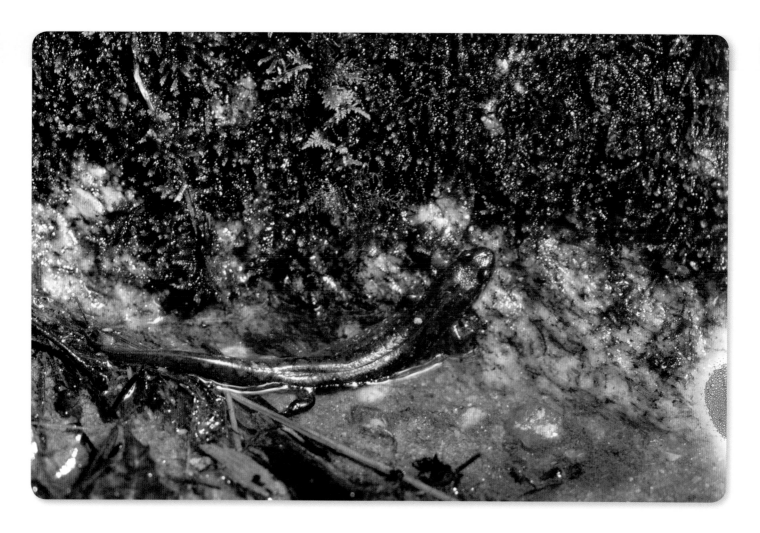

ABNER CREEK, 1991 *for Shawn*

Dawn Johnson Mitchell

WE GREW UP IN THE WATERY ARMS OF ABNER CREEK, WHICH WRAPPED AROUND THE RURAL ROADS WE CALLED HOME. WE DIDN'T HAVE BOUNDARIES MADE BY SIDEWALKS AND SUBDIVISION SIGNS, JUST THE NATURAL FLOW OF THE CREEK AND THE TWO MAJOR HIGHWAYS THAT MAMA WOULDN'T LET OUR BIKES CROSS.

Home was the stretch of land between Highway 101 and Highway 14 in rural Spartanburg County. Home was sloping hills dotted with hay bales, farm houses that held families like the Fowlers and Fishers for generations, worn-down but well-cared-for tractors and trailers, and small two-lane bridges that crossed the banks of Abner Creek and connected it all.

We had a few options that a bicycle afforded us growing up in the country. If Mama was home, we could ride our bikes toward Reidville to the edge of Highway 101 and go to Joe's Fishing Lake. We'd buy a hot dog with homemade chili and mustard and sit in the paneled diner under the mounted deer

and fish and watch what men would pull out of the murky lake. If Mama wasn't home, we could ride up the other direction toward Highway 14 and go to Donahue's Country Store. We'd look around at the dusty shelves filled with everything—Stren fishing line, rusty baling wire, shelves of potted meat, and yellow bagged Sunbeam bread. Usually, we'd fish out a bottle neck Pepsi swimming around in an ice chest, and if we had enough change, maybe a Little Debbie cake. Our other, preferred option was just a ways out the back door. We didn't need a bicycle or loose change to afford what Abner Creek offered us on sunny, summer days.

It was pale like dirty dishwater, and thin

like my brother's long legs, running in slow loops, carving our land with grainy banks and exposed tree roots. It had pockets deep enough for a few small horny heads and bream, filling up the green honey holes swirling with summer's catch. It was shallow enough so scrawny kids with matchstick legs jammed in soggy sneakers could walk upstream against the cool pull of the current all day and not grow tired.

We loved that creek, my brother and I. We loved it full of water moccasins and mud, giant poplars and pines towering over us, sandy secrets burrowing below the bottom. Coins, bottle tops, and an old whiskey jug were treasures we found half buried in the murky bed. We rinsed and filled that old jug with copper pennies that shined inside my brother's closet like the glittering mica he poured out.

We stumbled upon a painted turtle's nest one sun-speckled afternoon playing in the creek's shallow sections, eyes wide as we watched the tiger-striped mama on the bank carefully scratch sand over her rubbery eggs, hind legs moving like a rhythmic backhoe.

We washed red tomatoes, Better Boys and Park's Whoppers, grown in the field Daddy plowed with a tractor he shared with our neighbor, in the shallows. We'd wash the nose-burning tomato smell off our hands and wipe the slick skin on worn shirttails. We'd eat them like apples, climbing up the black walnut tree whose roots thrived in Abner's sandy soil.

We didn't have enough money or lumber to build a real tree house, but we nailed up a board for the two of us and we would use the branches to shimmy our skinny legs up to our board and we'd sit. We'd sit for the last dredges of an afternoon, legs dangling over the creek, tomato seeds in our grins, and shirts wet from Abner Creek's washing.

We fished its banks armed only with a rusty, worn-out Zebco 33 rod and the end pieces of week-old bread—if we were lucky, a can of Del Monte corn. We never boasted a big catch, but we didn't care. The promise of what we might reel up kept us busy and we took it seriously. We fought over whose turn it was to use the rod and criticized each other's casts. We loved the feel of pressing down the automatic reel with our thumbs, the tension of aiming toward just the right spot where green-gray depths met a circle of current, the whir of the line releasing, and the plop of the bait and bobber.

No matter how small the catch, we never threw anything back until we were done. We toted our fish around with us in a five-gallon paint bucket. Up and down the creek, we'd take turns toting the bucket, its plastic heft banging into our legs every time we lifted up a water-logged sneaker from the sand. We never caught anything big enough to fry, but along with that bucket, we carried inside us the shiny hope of what could be waiting for us around the next bend, hovering just below the surface under the exposed root of a tree or in the shadows of a fallen log.

We didn't need a bicycle or loose change to afford what Abner Creek offered us on sunny summer days.

When we grew tired and hungry, we climbed out and ate baloney and mustard sandwiches on warm white bread a few yards away with water puckered hands, river-washed clean, and Carolina clay crusted around our knees. We took showers, but our skin kept a red clay tinge, and we had a creek smell to us that didn't wash off. We lived like creek creatures and relished in it.

It's amazing that a place can become a part of you like flesh and bone. After so many breaths spent in and along this creek bank, it ceases to exist outside of you, but becomes a part of who you are like the Case pocket knife my brother always kept in the right front pocket of his jeans. It wore its place, its rectangle mark, into the fabric. You carry it around with you, the hard, true knowledge of a place. We didn't need to breathe the earthy smell of the creek bank or touch the paper thin bark of the birch tree rooted close by to know the texture of it between our fingers.

We know it by heart.

It's been awhile since we played in Abner's arms, trudging home with a tackle box and farmer's tans, two twin shadows separated only at dark, our laughter still caught in her currents.

OBSERVING

Pamela Burgess Shucker

Kirk Neely

Sabrina Moser

Jane Chew

Ernest Glenn

Joni Tevis

Russ Burns

MORE THAN OCONEE BELLS

Pamela Burgess Shucker

MY HUSBAND AND I LEAVE THIS EARLY SPRING DAY'S BRIGHT WARMTH AND DESCEND INTO THE TWILIGHT OF THE HUSHED PINE FOREST AT DEVILS FORK STATE PARK. OUR FEET SILENTLY TREAD THE NEEDLE-LAYERED TRAIL MEANDERING TOWARD THE CREEK.

We seek one of the most endangered and elusive wildflowers, *Shortia galacifolia*. This plant, commonly called Oconee bell, grows naturally only in the rugged Blue Ridge Escarpment and nowhere else on Earth.

Here in the South Carolina piedmont, in the nationally protected area of the Jocassee Gorges, French botanist Andre Michaux identified and named the plant in 1787. For almost one hundred years after, naturalists searched unsuccessfully for other plants until a boy discovered it once again in this area of the southern Appalachian Mountains.

Today's crisp air tingles, pungent with spring's promise. Through the quiet our ears soon detect the creek's gurgle, and we feel we are close. The plants thrive along damp stream edges, creeping up and down banks and gracefully draping them. The sheen of the emerald, half-dollar size leaves with ruffled borders makes the plant easy to recognize. In early spring pure white blooms hang bell-like, each of the five petals trimmed in exquisite lace fringe. Peeking from the bloom's center, five gold lace-skirted stamens contrast like golden sunlight on snow. It isn't easy to photograph the hanging blossom, which blooms profusely only where sunlight straggles through the tree cover. In rich, loose soil of damp areas *S. galacifolia* creates a lush carpet, but it does not tolerate footsteps that compact the soil. To protect these rare beauties, hikers must stay strictly on the trail. My husband and I step gingerly, following the winding stream to view and photograph this exquisite snowflake tapestry.

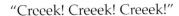

"Creeek! Creeek! Creeek!"

Incessant and shrill, the calls pierce our ears, diverting our attention. Our hunt for white lace-edged blooms meets a detour. "Night sounds" my husband and I call these chirps, clicks, hums, and drums. As spring weather warms the South Carolina piedmont, this joyful chorus tunes up for its annual performance.

But this is *mid*-March, *mid*day, and *mid*way on the Oconee Bell Trail at Devils Fork State Park. These are not *night sounds*. "What's going on here?" we wonder aloud.

Thrilled that I might improve my knowledge of various pitches, tones, and cadences created by each creature, I point my digital camera in the direction of the sounds. As I film through the camera lens, my peripheral vision picks up movement in the algae-dotted pond beside the shaded trail. The edges of the pond seem to be boiling! The surface churns and splashes, exploding in bubbles three feet from where I stand at the pond's edge. A brown- and white-splotched ball rolls, twists, and turns as it floats on the surface. Scanning my brain for what this mass could be, I call my husband to share the phenomenon.

Our eyes and minds finally focus, and we realize that a ball of toads floats and struggles on the water's surface, brown legs flailing in every direction. A single toad slips off and drags himself onto a moss-covered log jutting above the surface. We watch his cream-colored vocal sac swell and empty repeatedly. His voice rises above the chorus, almost bursting with longing for any female toad ears in his territory. My mind can label this: a toad calling for a mate.

The floating mass recaptures our attention. We interpret this to be a toad-mating ball. Five or six toads have successfully clambered onto and now cling in motley postures to the back of one female. Several additional males attempt to climb onto the mass of speckled brown legs and backs. The unlucky ones slide off into the water in a backwards somersault, flashing a white belly as they splash. We watch for fifteen minutes, but no male dominates and no eggs emerge from this female.

We follow the chorus around the grassed edges of the pond where scores more toads sonorously call seeking mates. Just beyond the pond's semicircle rim, dozens of stacked and mated pairs float together serenely. Other females, always larger than the males, struggle in the shallows as numerous males attempt to mount. Contesting males slide off or are kicked off by other better-situated legs. Each male vies to propel his genetic code into the future, competing for the privilege of fertilizing the female's eggs when she releases them into the water.

Curly transparent strands filled with black gelatinous eggs float in the water, catching among the pond grasses or swirling around stacked couples. We watch twin coiled strings of dark eggs emerge from several females as each accepts the male who has secured prime position on her brown splotched back.

From later research I learn this toad is *Bufo americanus*, the American toad. The American toad lives in the drier areas of the woods throughout the year. The mating urge arises during these first few days of spring, prompted by warmer weather, longer daylight, and rains that create or swell ponds. The males arrive and establish territories about a week before the females. They begin their incessant calls to attract mates who arrive ripe with eggs. The males compete to attach to the female's back using horny toe pads grown for this purpose. In a rear hug posture, called *amplexus*, the successful male holds the female as they float together in the reedy shallows of the pond's surface, ready to fertilize her eggs when she releases them.

> Our eyes and minds finally focus, and we realize that a ball of toads floats and struggles on the water's surface, brown legs flailing in every direction.

As we watch, no egg strings emerge from females involved in a struggle with the males. The female only releases her eggs when one male predominates and successfully attaches in amplexus. We conclude the male's successful dominance stimulates the female to lay her clutch, thus assuring that the genes of only one male fertilize her eggs.

Following this annual mating ritual, the adult toads hop back to the woods to live out the year. In three to twelve days the strings of eggs hatch into tadpoles, recognizable as *Bufo americanus* by skinny tails in relation to their heads. During the next thirty to forty days these tadpoles use gills to breathe oxygen dissolved in the pond's water, eventually growing legs and absorbing their tails. They mature into small toadlets, losing their gills and convert-

ing to breathing air. Soon they, too, move into the drier woods where they continue to grow, shedding and eating their outgrown skins as they develop to full size.

I return to this spot three days later. The magic has vanished. The pond holds only silence and a few decomposing toads. No tadpoles have yet hatched. Some strings of eggs still float, clear streamers with black dots weaving among the golden grasses. Many have sunk and lie on the sandy pond bottom. Some eggs have turned an iridescent white within their strands, glowing as the sun shines through the shallow water on the thousands of coils. I wonder if these near hatching. The pond has resumed its quiet routine, its borders secretly cradling this future generation of *Bufo americanus*.

During the hours of our vigil, no other trail walkers passed to share the encounter. We humans often consider ourselves the most prevailing members of creation. But on that day we witnessed in wonder a ritual that developed without human technology or intervention. Using knowledge passed down through the millennia, these toads perfectly enacted their roles in nature's reoccurring drama. Being the audience for these performances, we captured not only the beauty of the pure white Oconee bell blooms with our senses and our camera, but recorded Earth's awesome natural rhythms: life recreating itself. 🖎

SNAKE HANDLING WITH RUDY MANCKE
Kirk H. Neely

IN 1909, THE REVEREND GEORGE HENSLEY DELIVERED A SERMON USING THE LAST SEVEN VERSES OF THE GOSPEL OF MARK AS HIS TEXT.

The phrase "they shall take up serpents" made such an impression on the preacher, he chased down a timber rattler, assembled his church members for a meeting, and passed the venomous rattlesnake among them. In the southern Appalachian Mountains, this was the beginning of snake handling as a religious ritual.

Rudy Mancke and I grew up together in the Duncan Park area of Spartanburg. Many know Rudy from *Nature Scene*, a television program on South Carolina Educational Television. Rudy teaches at the University of South Carolina.

Soon after I learned to drive, Rudy and I decided we were going to stay out all night. I was fourteen, the legal age for driving in South Carolina in those days. Rudy was one year younger. We planned to camp and fish at a farm pond near Walnut Grove.

We fished awhile, catching several good-sized bream. We put them on an old chain stringer in the edge of the water. As darkness surrounded us, we cooked our supper over a campfire. On a clear moonless night, the air was filled with the sounds of bullfrogs, tree frogs, crickets, and a pair of owls. Above the evening serenade, we heard the discordant note of the chain stringer rattling.

I whispered, "Something's trying to get our fish."

We couldn't see through the dark, but something was definitely messing with our bream. We heard the rattling of the chain again.

Scrambling to his feet, Rudy grabbed his flashlight. We ran to the water's edge to investigate. Caught in the beam of light was the largest snake I had ever seen. The reptile had a bluegill halfway down his throat. Rudy identified the culprit as a red-bellied water snake.

"Look! His lips are red!"

I did not care what kind of snake it was. I surely wasn't interested in his lips. As far as I was concerned, the snake was an unwelcome intruder. Not so for Rudy! For Rudy, catching snakes was better than catching fish any time of the day or night.

Years later, Rudy informed me, "That night was a history-making event." Ever the teacher, Rudy said, "Nobody had ever reported a red-bellied water snake that far north. If you look in *A Field Guide to Amphibians and Reptiles* by Roger Conant, you will see that the range for this snake now goes into Spartanburg County. Kirk, that is because we identified the red-bellied water snake in Spartanburg County as teenagers. Before our discovery that night, everyone thought those particular snakes did not live in areas north of Columbia."

On the night Rudy saw that big snake in his flashlight beam, he took charge.

"Get your pillowcase!"

He grabbed the snake behind the neck—I should say behind the head, since a snake is almost all neck—and pulled the bream out of its mouth. The snake did not like Rudy rudely grabbing him and stealing his supper. The powerful serpent threw three coils around Rudy's arm. I cautiously opened the pillowcase. Rudy dropped in the gigantic snake, still writhing in anger. Dismayed, I stood, literally left holding the bag!

Rudy turned around, looked at me, and exclaimed, "We could do this all night!"

I do not know how many fish we caught that Friday night. I do know we filled two pillowcases with thirty-eight snakes.

Returning home right after daylight, we met my dad on his way to work.

"Dad, look!" I opened one of the pillowcases. A banded water snake thrust itself to the top, biting me on the thumb. I quickly closed the sack of snakes.

Dad asked, "What do you have there?"

"Thirty-eight snakes!"

"What are you going to do with them?"

"We're going to keep them."

"Not here, you're not! It'd be alright with me but not with your mama."

Rudy and I took the snakes to the basement of his home, a short walk down the road and around the bend from my house. Rudy's saintly parents had grown accustomed to critters as houseguests.

We kept the snakes in a big terrarium covered with framed hardware cloth. Through the summer, I noticed the number of snakes diminishing.

"Rudy, some of the snakes are getting out!" I told him one day.

"They're not getting out. Haven't you noticed how big that water snake has grown?"

The snakes were eating each other!

By early October, one snake remained, the big red-bellied water snake, bigger than ever. Before the first day of autumn, Rudy and I took the last snake to Duncan Park Lake and let it swim to freedom.

That night at Walnut Grove was my only snake-hunting expedition. Before long, Rudy graduated to seeking copperheads and rattlesnakes. He has been bitten a time or two.

Through the years, I've seen many snakes. I've handled a few, all nonpoisonous. My rule of thumb, my snake-bitten thumb, is to let them be.

Reverend George Hensley was supposedly bitten 446 times by the venomous vipers he handled in worship. He finally died after bite 447, at age 75, steadfastly refusing medical treatment.

Be careful out there, Rudy!

SOMEZING'S BUGGING ME

Sabrina Moser

WHEN I FIRST CAME TO LIVE IN THE UPSTATE WITH MY GERMAN HUSBAND, I THOUGHT THEY WERE NUTS. ALL THESE GERMANS, THAT IS.

Unlike me, a returning native, they had been sent here for a few years on foreign assignment to manage big companies during the week and to bask, on the weekends, in the exotically hot Carolina sun. Certainly they marveled at their new surroundings: at how fast the plants grew, at how friendly folks were, at the expanse of the parking lots and the breadth of the cars. But the thing that seemed to impress them most of all, the thing they never tired of re-marking upon, was the sheer size of our bugs. "Ooo, ze bugs in Southz Carolina are wery, wery large," they would assure me before launching into colorful accounts of things that they had seen. Or things that friends had seen. Or things that friends of friends had report-edly seen. There were tales of gigantic snakes and six-foot lizards and man-eating palmetto bugs. To hear them talk, you would think they had moved to the Amazon.

At home with my husband, the conversation tended to revolve around the somewhat more benign matter of Upstate mosquitoes. Already within his first weeks here he had developed an abiding dread of them, and he now refuses to go outside, even for a few minutes, unprotected. "But you have mosquitoes in Germany too!" I always remind him. "Yes, but zey are nothz-ing like ze ones here," is his standard reply as he douses himself with yet more foul-smelling bug spray. Since moving into our home a year ago, we have acquired such a spectacular array of mosquito-repelling gear that I am considering adding on an extra room to accommodate it all. The collection ranges from outdoor misting fans guaranteed to blow faster than a mosquito can fly to cases of citronella candles, a lively assortment of tiki torches, and a butane-powered gadget that releases a musty smell reminiscent of two sweaty men huddled together in a duck blind. The fumes drive the mosquitoes away alright—while also driving me straight indoors.

The crown jewel of my husband's collection, however, is a little vibrating clip-on gizmo that we recently learned about from a neighbor, a stately German lady who has been living here for at least the past twenty years. "It iz great for work in ze garden," she avowed while smugly displaying the blue plastic device dangling from her pocket. Needless to say, we hopped into our car and raced off in search of one, but, alas, the stores were all sold out. Apparently, the Germans had already spread ze word. Finally, weeks later, I have managed to secure one for my husband in the hope that he will now do his gardening dressed like a normal human being in a t-shirt and shorts rather than covered up from head to toe in a thick cloaking of mosquito-proof denim. Personally, I would rather spend the entire rest of the day manically scratching than go out into the ninety-degree South Carolina heat dressed for a cool day on a lake in Wisconsin.

Secretly, of course, I have been thinking to myself all along that these Germans, my husband included, are hopeless drama queens. How could anyone be truly afraid of a palmetto bug, after all? No, they seem intent on blowing the animal life here wildly out of proportion for the sake of a good story. Certainly detailed accounts of fantastical creatures, of sea monsters and fire-breathing dragons, are more interesting to the folks back home than bland reports on how friendly the people are or how nice the weather is.

But daggum it, now that I have listened to their stories all summer long, now that I have encountered first-hand some of the insects winging their merry way through the Upstate, I seem to have come down with a major case of the heebie-jeebies myself. Whereas before I could march right into the bushes to get to the garden hose without even a thought of what might be lurking there, I now proceed tentatively. My eyes are on the ground scanning for fire ants while my ears are alert for the buzzing of a belligerent wasp. Whereas before I cavalierly flung open the doors of the garden shed to grab a shovel or a flowerpot, I now open them

carefully and stare into the darkness, my eyes straining to catch movement in the shadows. If I should determine that all is clear, I snatch what I need, slam the doors shut, and run like hell in the opposite direction. My brief intrusion, after all, might have awakened a whole host of sleeping cave crickets.

And just the other night, as we were setting the table out on the deck for dinner, something brushed against my flip-flopped foot. "Ooo!" I cried and jumped in the air. When I looked down, I did not encounter a gigantic wolf spider lurking under the table, his eight eyes studying me intently before going in for the kill, but rather, I found only a desiccated leaf that had dropped innocently from a nearby hibiscus plant.

How do I cure myself of this sudden case of the willies? I am not so certain. Perhaps the key lies simply in repeated exposure to the things that have been spooking me. I forced myself a few days ago, for example, to pick up and take home a dead beetle I found in a parking lot. It is about two inches long, speckled, has a gigantic rhinocerial horn and, at the moment, is lying belly up in my garage in case anyone would like to come over and see it or maybe identify it for me.

Because cure myself I must. It would be an inexcusable shame to spend the summers indoors and frightened of what is going on outside. And I certainly do not want my son to learn to be afraid. No, I want him to grow up in the Upstate loving the things about the hot and humid South that I have always treasured: the flicker of fireflies in the woods on a soft summer night, the deafening swell of the cicada calls in late July, the slow progression of a black snake through the ivy leaves. These are the things that, for me, define life in the Upstate just as much as our vibrant expatriate community does. The abundance of wildlife here—even in the suburbs—is startling, and I am proud that my German friends will return to their home country and report on it in vivid detail. For it is this unique constellation of an international community putting down roots and learning to thrive in Southern soil that makes me want to call the Upstate my permanent home. 🖎

A BIRD'S-EYE VIEW OF THE UPSTATE

Jane Chew

ADIEU! ADIEU! THY PLAINTIVE ANTHEM FADES
PAST THE NEAR MEADOWS, OVER THE STILL STREAM,
UP THE HILL-SIDE; AND NOW 'TIS BURIED DEEP
IN THE NEXT VALLEY-GLADES:
WAS IT A VISION, OR A WAKING DREAM?
FLED IS THAT MUSIC:—DO I WAKE OR SLEEP?

—John Keats, "Ode to a Nightingale"

In 1996 my husband, Jim, looked out the window into the bald winter landscape of our woods on Paris Mountain and saw a bird—a small bird, what birders call "a little brown job"—flitting around the understory. For years we had ignored the variety of birds that visited our yard, but suddenly that kind of inattention would no longer do. Jim had to know what it was. We conducted a search, located *Peterson's Field Guide*, and found our laughable binoculars, and all the while, the bird continued to bounce around within view. Small, grayish-green, wingbars, yellow on a striped head: a

golden-crowned kinglet! We were so proud of ourselves, but more important, we realized there was a shadow world lurking out there, populated by feathered jewels, and suddenly we wanted to experience that world.

In that spirit, with Christmas approaching, I thought it was time to invest in some good binoculars. So I went to Wolf Camera and bought what I thought were serious binoculars—after all, they cost $150 long on magnification and short on field-of-view, which I didn't understand anyway. I figured we wanted these birds blown up big; it didn't occur to me that locating them in the first place might be difficult. The presentation was made Christmas Day and was duly appreciated, but the binoculars were soon consigned to storage and never made it into the field. This was my first lesson in birding: good optics are essential, expensive, and aren't usually available at Wolf Camera at the mall. So, after an Internet search, some solid gold Leica binoculars were on the way. Then, it turned out one couldn't share binoculars in the field, so a pair of more affordable Nikons was ordered for me, but ten-power—I was still enthralled by magnification at the price of field-of-view. Armed with this equipment, we started looking for local birding sites.

One of the first places I found was the Bunched Arrowhead Heritage Preserve, northeast of Travelers Rest. Bunched arrowhead is a very rare plant discovered by the late Leland Rogers, a longtime professor of botany at Furman University (and, coincidentally, Jim's teacher in his long-ago undergraduate days). It needs very special conditions that provide continual seepage, and it is known to grow in only three locations: at the Preserve, on the Furman University campus, and in Henderson County, North Carolina. The Preserve features a maintained loop trail, which traverses a variety of habitats: short scrub, open fields, deep woods, a pond (depending on rainfall), and streams. I have never found the Preserve to be particularly good during migration, but it is home to most of the Upstate's resident birds. In addition to bird-feeder birds, I've found indigo buntings, ruby-crowned kinglets, savannah sparrows, field sparrows, eastern towhees, downy and hairy woodpeckers, bluebirds, goldfinches, red-tailed hawks and red-shouldered hawks, common yellowthroats, yellow-breasted chats, wood ducks, and once I startled a woodcock. About halfway around the loop, especially in spring, one frequently encounters contorted photographers trying to get a good shot of the bunched arrowhead plants. But rarely have we seen other birders or hikers. You have the place pretty much to yourself, although there is often evidence of all-terrain vehicles (forbidden) and horses (also forbidden).

The Bunched Arrowhead Preserve was important to me because there I learned something of the skill of birding, which involves training both the eye and the ear. Getting the binoculars, even good ones, on the birds is not a trivial matter, and I had made the task more difficult with my ten-power glasses. With the greater magnification, I could only focus on a very small spot in my field of vision, and if the bird wasn't exactly there, I wasn't going to see it. Also, the increased power magnified the unsteadiness of my hands and feet and dimmed the color of what I was looking at. Yet even with this disadvantage, I learned to move the binoculars up to my eyes slowly while keeping the bird in view, and to note the bird's surroundings and other nearby landmarks that could guide me to the bird in the glasses' field-of-view. My instinct early on was to scan the landscape with my binoculars looking for birds, but that yielded few results. Better to look with the eye for movement, and then to get binoculars on the movement. We also had to learn how to tell each other where to locate birds—two o'clock on the largest tree on the horizon—and fast. I had to hone my powers of observation, to note the aspects of the bird that would allow me to identify it if I had to resort to a field guide: eye-ring, wingbars, and head and breast pattern are far more reliable than color or size.

But the most important and counterintuitive lesson of our Bunched Arrowhead field experience was the value of the ear over the eye. You hear birds long before you see them, and they have distinctive songs during nesting season and call notes or chip notes the rest of the year. Professional birders can walk along and identify every note in the dawn chorus. I worked on the songs, but I still have to refresh myself every year, because it takes a kind of memory I rarely have call to use. So while I didn't find an ivory-billed woodpecker at Bunched Arrowhead Preserve, I got valuable field experience there.

Perhaps the most exciting birding in the Upstate is to be found near Townville, in Anderson County near Lake Hartwell. Behind Mac

Praytor's house, I've seen fields crowded with meadow larks, American kestrels perched on the power lines, and northern harriers eerily wafting low over the ground in the dawn's early light. A nearby field is a rich source of Townville's five regular sparrows: song, white-throated, savannah, swamp, and grasshopper—the last an increasingly rare flat-headed species with a buzzy, insect-like call. I discovered my first Upstate Eurasian collared doves here, an introduced species now spreading rapidly. Once we gave Mr. Praytor five dollars to roust a barn owl out of one of his outbuildings; he was only too willing to indulge our nuttiness.

But the Holy Grail of Townville is a three-to-four mile loop road that runs through Fred Dobbins' farm and along the edge of the Beaverdam Wildlife Management Area. I usually park first at the corner near the old school house. In the field across from the school we scared up close to fifty woodcocks at dawn during a Christmas count led by the Clemson ornithologist, Sid Gauthreaux, each one barking its metallic "peent peent." I saw my first yellow warbler from the nearby bridge, radiating like a little sun in the gloom of the swamp. A brick-colored orchard oriole nests in the scrub at the corner each year. I think of the road in front of the schoolhouse as the blue grosbeak road because the grosbeaks reliably perch on the wires along that road in the summer. One can always hear a red-shouldered hawk shrieking throughout the Townville area. These birds are residents, mostly during the summer, there for the looking.

The thrill of occasional migrants is also to be found along Fred Dobbins Road. On one side are Mr. Dobbins's cow pastures, and on the other side he grows rotating crops to feed his livestock. When we visited, Mr. Dobbins, a product of the Clemson agricultural program and now near ninety, occasionally rode by, sometimes with his wife (now, sadly, deceased), curious about our enthusiasms and quite proud that his farm lured such unusual bird (and birder) life. The weeds and rivulets around his barn attract snipe and migrating

shorebirds like least, semipalmated, spotted, solitary, and pectoral sandpipers. In the stubble of his harvested corn we've seen horned larks and American pipits on their way to the Arctic, and before the harvest his hay has been weighted down with flocks of dickcissels and bobolinks—fun words to say. His ponds are an abundant source of ducks in winter, and one winter a pair of short-eared owls paid a brief visit, prowling the fields in the dim light. One fall, Jim came upon three sandhill cranes, storing up on food on their way to Florida. Another time, a lone snow goose brought birders from near and far, which tickled Mr. Dobbins.

But our greatest find on the Dobbinses' farm was a Say's phoebe, clearly distinguished from our common eastern phoebe by its rufous flanks and vent, and a rare find east of the Mississippi. Jim spotted it first, perched on a fence perpendicular to the road. We had a friend along, so there were three of us to confirm the bird, and it turned out to be only the third sighting of a Say's phoebe in South Carolina. We posted it on the Carolinabirds' Internet birdline as soon as we got home, and some other birders went out that afternoon, without luck. That is the nature of migrants— pure serendipity, but I don't think we have ever gone to Townville without finding something unexpected. And Fred Dobbins's farm is its own vanishing rarity, gently rolling pastures dotted with trees and ponds, a place where work and wildlife coexist in harmony; once I even saw a coyote who had found a home there. The early morning stillness of that landscape, bathed in golden winter sunlight, as the Psalm says, "restoreth my soul." Mr. Dobbins's sons run the farm now, but still I worry: when might it fall victim to rapacious earth-moving equipment in the construction of yet another housing development?

On Sassafras Mountain in Pickens County, South Carolina's highest peak (3,650 feet), one can follow spring bird migration as it progresses week by week up the mountain. Beginning at Rocky Bottom, the first arrivals are Louisiana waterthrushes, pumping their tails to the beat of their trills in the streams that border the ascending road. Next comes the ovenbird, as loud as he is reclusive, whose bold eye-ring gives him a look of permanent astonishment. Farther up squeaks the black-and-white warbler, shimmying up and down the trunks of trees like a nuthatch, and nearby are to my mind the most fashionable birds in birddom: the rose-breasted grosbeaks, with a prominent splash of exquisite rose against a white breast enveloped by jet-black wings. It is best to ascend Sassafras with the car windows open, listening for whatever you can hear.

I park about halfway up on the left and hike along an old logging road that runs along a ridge. Along that road, I can chart the arrival of spring warblers. First come the black-throated greens (to my eye, quite yellow, but these birds were named by men, who are notoriously color-blind), whose song, like the Pony Express, passes from cove to cove along the winding road. A little later, the furtive hooded warblers turn up, denizens of rhododendron hells, who with their black hoods and yellow bodies look like monks gone to carnival. They let you look once, but only once. About the same time, redstarts appear, flashing coral as they fan their tails. In late spring the natty worm-eating warblers take up residence every year in the same curve in the logging road. The last warblers to arrive are the black-throated blues (yes, these are blue), who can make a mighty sound with their tiny bodies. In the background, one can hear the "Who cooks for you?" call of a resident barred owl, one of the more diurnal owls. And surprises are possible: I've seen both a Cape May and a Blackburnian warbler passing through.

Close encounters of the non-bird kind are also possible on Sassafras. Jim was up there one day by himself on the logging road when he came around a curve to behold a mother bear with two cubs on the road. The mother headed downhill, while the two cubs ran up two adjacent trees. Jim stood a while looking at the cubs and trying to decide whether to go on or not, concerned about getting between a mother and her cubs. Suddenly he heard some snuffling

noises behind him, and, fearing an irate mother bear, he turned around slowly, only to discover some jostling dogs who had no interest in him. Still, returning to the safety of the car seemed like the best course at that point.

Whether I'm seeing old friends, itinerant migrants, or even if the whole outing is a complete bust, birding orients me in the world in a way nothing else has. I've been to the four corners of the North American continent in search of birds: west to the Yupik village of Gambell on the St. Lawrence Island in the Bering Sea (I really have seen Russia from Alaska); north to Point Barrow, Alaska; east to Cape Spear in Newfoundland; south to the Dry Tortugas near Key West. I've learned birding etiquette—be quiet, share the scope, don't be too emphatic with your identifications. I've honed my skills so that I can hold my own even in expert birding circles. But I reserve particular affection for my local birding sites in the Upstate. They help me to relate to my adopted state of South Carolina in a way that transcends the vagaries of culture or politics. The rewards of birding are also deeply personal, for in paying attention to birds in their habitat, I come to terms with my own inevitable flight. When people hear that I am a "bird watcher," they always ask if I take photographs of the birds, which, of course, would be a way of pinning them down, of holding on to them, of defying their flight. But it is the transience of the experience I have come to value, when as from a palimpsest, the shadow of a bird emerges from a familiar landscape. Movement in the fir tree reveals a shape: hyperactive, yellow on the head, a flash of orange, a high-pitched note of agitation. A golden-crowned kinglet! And then it is gone. In that moment, I feel I bear witness to what passes but also returns, and to my own participation in this cycle of death and renewal. It is the fleeting moment Keats describes in his poem that I treasure, something that can't be captured in a photograph, which places the birds and me in the cosmic scheme of things. In short, the birds of the Upstate have taught me to let go, a valuable lesson in this world. 🍃

THE RAVEN REPLIES
Ernest Glenn

THE QUESTION WAS SIMPLE ENOUGH: "DO BIRDS EVER TURN FLIPS?"

My son Tom and I had hiked to the top of Table Rock. We were sitting out to the north of the main part of the table, looking over Greenville County. From that spot I have on occasion seen one of the local peregrine falcons soaring above the valley, so I was hoping we might catch a glimpse of that lovely bird on this trip.

A turkey vulture cruised by, tipping and tilting in the drafts of air. That sight—for we both saw the vulture—was surely what prompted Tom's question. A slightly stronger-than-normal gust may have hit the vulture, or maybe something about being close to the rock face made the wind behave in an unusual manner. Whatever it was, the vulture tilted more than usual, suggesting to us that it might tip past the ninety-degree point and turn over.

I responded casually, by no means in a know-it-all manner. Tom was a high schooler at the time, and I was used to questions. Good, intelligent questions. I had learned from experience to avoid too many all-or-nothing statements when I answer my children. Or, to put it another way, to remember what I don't know. Still, I felt fairly certain.

"No," I said. "Why would they? I can't think of any reason for them to have to do such a thing."

Simple question. Simple answer.

I don't claim to know a lot about bird behavior. I describe myself as a bird lover, among other things, but a hobbyist for the most part. My answer was a safe one, I thought. Consider purpose, need, things of that sort. There have to be reasons, probably attributable to survival and all that, for everything that birds do. Why would they *need* to turn a flip?

I hadn't counted on the raven.

We sat there a few more minutes and then walked toward the top of the rock to pick up the trail and go back down the mountain. At the last part of open rock before we re-entered the woods, we stopped to take in the view one more time. A pleasant, stiff breeze swept across our faces from the south. And the raven came by to nonchalantly—but profoundly—teach me a lesson. As we were standing there taking in the scene from Caesars Head down toward Paris Mountain and Greenville, a raven flew above us, moving from south to north, probably no more than ten feet from our heads.

And it flipped.

I believe acrobatic pilots would call what the raven performed a barrel roll: a three-hundred-and-sixty-degree rotation on its long axis, keeping its head zooming forward, never slowing down. And then it was gone. The raven was so close we heard the wind ripple through its feathers with loud pops as it rolled above us. I thought of the sound a kite makes when it catches a gust and tugs hard on the string.

If you are going to have one of Mother Nature's great teaching moments, and at the same time by good fortune avert what could have been one of life's great embarrassing moments, you could be a lot less fortunate than to have such a moment occur on a mountaintop with your son. He loves me, after all, and decided to go easy on me. Lessons, both nature's and life's, sometimes take years to piece together from observation, hard experience, and trial and error. This lesson took about five minutes. Shall we call the lesson I learned something like: appreciate the fullness of nature and acknowledge that you don't know everything? Succinct enough, I think. The raven seemed to be speaking directly to me. I could easily imagine it scoffing as it looked down on us from some point in its roll and saying, "You don't know everything about me. You can't." It isn't hard to imagine the raven saying something like that. And aren't mountaintops known for revelations?

Tom and I both saw the raven perform its flip. Tom was the one with the arched brow, I the one with the slack jaw. We exchanged a glance, but I am not sure we even exchanged a word. I may have smiled sheepishly and muttered something like, "Okay, so much for what I know."

That episode—just about the right mix of awe and humility for a summer afternoon on Table Rock—took place several years ago. Since that time I have seen the Upstate's local population of ravens perform a variety of tricks, including more flips, to the point that I almost expect some sort of amazement most times I see them. And though that little lesson—about not limiting or confining any aspect of nature with my own ignorance—took place in just a few minutes, its repercussions have stayed with me from that time onward.

Ravens live in the "upper" part of the Upstate, in the tops of the mountain counties of Greenville, Pickens, and Oconee. They are not common but are not hard to encounter. If you are not acquainted with them, they are large black birds, considerably larger than the crow, with black beaks, a characteristic wedge-shaped tail, and a deeper, croakier voice than the crow. In the eastern United States they live in the mountains, following the ranges all the way up to the great forests of Maine. According to some accounts I have read, they are becoming more urbanized here in the east. They are more common, and more urbanized, in the western United States. I have seen them hanging out in the parking lots of strip malls in Sedona and Flagstaff, Arizona, and they are easy to see at the Grand Canyon. Tom has encountered them on various expeditions he has made since the Table Rock episode, at high altitudes on Mount Rainer in Washington state and Mount Shasta in California.

A good place to watch ravens and to see them perform—and somehow I think they know this—is at the observation area at Caesars Head State Park. At just about any time you can catch the local ravens soaring over the valley between Caesars Head, Table Rock, and the Dismal out to the right. (It is the Dismal, of course, that has the appropriately named Raven Cliff Falls.) That observation area is where people gather every September for the hawk migration. The main attractions at that time are, naturally, the hawks. Thousands of broad-winged hawks, a single species, pass through that area over a period of several weeks. They are taking advantage of the great warm air drafts rising up from the Piedmont, using those drafts to gain altitude to help send them on their way south and west to Central America for the winter. Many other hawk species come through as well, but the broad-winged account for the large numbers. Some hawks soar directly overhead. Others are mere flecks of pepper, spotted by some very skilled eyes scanning the horizon—from Paris Mountain, way down to the south or left, to Panther Mountain in North Carolina to the north and right.

On more than one occasion when I have been at Caesars Head to watch the hawks, the ravens have not passed up the opportunity to perform for the crowd. I don't really know if they are doing such a thing, of course, though I would not put it past them. They offer their own spectacle during some of the hawk watches and add to the excitement and joy we feel while watching the migrating hawks.

One great September afternoon I saw a raven display another gem from its repertoire of tricks by performing a second type of flip. There we all were at the top of Caesars Head, binoculars ready to count hawks, when a solitary raven cruised by at eye level, probably fifty feet from the fenced rock platform where we were all standing. This wag proceeded to do a forward somersault, pausing for a split second with its head pointing backward, and then returned to its original position by reversing the flip it had just made, all with seemingly no effort, still maintaining a lazy cruising attitude. I shook my head and looked around at the other hawk watchers to verify what I had just witnessed. The consensus of the group, many of them seasoned birders with much more experience and knowledge than I, was a rather casual, "Yep, that's our ravens. That's what they do." All in an afternoon's entertainment.

I won't attempt—remembering in part my humbling experience from a few years back—to really explain this behavior of the raven. I have no idea whether or not it was performing for those of us who were looking on. But it is fun to think about. Take it for what it is, or might be: acrobatics, sport, play, performance. Choose from the list. The behavior certainly seems to be entertainment, for themselves at the least, if not intentionally for us as well. The naturalist and author Bernd Heinrich has a book about ravens called *Mind of the Raven* in which he describes many experiments proving how intelligent these birds are. He talks about how humans have for centuries imbued ravens with all sorts of special powers. I don't, however, remember anything about flips.

The air currents around Caesars Head and Table Rock must be particularly conducive to "sporting about." While the migrating hawks are using the currents to gain height for their long trip to the south and west, even the local red-tailed hawks get into the act of enjoying the winds. The other hawk watchers have pointed out to me the resident red-tails playfully charging each other and frolicking in the breezes on sunny days in the fall.

Looking back over some of my notes from past hawk watches, I was struck by a brief sentence at the end of my list of one day's count of broad-winged, red-tailed, sharp-shinned, and other raptors. "More raven flips," I tacked on at the end of the list, in what seemed like an afterthought. Then I also scribbled, "Very routine." I suppose the wonderful can indeed become routine if you see it often enough. Or perhaps I should say, if you let it. If you work at the Grand Canyon or at Machu Picchu maybe those sights become

> I have no idea whether or not it was performing for those of us who were looking on. But it is fun to think about.

routine. But it would be your loss. The fact that I have been enjoying ravens in our mountains for quite a few years convinces me that I really don't consider those wonderful sights to be humdrum. I'll just blame my tone in that list on the brevity of my note taking. Ravens are hardly an afterthought for me now.

In fact, the last time I was in the Caesars Head area—just a few weeks ago—I made a special stop at the state park to look for them. I had heard ravens on my hike in Jones Gap earlier that morning but had not seen them all day. I was not to be disappointed. As I walked slowly toward the observation area I saw a pair perched on the railing. They of course noticed me immediately, even though I was still behind the small trees along the approach. I was not exactly sure what they were doing there, but from the look they gave me I concluded that at least one of the things they had been doing was enjoying the absence of humans. As I took the step that became too close, the ravens simply lifted their wings in the strong wind coming from the direction of the Dismal, rose vertically for several feet, and then, continuing to watch me, trailed away, backwards, without ever flapping their wings. After receding like this for several more sec-

onds they turned to go with the wind, changing to a shape more falcon-like, and disappeared quickly out of sight.

Tom is now in graduate school—in biology. He isn't studying birds, but he is becoming a real scientist. I remain an amateur. We descended Table Rock that day years ago wiser than when we had hiked up. As we walked down the mountain I was still thinking about what we had seen, trying to enlarge my grasp of several things—things which began with the behavior of the raven—but also included humility, wonder, motivation to keep observing and learning, even parenting. My brain was stretching, thanks to a large black bird. Can you ask much more from a walk in the woods? I can only try to keep my eyes as open on every other walk, so that I see as much at which to marvel.

"Any other questions I can answer for you?" I asked Tom as we headed toward the parking lot.

He had lagged a bit behind me to get one last look at the creek before we left the park. As he trotted to catch up with me, he pretended he had not heard me. "Was that you talking," he said, "or the raven?"

JEREMIAD OF A BAD DROUGHT YEAR

Joni Tevis

1. IN A WET SEASON, THE TULIP-TREE PROSPERS, ROOTS WRIGGLING THROUGH HUMUS AND PINCHING SLICK CLAY, BRANCHES FORCING OUT WRINKLED LEAVES THAT UNFURL, STRETCH TAUT, SHAKE DOWN SHADE ON TRAILING SQUAW-WEED AND DARK PIPSISSEWA.

And the sunlight through leaves is green and gutters when the wind blows. Some, pressing stethoscopes to trunk, say it's possible to hear sap rise; veins groan as they strain, they say, laboring.

In a wet season, the tulip-tree swallows sun, is the Appalachian forests' prize. Straight and thick-boled, it would make a good canoe; its fibrous bark Cherokee twisted into fish nets, plaited into strong rope. Early in the season it drops painted buds to the ground, tender petals dipped in orange, and by this token makes its lineage known: magnolia. The blooms of the famous Southern magnolia, white and peach-smelling, are so delicate they cannot be touched; even careful fingers burn the petals brown.

But in August of a bad drought year, I watched the tulip-tree choke on sap curdled from want of rain. Too soon it dropped leaves, bone-colored, to litter the trail like tossed paper; its naked branches rattled. In August of a bad drought year I hiked to the mountaintop, and under my feet frazzled grass crunched, and no beetle buzzed, no snake rustled. My shoes left no print on the hardpack clay. In a wet season, I had seen clouds darken to charcoal there, seen rivers of rain flush the bald clean of ground quartz and pine straw. But there was no rain this year. The trail smelled of earth baking. My feet pounded leaves to dust, and I could not count the dying trees.

2.

He wakes in a dream, tongue thick with dust, robe sweat-damp. He knows where he is: a battleground outside the city, the valley of dry bones. Squinting against the sun, he stares across the plain at the skeleton-stacked canyon, waiting. Then the voice of the Lord rockets across the noontime desert, howling around hoodoos, asking: *O man, will these bones rise again?* What can he say? Ezekiel answers, wisely, *Lord, thou knowest.*

Then it happens: wind blasts down the valley and knocks the bones to the ground. They clatter as they fall, raising dust, and as the wind gusts the bones rise and pair, sorting themselves from their stacks. Bone to bone, they twirl and knit, dance like leaves, figure the old fit. Pale at first, sun-bleached, the bones redden and sprout sinew, thick cords of muscle, unwrinkled skin.

In the valley of dry bones stands a blank-eyed army. They are the standing dead; their placid faces do not crease in shock, their limp arms do not clutch their chests. Then another, softer wind steals through the valley, and the army of men does live. What they do next we are not told.

3.

On a short summer night in the bad drought year, I walked through dark woods that shivered with lust for the burning. Stars glinted in an obsidian sky, the air too dry to tat a cloud. I kept to the trail, the day's heat still rising from it, and in the darkness saw a lighter stretch ahead. As I walked toward it, the sound of rasping and grinding, quiet at first, grew loud. When I stepped from dark woods into gray light, I saw that I was in a clear-cut, pines stacked in ragged piles, snarled roots upended. All around me was the sound of chewing, millions of mouths crunching wood: pine beetles. No bigger than a pencil point, but capable of killing thousands of acres of pine woods, pine beetles love dry years; drought-weakened trees can't fight. To slow the beetles' spread, foresters cut infested trees; when the tree dies, the beetles starve. It stopped me short: the hole in the forest, piles of uprooted trees, and worst, the infested pines that still stood, their needles

tinder-dry, an army of the dead. I haven't walked through that clear-cut in years, haven't seen the skinny pioneer species (by the creek, alder; in the sun, Virginia pine) that must be, already, turning the scar into something like forest, but I can't shake the vision I had, gnawing mouths and drifts of sawdust, on a blighted midsummer night.

4.

Once, in a wet season, a summer storm caught me on the mountain ridge. Storms can cook up fast in the lower Smokies and this one had, stalling above the creased gorges; I didn't notice until the air darkened and thunder knocked. Say the sky was a glass of milk and the storm a root-clutch steeping there; say the sky drained of color as it will in the long summer dusk. Say the sky thickened and piled like a bolt of denim at the textile mill down the road, the one that shut down after forty hard years: now bearded grasses crack open the parking lot, lay raw clay bare. Say the sky unburdened itself like the mill on its last day, when workers packed looms on flatbeds and wrapped them in yellow tarps, and drivers tightened the straps to secure the machines for the long haul down to Mexico. The newly out-of-work watched the trucks pull out of the lot, making for the freeway, and long after the trucks disappeared, the diesel they burned hung heavy in the air. The people tasted the hard time come upon them, and it tasted like diesel. Say the sky above the mountains turned dark as the abandoned mill's blind exhaust vent, that the screaming of crows was like skittering claws on metal. And then the rains came.

The storm clamped down like a heavy thing and set to pounding. Wind ripped through the gorge, bending and shaking the trees, and thunder hummed low like big trucks rolling. Lightning flashed its keen steel scissors. A town girl caught without shelter, I ran down the trail looking for a place to ride it out, found a crevice under an overhang and crawled in. Ant lions' conical traps dotted the powdery ground, and dark lampshade spiders crouched against the granite ceiling. Hunched in last year's leaves, I watched the storm erase the trees across the gorge, turn the nearby hemlocks into dark thrashing shapes, sheet the trail next to me with water. Cold rain blew in, and I hugged myself, scared, when thunder split with a sound not like a slammed door or a dropped dictionary, not like a kerosene bomb or a bulldozed wall, not like bent metal screaming: like something inside my head, a nightmare cry pushing out. Lightning flashed close, closer, and when it struck a near hemlock I heard sap sizzle and smelled ozone, and then the thunder cracked loud with a sound like earth breaking, and I screamed.

Then the storm passed, strips of blue showing in the torn sky, and I crawled out of my hiding place to hike the slippery trail (broken branches, split trees) down the gorge, where the creek ran thick and fast, yellow with mud, over swelling boulders. Carefully I pulled myself up to the cable crossing and tight-roped over the roiling creek, and if I had shouted I could not have made myself heard over the water's roar. In the bad drought year I prayed for this, the violence of rain, to be alone in the wilderness when everything came crashing down.

5.

 Who will stand witness to the miracles of our time? Who will tell of the workers who loomed sheets, spindled thread, edged the millions of towels that once dried dinner dishes and damp bodies all over the world? The people learn to drive postal routes, serve coffee and fried eggs, restock shelves at the discount store. Or they look for work and cannot find it, and when their socks wear thin they darn them, and when the patches wear through they tear the fabric into strips, knot strips into rope, stitch rope into rugs. They move in with relatives. They halve dosages, stop subscriptions, fix beans. Boil a bone, make a soup. They know how to make things last. And some nights, to save electricity, they sit in the dark, as my grandfather used to do. He sat on the old brown davenport as night fell, and would not light the lamp. Like him they sit in the dark, figuring, wrapping themselves in hard hope.

In a faithless time I have gone to the desert and seen there ocotillo, devil's buggy whip, naked canes rising from the stony ground. Gray, stippled with thorns, it rattled in the wind, and no plant has ever looked so dead to me. But I've seen, too, the desert after rain, when the ocotillo's tips force out petals red as any cosseted rose. The ocotillo plays at death, crying a song to the cold desert wind; the ocotillo in bloom is a god's hair ablaze with fire, or blood.

This was my vision: Go to the tulip-tree in the depth of the bad drought year, carrying a pick if you can find one, or a sharp stone, or a spade. Clear the fallen leaves; bear down on the spade until your arch blisters; dig a trench in the brick-hard clay. Take off your shoes (cracked from walking); bury them there. Cover them with earth. Tamp it down. Leave your footprints there, dancing.

The night after I did this, clouds gathered and flung down rain. The drought broke as the Baptists, the Methodists, the Presbyterians had all prayed; as I had. Then I went to the place on the mountain's flank where bright water poured from a jutting pipe. People fill their jugs there, say that water heals, those minerals make bones strong. Where granite gleamed with wet and moss sparkled with mist, where water gushed from a dark stub, I cupped my hands and drank. I buried my shoes at the foot of a mountain tree. Let its roots, well-watered, twine around those rusting buckles; let rain crumble that old metal into strength.

6.

There was a break in the battle: not a truce, but a pause during which both sides admitted their exhaustion. The factions retreated: David and his men into the cave of Adullam, his enemy into Rephaim Valley. The late sun shone red on the wall of David's cave. The men

> In August of a bad drought year I hiked to the mountaintop, and under my feet frazzled grass crunched, and no beetle buzzed, no snake rustled.

kindled fires of dried dung and thorny branch-es, husbanding the scarce wood; they scrubbed their blood-caked bodies and swords with sand, roasted a snared goat and ate of it, gulped their rationed water. The watchmen took their places. The others, weary unto collapse, unrolled their mats but would not lie down before David.

He sat on the dusty cave floor, staring at the dwindling fire. Something about fire can make a man nostalgic. Perhaps he thought of how he came to fight his first battle. He had gone to the encampment on an errand, taking provisions to his brothers; he had been a boy then, and eager to go. He was sick of his town, knowing every dwelling and rut in the road, how the market-place smelled of sour milk and the tannery. He walked out the gate with a cloth-wrapped bundle: cheese to bribe the commander, bread his mother had baked, a bag of dates for her favorite son. How well she had known the commander and what he would demand. But when David arrived at the encampment the tents were filled with the groaning wounded, and the place resounded with the enemy's daily taunts. He had not had time for homesickness; that would come later, when even the stars and sky seemed different than they had when he had lain in the field, surrounded by his father's herds, insulated from the dew by a blanket his mother had woven for him.

Would that I could drink the water of the well of Bethlehem! he said, suddenly, startling the men from reverie. *To taste once more those sweet waters.* The others nodded their heads gravely, keeping their eyes on the fire, looking at him and then at each other. And to each other their eyes asked, *Is this a test?* But he did not see their glance, and gazed at the fire a long time before stretching out on his blanket. Soon he was sleeping the heavy, silent sleep of the career soldier.

They were three, even then his most trusted, those permitted to rest near him. But that night they did not sleep. Smothering the fire with sand, they passed the guards with a silent nod, picked their careful way down the canyon, and ran a looping oxbow around the enemy camp, their sandals' slap the only sound. The sleeping town of Bethlehem was strange with the pres-ence of enemy invaders. No snores or muffled love-cries came from the cloth-draped windows; no dog shambled down the street. Clay ovens ticked in the cool midnight air. Did they silence the enemy guards with their swords? Did they glide past so skillfully, keeping to the dark places between houses, that no one detected them? Somehow they made their way to the well, lifted the heavy lid that dripped with condensation, and hauled up the bucket. Did they drink? They had no time; wrapping the jar in a worn tunic, they turned to go. The moon sank as they ran across the desert, and they were keenly aware of every stone's shadow that could hide a man, every gully where a spy might crouch. Would they have heard the whicker of an arrow over the pounding of their breath? Would they have noticed if one of their group fell? The sky light-ened as they ran into their own camp. They waited outside the cave until he rose.

Where have you been this night? he asked. *I heard the three of you rise and run down the canyon path.* His face was weary; he looked like someone who, a betrayer himself, knows he will never be able to trust anyone. And one of the three pulled a bundle from his side, unwrapped a cloth, and held up a jar. *Water from the well of Bethlehem*, he said, and sat down, feet still dusty, shins thorn-scratched. David held the jar ten-tatively, as though it were a serpent that might strike if not carefully handled.

Stand up, he said. Taking each man's face in his hands, he pressed his mouth to their stubbled cheeks. *I cannot drink this*, he said. *This could as well be your blood, my men, you who risked your lives for my pleasure.* The sun rose over the edge of the desert, and in the valley below, the enemy girded for battle. David fell to his knees, holding the jar to his chest, and the men instinc-tively put out their hands, shielding the vessel from harm. He raised his hands above his head and brought the jar crashing to the ground. The water seeped into the dry sand. *This is my offer-ing to the God of Israel*, he said. *This blood of my men, these waters of my home.* Clay shards shiny with water, and the sun drying them. The dark patch shrank, lightened, disappeared.

After that morning they were good as be-trothed, David and his men, filial and pledged, they who would make together a history to be remembered long after their passing. They risked their lives to slake his thirst; they carried his home in a jar. He poured it out as the only use worthy of a holy thing. Did this offering please his God? The sun licked up the water and it rose invisibly on its long journey, gone as though it had never been, until clouds gathered over the desert and dropped down rain. For water is a thing used hard, and used again; water is older than the bodies it laves; water is a relic scrubbed by charcoal and root, and sparkling still as on its first bright day. Thousands of years later, the story survives; can't you see the cup outpoured? Can it be that even now, at this late hour, the very blood that swells your veins carries something of the waters of Bethlehem?

SUCCESSION

Russ Burns

MOTHER NATURE HAS ENDLESS PATIENCE. I ONLY HAVE A LIFETIME.

The drone of the multi-blade mower sounds like a cross between bacon frying and an angry hive of bees. It is hypnotic, this mower music, and after a bit I find myself lapsing into a reverie. Pleasant images float up and stream away like the seeds of a dandelion in a breeze—scenes from a vacation in the tropics, snatches of a love sonnet, the sound of Enya singing her latest sad, Irish tune. The grass of my hay field streams through the mower.

Thump.

Slowing, then quickly rebounding, the mower regains its music. A young persimmon tree is ejected from the rear of the mower. Up ahead I see another three-foot sapling marching toward my tractor. The mower skitters through the grass and slashes down the interloper. Another *thump*. Another tree-to-be is spit out atop the swath.

Tree seedlings invading my hay field are constant nuisances. Their trunks and branches get rolled into the hay bales, lowering the quality of the hay. In the northwest corner, the persimmons pop up yearly. Along the woods on the northeast, the ubiquitous sweet gums plague my field. On the south, it's invasive chinaberries. No matter how many times I decapitate them, they find the strength for resurrection. I cut them and curse them, but each year they come back.

Yet I know this is nature's plan (not the cutting and cursing; just the invasion). For each type of landscape, nature has decreed an optimum botanical mix. Here on my farm just north of Laurens in the piedmont of South Carolina, the land should be cloaked in trees of all types, but mostly oaks and hickories. My field of grass goes against nature's plan. Grass is for the great plains of the American West, for the East African plateau, and for the steppes of Russia—to name a few. But the grand design for my farm is trees, trees, and more trees. I have chosen to violate this master strategy by imposing a grassland where temperature, rainfall, and soil type command domination by hardwoods.

I pay the wages of my transgression by having to fight a constant war. The enemy forces keep coming, launched onto the battlefield through myriad devices. Robins and their ilk spread the chinaberries in their droppings. Opossums, raccoons, coyotes, and other mammals transport the persimmon seeds, planting them wherever their gut feels the urge. The sweet gum seeds take the direct approach, blowing in on the winter wind. Other botanical interlopers have their variations on the invasion theme. Next spring, the green army will raise up its new recruits and the battle will be rejoined. The enemy forces seem inexhaustible, and I am growing older. The ultimate outcome seems assured.

Thump. This time it is a small cedar, no doubt the beneficiary of an avian digestive system. The spicy aroma of this juniper wafts across my line-of-mow before dispersing under the hot, spring sun. I savor the smell before it is gone.

The scent spurs me to consider how our pioneering ancestors misnamed so many things, the eastern red cedar being a prime example. It is not a cedar at all, but a juniper. The Biblical cedars of Lebanon looked nothing like the cedars of my farm. Likewise, the poplars in the woodlands beside the field are not poplars, but rather tulip trees. The poplar family includes trees like the aspens of the American West, but the tulip tree, *faux* poplar, is a relative of the magnolias. We humans seem to have a propensity for screwing up relationships, botanical and otherwise.

Following the last ice age when the great conifer forests had retreated to the north, the dynamic relationships of the various biomes of the United States were established. Grasslands of varying heights filled the center of the continent. Hardwoods cloaked the higher lands of the east. Conifers dominated along the east coast and in the western highlands. Desert vegetation claimed the southwest flatlands. The flora and fauna of the United States as we know it (or, at least, as our pioneering ancestors knew it) had settled into comfortable, long-term relationships.

Even the presence of Native Americans did little to alter the natural scheme of things. When these early Americans did wreck some portion of the landscape, such as by using fire to clear patches in the forest for planting or to stampede grazing herds on the plains, nature quickly repaired the damage through a series of successional stages. Here in the eastern piedmont, openings in the forest usually were closed by a patchwork of low-growing shrubs and grasses that provided cover for young pines and cedars that in turn sheltered sprouting hardwoods. The hardwoods then jostled among themselves for dominance until the oaks, hickories, and chestnuts would win out. Botanists estimate that this terminal phase of succession in the piedmont, called the climax forest, takes about three hundred years to achieve.

As another sapling rattles through my mower, I muse that my work in the hay field is derailing a three-century plan that nature has for my farm. Left alone, my hay field on the broad plateau between the Saluda and Enoree Rivers would soon be overgrown in plum thickets and young pines. The invasive sweet gums would vie with the persimmons for a place in the emerging forest. The chinaberries would lose out quickly. In time the pines and sweet gums would reign supreme as the plums and grasses met their demise in the growing shade. But their dominance would be short-lived. In their shadows, willow and water oaks, as well as white and post oaks, would be gaining a foothold. Hickories would also be moving into

As a small pine clad in catbrier whooshes through the mower, I survey my hay field. Nature is sending me a message.

my field, courtesy of thoughtful squirrels. Unfortunately, the magnificent American chestnut would not be in the mix because of the disease we humans carelessly brought into its range.

The great eastern hardwood forests in which the chestnut stood supreme are no more. Only a few chestnuts remain that are resistant to the disease that we introduced when we planted Chinese chestnuts in our yards and parks. Dissatisfied by the bounty of our native chestnut, we opted for more, and like the dog that saw the reflection of the bone in its mouth, we grabbed for the bone mirrored in the pond and lost the prize that we already possessed. In so doing, we destroyed a relationship established by nature.

The clatter of a tough sweet gum spinning through my mower reminds me that nature is resilient. The climax oaks and hickories, along with the poplars, sweet and black gums, sassafras, sourwoods, and other hardwoods and conifers will establish a new balance. Diversity is the key to nature's success. Disease and other elements of destruction spread more slowly through a diverse population—where one member is weak, another is resistant. The forest continues.

We humans seem to have difficulty with the biodiversity concept. We clear-cut the old forests and replant a monoculture of pines. Then we anguish over the millions of dollars of

damage done to our enterprise when the pine bark beetles ravage our pine plantations. To the beetles, a thousand acres of pines is an endless cafeteria line. If pines are intermixed with hardwoods, the beetles have a much more difficult time locating lunch and spreading their kind to the next pine patch.

But we are slow learners, or just plain stubborn. We keep trying to improve on nature, and we continue to pay the price. We introduced kudzu in the East to control the erosion that our poor stewardship of the land had created and, in the process, unleashed a voracious vine that is overwhelming our forests in places. We released starlings from Europe, where they are well-behaved, and the birds erupted into an aerial plague here. Add to the list of unwelcome immigrants: fire ants, tiger mosquitoes, Japanese honeysuckle, horse nettle, walking catfish, and just about every noxious weed that ravages our lawns and farm fields. We alone have created these plagues, intentionally or inadvertently, by upsetting the relationships that nature established.

As a small pine clad in catbrier whooshes through the mower, I survey my hay field. Nature is sending me a message. The hay field itself is a manmade landscape, an aberration in the normal biota of the area. If I let nature have its way, the hay field would begin the long successional trek toward a climax forest. In the process, pine bark beetles, fire ants, noxious weeds, starlings, plum thickets, and honeysuckles would virtually disappear because they can't live in deep woodlands. Who knows, maybe even kudzu would succumb to the shade.

Turning my tractor around at the top of the hill, I look back across my forty acres of out-of-place grassland and I contemplate the future. When I can no longer mow this field and no one else takes up the challenge, the hay field will rejoin nature's plan.

And I wonder if my great-great grandchildren—my successors—will enjoy walking in the biodiversity of the emerging oak and hickory forest where I once did battle with succession. ⮑

Ned Barrett has run in almost every state and in at least two foreign countries during the past twenty-five years. He lives in Spartanburg with his wife, Christy, and two children, Lydia and Quinn, their cats, and Bristol the Enduro-Dog. He works for Partners for Active Living, a non-profit working to make Spartanburg County a healthier and more livable community.

The Reverend Rob Brown serves as rector of Saint Matthew's Episcopal Church in Spartanburg. He and his wife, Sandra, have two children, Zach and Becca, and a black Lab named Gracie. Sandra patiently tolerates his obsession with the outdoors and even acts interested when he practices turkey calls and waxes poetic about lunar cycles and their influence on deer movement and patterns. He has been published in *The Southerner*, an online literary magazine, and *In Morgan's Shadow* (Hub City, 2001).

Russ Burns is a retired public school educator and former supervisor of the Science Museum in Columbia. With a life-long love of nature and formal training in wildlife biology, he has written extensively of his observations of the interactions of humans and the natural world. He and his wife and daughter operate Foxbrier Farm (www.foxbrierfarm.com), a multi-use facility featuring cattle ranching, equestrian events, teacher training, and wildlife conservation, in Laurens County.

Hunter S. Bridges is a wildlife biologist from Greenville. He has spent years hunting, fishing, and observing wildlife all over the Southeast, but it was the works of Aldo Leopold that inspired him to begin writing in his early twenties.

Jane Chew is a professor of German at Furman University and has lived in Greenville since 1980.

Emma Chisolm, a seventh-generation South Carolinian, lives in the foothills of South Carolina, where her paternal ancestors settled in what is known as "The Dark Corner." A poet who's just completed her first novel, Emma lives beside, honors, and fly-fishes her nearby mountain rivers and streams.

D.W. Damrel lives in Spartanburg and came to the Upstate four years ago by way of Texas and Arizona. He teaches world religions locally and volunteers at the Clemson Herbarium.

Sterling (Skip) Eisiminger was born in Washington, D.C., in 1941. The son of an Army officer, he traveled widely but often reluctantly with his family in the United States and Europe. After he finished a master's degree at Auburn and took a job at Clemson University in 1968, he put down deep roots in the red Carolina clay. In 1974 he received a Ph.D. from the University of South Carolina where James Dickey "guided" his creative dissertation. His publications include *Non-Prescription Medicine* (poems) and *Felix Academicus* (personal essays). He is married to the former Ingrid (Omi) Barmwater, a German native, and is the proud father of a son, Shane, and a daughter, Anja.

John Faris's dad taught him to hunt, fish, and enjoy the outdoors. By the age of eight, John's greatest love was following his dad through the rolling hills and hardwood river bottoms of Laurens County. Georgia Tech, the U.S. Navy, and graduate school took him away until 1978 when he and his wife, Claudia, purchased Oilmen's Equipment Company in Spartanburg. More than thirty years later he continues to manage the company, but still spends many happy hours enjoying his first love with his dad, his son, and his grandchildren. This is his first publication.

Ernest Glenn grew up in Greenville and lived elsewhere for many years. He has been back in the Upstate since the mid-90s. He teaches classes on software for building control and energy management. This is his first published essay. He has been a nature lover most of his life.

When in America, **Peter Godfrey** lives with his wife and two children in Pickens County's Talley Valley at what used to be Wattacoo Post Office. A professional actor who studied at the Royal Academy of Dramatic Art, he has also worked as a teacher (Christ Church Episcopal School, The Governor's School, Stanmore College) journalist (*Creative Loafing*, *Visual Education*, *Performance* magazine) artistic director

(Rational Theatre Company, RT productions), and arts administrator (Arun District Council, TRAM/Trillium). He has written/directed four short films, two dozen stage plays, and is currently working on "The Great Welsh Novel," while also running Blue Wall Group, an arts non-profit in the Slater-Marietta area.

Scott Gould's fiction, poetry, and nonfiction have appeared in *Kenyon Review, Blood Orange Review, Carolina Quarterly, Black Warrior Review, Yemassee, New Stories from the South*, and *New Southern Harmonies* (Hub City, 1998), among others. He is a past winner of the Literature Fellowship from the South Carolina Arts Commission and the Fiction Fellowship from the South Carolina Academy of Authors. Gould teaches creative writing at the S.C. Governor's School for the Arts & Humanities in Greenville.

Ellen E. Hyatt lives in Summerville and is a professor of English. She writes a monthly column for *The Summerville Journal Scene* and has had poems published in a variety of journals. The South Carolina Poetry Initiative has published poems from her chapbook *Leaving* on its web site.

M. Jill Jones is a clinical social worker, writer, and poetry therapist living in Anderson. She maintains a private practice in Due West and enjoys leading poetry therapy groups and workshops in the Upstate area. Jill has published in various regional journals, anthologies, and newspapers.

John Lane teaches English and environmental studies at Wofford College, where he is the director of the Goodall Environmental Studies Center at Glendale Shoals. He is the author of numerous books of poetry and prose, including *Waist Deep in Black Water* (2002), *Chattooga: Descending into the Myth of Deliverance River* (2004), and *Circling Home* (2007), all published by the University of Georgia Press. His weekly newspaper columns were collected in *The Best of the Kudzu Telegraph* (Hub City, 2008).

J. Drew Lanham is a professor of wildlife ecology at Clemson University, where he studies a variety of subjects, including bird conservation, hunting ethics, and African-American land ethic. His published essays include "Towards Home: A Search for Place and Land Ethic" in *American Crisis, Southern Solutions: From Where We Stand, Peril and Promise* (NewSouth Books, 2008), and "Bartram on Blacktop" in *Bartram's Living Legacy: The Travels and the Nature of the South* (Mercer University Press, 2010). Drew's first book, *The Home Place:Memoirs of a Colored Man's Search for Self in Nature* is scheduled for publication by Milkweed Editions in 2011. A native of Edgefield, Drew lives in Seneca with his wife, Janice, and children, Alexis and Colby.

Sabrina Broselow Moser holds a Ph.D. in German literature and wrote her dissertation on the history of German food in the eighteenth century. She has lived in Germany and in Spain, but she is now a full-time mother in Simpsonville. Her work has appeared in academic newsletters, and she currently writes a culinary blog for Aga Ranges.

Heather Magruder is a freelance writer and teaching artist living in Greenville with her husband, three children, two dogs, cat, and Great Highland Bagpipes. She is the recipient of the 2009 Sue Lile Inman Prize for Excellence in the Art of the Short Story. Her flash fiction has twice won the Piccolo Fiction Open. Heather's work is published in a variety of periodicals, including the *Emrys Journal, Literary Mama*, and *Main Street Rag*.

Jim Magruder works as a network specialist and races throughout the Carolinas in the Masters 40+ cycling category. He lives with his wife, two teens, two dogs, and a cat in Greenville. He is currently lobbying USA Cycling to give parent-racers a two-place handicap for every child under the age of thirty-two. His shorts get washed after every ride, Shroud of Turin salt stain or not. This is his first publication.

For almost twenty years, **Jeanne Malmgren** was an award-winning feature writer and editor at the *St. Petersburg Times*, Florida's largest newspaper. She has co-authored one book of nonfiction, *Journey to Mindfulness*. Her essay in this book was written during an artist's residency she won in 2009 from the Emrys Foundation. She lives in

Clemson and is working on a novel with Oconee bells as a leitmotif.

Diane Milks lives with her husband and three children in Greer, where she owns a real estate development company. She is a former writer and project coordinator for the Palmetto Conservation Foundation. Previous publications include *The Catawba River Companion* and articles for *South Carolina Wildlife* and *Upstate Lakes* magazines. Diane enjoys writing and oil painting in her free time.

Dawn Mitchell is the partnership director of the Spartanburg Writing Project, housed at USC Upstate, where she works with teachers and students across Spartanburg County to improve writing instruction through school partnerships and graduate courses. She has been a classroom teacher and instructor for the last ten years, including adjunct teaching at Spartanburg Methodist College, Furman University, and USC Upstate. She grew up and continues to live near Reidville in Spartanburg County.

Craig Murphy has been living in Cairo, Amman, and Baghdad for the last two years, working for the International Organization for Migration (IOM) on an Iraqi refugee resettlement program. He is in the process of relocating to Abeche, Chad, as IOM Head-of-Sub-Office to work on a Darfuri refugee program that falls under the U.S. Department of State. He has published occasional op-ed pieces in the Spartanburg *Herald-Journal* and in the BBC *Focus on Africa* magazine.

Kirk Neely is senior pastor of Morningside Baptist Church in Spartanburg. He has published *Comfort and Joy: Nine Stories for Christmas* (Hub City, 2006), *When Grief Comes: Finding Strength for Today and Hope for Tomorrow* (Baker Books, 2007), and *A Good Mule is Hard to Find and Other Tales from Red Clay Country,* (Hub City, 2009), among other books. Kirk is a frequent writer for the religion page of the Spartanburg *Herald-Journal*. He writes a weekly column for *H-J Weekly* and has written for *Sandlapper* magazine and *Spartanburg* magazine.

Missy Nicholson is a full-time mom and part-time CPA living in Greer. She spends her "free time" volunteering at her children's schools while dreaming of hiking and writing. Her essay "Sudden Death" was recently published in *The Pettigru Review*, and *The Greenville Journal* published her Lenten essay, "Forty Days without Facebook" in spring 2009.

Wilson Peden is a teacher and writer from Greenville. He holds a bachelor's degree from Wofford College and an MFA in creative writing from the University of Minnesota. He currently lives in Minneapolis.

Ron Rash is the author of eleven books, the most recent being *Burning Bright*, a book of short stories. He teaches at Western Carolina University where he is the Parris Distinguished Professor of Appalachian Cultural Studies.

Pat Robertson, retired outdoors writer and columnist for *The State* newspaper in Columbia, has produced freelance articles on the outdoors for several magazines and websites, including *South Carolina Wildlife, South Carolina Sportsman,* and AnglersChannel.com. He also produces a regular travel column for *South Carolina Living* magazine. He and his wife, Jan, live in Blythewood, where they raise beagles and compete in field trials across the Southeast.

Pam Shucker taught for more than twenty-five years in Greenville County schools as a teacher-naturalist, often immersed in Roper Mountain Science Center's Rainforest and Sea Life Touch Tank. She continues to share her wonder in and exploration of the natural environment with hundreds of children through the Furman University Summer Scopes program. In 2001 she published *Symbols of our Faith*, a photo essay on the symbols incorporated in worship at First Baptist Greenville.

Charlie Sowell lives outside of Greer, near Lake Robinson, and within sight of Hogback Mountain. For more than thirty years he's worked as a writer, editor, and columnist at newspapers stretching from the East Coast to Honolulu. He currently plies his craft at Community Journals, a media company headquartered in

Greenville. He is shopping for publishers for his first novel and has started a second.

Shandi Stevenson lives in Travelers Rest. She works as a teacher, tutor, and freelance writer. Her poetry and nonfiction have appeared in local, national, and international publications, including *South Carolina* magazine, *G* magazine, and the Spartanburg *Herald-Journal*.

Gerald Teaster grew up in the Pacolet area and graduated from Pacolet High School. He is a graduate of the University of South Carolina and is a retired professional engineer. He is the author of *The Confederate Submarine H.L. Hunley*, *The Confederate Steam Torpedo Boat CSS DAVID*, *Confederates Courageous: The Story of the Confederate Submarine H.L. Hunley*, and *Spirit Up the People: Four Days to the Cowpens*. He lives in Summerville.

Joni Tevis teaches creative writing and literature at Furman University. Her book of lyric essays, *The Wet Collection*, was published by Milkweed Editions in 2007. She is at work on a new book of nonfiction about ghost towns, tourist traps, and atomic dread.

Gerald Thurmond is a sociology professor at Wofford College with an avid interest in canoeing, hiking, bird watching, and natural history in general. He is the editor, with John Lane, of the anthology *The Woods Stretched for Miles: New Nature Writing from the South*. He has published nature essays in *Pride of Place,* an anthology of Texas nature writing; in the journal *Isle*; and in Mercer University's reissued edition of *Bartram's Travels*. This is Thurmond's third essay to be included in a Hub City book.

Previous Publications

Russ Burns' essay "Succession" was first published in the 2003 edition of *Catfish Stew*, the annual anthology of the South Carolina Writers Workshop.

A longer version of John Lane's "Looking for Wildness in a Damaged Southern Landscape" was published in *Watershed Journal* (Brown University) under the title "ReGenesis" in its fall/winter 2006 issue.

Kirk Neely's piece, "Snake Handling with Rudy Mancke," appeared in *Sandlapper* magazine, fall 2005.

"Exotic Fishing" by Ron Rash was originally published by *Oxford American*.

A version of Pat Robertson's essay, "Noodlin' and Canoodlin'" was first published in *The Country Chronicle*, a weekly newspaper in Blythewood.

"Jeremiad of a Bad Drought Year" by Joni Tevis was originally published in *The Wet Collection* (Milkweed Editions, 2007).

Michel Stone has published about a dozen short stories and is a winner of the Hub City Prize for Fiction as well as *South Carolina Magazine*'s Very Short Fiction Contest. Her work has appeared numerous times in the *Raleigh News and Observer*'s emerging Southern Writer Series, and one of her short stories was the title story in Hub City's award winning collection *Expecting Goodness and Other Stories*, edited by C. Michael Curtis. Michel is an alumna of the Sewanee Writers' Conference and lives in Spartanburg with her husband and three children. She is at work on her second novel.

 Ted Borg is former chief photographer of *South Carolina Wildlife* and *South Carolina Home & Garden* magazines. His field assignments have covered nearly every natural setting in the state and most types of nature-based recreation. A native of Mobile, Alabama, he now lives with his wife, Martha, and dog, Sandy, in a wildwood setting near Chapin, South Carolina.

 Lydia Dishman has been the editor of the *Emrys Journal* literary magazine since 2003. She is a contributing editor of *G, the Magazine of Greenville*, and feature writer for CBS Interactive's BNET, Entrepreneur, Fast Company, and others.

Hub City Press is an independent press in Spartanburg, South Carolina, that publishes well-crafted, high-quality works by new and established authors, with an emphasis on the Southern experience. We are committed to high-caliber novels, short stories, poetry, plays, memoir, and works emphasizing regional culture and history. We are particularly interested in books with a strong sense of place.

Hub City Press is an imprint of the non-profit Hub City Writers Project, founded in 1995 to foster a sense of community through the literary arts. Our metaphor of organization purposely looks backward to the nineteenth century when Spartanburg was known as the "hub city," a place where railroads converged and departed.

Nature Titles

Family Trees • Mike Corbin

The Seasons of Harold Hatcher • Mike Hembree

The Lawson's Fork • Gary Henderson, David Taylor

Noble Trees • Mike Dirr, John Lane

Cottonwood Trail • Thomas Webster

Best of the Kudzu Telegraph • John Lane